THOMAS TALLIS
AND HIS MUSIC IN
VICTORIAN ENGLAND

Music in Britain, 1600–1900

ISSN 1752-1904

Series Editors:
RACHEL COWGILL & PETER HOLMAN
(Leeds University Centre for English Music)

This series provides a forum for the best new work in this area; it takes a deliberately inclusive approach, covering immigrants and emigrants as well as native musicians. Contributions on all aspects of seventeenth-, eighteenth- and nineteenth-century British music studies are welcomed, particularly those placing music in its social and historical contexts, and addressing Britain's musical links with Europe and the rest of the globe.

Proposals or queries should be sent in the first instance to Dr Rachel Cowgill, Professor Peter Holman or Boydell & Brewer at the addresses shown below. All submissions will receive prompt and informed consideration.

Dr Rachel Cowgill, School of Music, University of Leeds, Leeds, LS2 9JT
email: r.e.cowgill@leeds.ac.uk

Professor Peter Holman, School of Music, University of Leeds, Leeds, LS2 9JT
email: p.k.holman@leeds.ac.uk

Boydell & Brewer, PO Box 9, Woodbridge, Suffolk, IP12 3DF
email: editorial@boydell.co.uk

ALREADY PUBLISHED

Lectures on Musical Life
William Sterndale Bennett
edited by Nicholas Temperley, with Yunchung Yang

John Stainer: A Life in Music
Jeremy Dibble

*The Pursuit of High Culture: John Ella and
Chamber Music in Victorian London*
Christina Bashford

THOMAS TALLIS
AND HIS MUSIC IN
VICTORIAN ENGLAND

Suzanne Cole

THE BOYDELL PRESS

First published 2008
The Boydell Press, Woodbridge

ISBN 978-1-84383-380-2

The Boydell Press is an imprint of Boydell & Brewer Ltd
PO Box 9, Woodbridge, Suffolk IP12 3DF, UK
and of Boydell & Brewer Inc.
668 Mt Hope Avenue, Rochester, NY 14620, USA
website: www.boydellandbrewer.com

A catalogue record of this publication is available
from the British Library

This publication is printed on acid-free paper

Designed and typeset in Adobe Minion Pro by
David Roberts, Pershore, Worcestershire

Printed in Great Britain by
Antony Rowe Ltd, Chippenham, Wiltshire

❧ Contents

List of Illustrations

List of Tables

For Thomas and Hilary

Acknowledgments

In 1980 I started organ lessons with the late Rev. Paul Harvie, who several years later somewhat reluctantly took me on (in the absence of any suitable male candidates) as his assistant organist. The origins of this book can be traced directly to my encounter with Paul's absolute, if eccentric, dedication to the preservation of the Anglican choral tradition in working-class inner-suburban Melbourne. I owe him an immense debt of gratitude.

I am also deeply indebted to my mentor and friend, Kerry Murphy, who has provided every possible support, advice and encouragement over the last ten years. I also wish to thank her, along with my fellows members of the 'Melbourne School of Reception', particularly Elizabeth Kertesz and Megan Prictor, for providing the intellectual stimulus behind this study.

My thanks go to the endlessly patient staff of the Music Library at the University of Melbourne; to the staff at the British Library, and to Oliver Davies at the Royal College of Music for their assistance in locating material; to David Coppen from the Sibley Music Library at the Eastman School of Music, University of Rochester, for providing me with a copy of the *Musical Library* article on the 1836 performance of *Spem in alium*, and to James Hobson for bringing this article to my attention. I am grateful to Ann Royle and Rachel Milestone for research assistance; to Kate Watson both for her persistent detective work and hospitality; to Ian Burk for sharing treasures unearthed in the Floyd archive; to Alan Davison and Trish Shaw for technical advice; to Peter Campbell and Jeanne Roberts for typesetting the musical examples; and to Jennifer Hill, Suzanne Robinson and Paul Watt for proof-reading and moral support. I would like to thank Richard Turbet for his many stimulating emails over the last eighteen months, and for generously sharing his immense knowledge of early English choral music and its revivals.

Part of Chapter 5 was originally published as ' "Enriched with the Englishman's harmony": Reading the History of Anglican Church Music' in *Context: A Journal of Music Research* 19 (2000): 73–9. Similarly, an earlier version of the discussion of the early performances of *Spem in alium* in Chapter 3 was published as ' "This mistake of a barbarous age": Performances and Perceptions of Tallis's *Spem in alium* in Nineteenth-Century England', *Context: A Journal of Music Research* 15/16 (1998): 21–31. A version of the discussion of the early score copies of the same work appeared as ' "Often seene, but seldome sung": 18th- and 19th-century manuscripts of Thomas Tallis's *Spem in alium*' in *Nineteenth-Century British Music Studies*, vol. 2, edited by Jeremy Dibble and Bennett Zon (Aldershot: Ashgate,

2002), 154–68. I am grateful to Christ Church, Oxford, for permission to reproduce part of Dean Henry Aldrich's Mus. 16; to the British Museum for permission to reproduce the Van der Gucht engraving of Tallis and Byrd, to the Royal Parks for permission to use the photographs of the Albert Memorial and to the Royal College of Music for allowing me to reproduce the handbill of the 1835 Madrigal Society Festival.

On a personal note, I wish to thank my parents, Bill and Bev Craven, for their ongoing support and for looking after the grandchildren when they still needed looking after, and my children, Thomas and Hilary, who can't really remember life without Tallis.

List of Abbreviations

EECM	Early English Church Music
TCM	Tudor Church Music

LIBRARY SIGLA

GB-Ckc	Rowe Music Library, King's College, Cambridge
GB-Cp	Peterhouse College Library, Cambridge
GB-Cpc	Pembroke College Library, Cambridge
GB-CF	Essex County Records Office, Chelmsford
GB-DRc	Cathedral Library, Durham
GB-Lbl	British Library, London
GB-Lcm	Royal College of Music, London
GB-Lgc	Gresham College Collection, Guildhall Library, London
GB-Ob	Bodleian Library, Oxford
GB-Och	Christ Church Library, Oxford
GB-WRch	St George's Chapel Archives and Chapter Library, Windsor

Introduction

IN an interview with Anna King Murdoch in the Melbourne daily newspaper *The Age*, Peter Phillips, director of the Tallis Scholars, observed that neither he himself, nor any of his singers, was a practising Christian. He explained: 'We're a professional concert-giving ensemble which happens to do sacred music. It's just very good music.'[1] He also questioned whether the composers of Renaissance sacred music were 'religious themselves', pointing out that laws against heresy would have made them think twice about admitting to atheism. He implies that his belief that music should be approached as 'just very good music' would have been shared by the composers themselves, that it represents a position that exists outside of history and was as true when the music he is discussing was first written as it is today.[2] Phillips's belief that music should be approached in purely aesthetic terms is, however, a product of what has been termed the 'project of autonomy' of the nineteenth century,[3] and of the early music movement of the twentieth, and is neither self-evident nor ideologically neutral. Despite its current widespread acceptance, it is just one of the possible stories that can be told about the music of the Renaissance and our relationship to it. In this study of the reception of Thomas Tallis and his music I wish to examine some of the other stories that have been told about the music – and especially the sacred music – of earlier eras.

The plainsong of the early Church has been configured as the wellspring of the Western European Classical Tradition,[4] leading inexorably to the symphonies of Beethoven;[5] and a quick glance through any undergraduate survey of pre-Classical

---

[1] Anna King Murdoch, 'A Vocation of Intoxication', *The Age*, 7 July 1995, 18. This interview was conducted while the Tallis Scholars were on tour in Australia.

[2] It is possibly unfair to read too much into Phillips's comments – he may simply have been trying to increase the appeal of his concerts to the largely non-church-going Australian public – but his statement does act as a succinct summary of the dominant contemporary attitude towards church music.

[3] Jim Samson, 'The Musical Work and Nineteenth-Century History', *The Cambridge History of Nineteenth-Century Music*, ed. Jim Samson (Cambridge: Cambridge University Press, 2001), 9.

[4] Leo Treitler, 'Toward a Desegregated Music Historiography', *Black Music Research Journal* 16 (1996): 3.

[5] For a discussion of the role of plainchant in construction of music history, see Leo Treitler, 'The Historiography of Music: Issues of Past and Present', *Rethinking Music*, ed. Nicholas Cook and Mark Everist (Oxford: Oxford University Press, 1999), 360.

music will show the integral role played by the music of the church in conventional histories of music. And yet the emphasis placed upon aesthetic autonomy in the nineteenth century rendered church music increasingly irrelevant to the study of music as art, even as the nascent historicism of the late eighteenth and nineteenth centuries led to a renewed interest in the music of the past.

A blunt statement of the inherent incompatibility between church music and 'art' in the Victorian era is found in Nicholas Temperley's *The Lost Chord*:

> sooner or later it becomes necessary to deal with the music itself: to evaluate Victorian music as art. Naturally this side of the matter is concerned with art music. Popular and functional music, almost by definition, do not invite critical evaluation; instead they are judged by their popularity or their functional utility, as the case may be.

In a footnote he defines functional music as 'designed as an accompaniment to other activity such as dancing, marching, or worship'; art music, on the other hand, is 'composed [...] for a restricted population that will accept intellectual challenge on the basis of its familiarity with a body of established classics'.[6] The problematic nature of this distinction with respect to church music is highlighted in the volume of the Music in Britain series dedicated to *The Romantic Age*, also edited by Temperley. It is divided into three parts: 'Music in Society'; 'Popular and Functional Music'; and 'Art Music'. Two chapters are dedicated to church music: 'Parochial and Nonconformist Church Music' is relegated to the second section, while 'Cathedral Music' is in the third. Temperley justifies this decision by acknowledging in the introduction that 'Cathedral music, though strictly speaking only an accompaniment to worship, had for long been treated as an artistic performance'.[7] Even more curiously, Temperley begins the 'Cathedral Music' chapter with the note that 'As it is often impossible to distinguish cathedral and parochial music in this period, all liturgical music for trained and rehearsed choirs is covered in the present chapter'.[8]

---

[6] Nicholas Temperley, *The Lost Chord* (Bloomington, IL: Indiana University Press, 1989), 5. As scholars such as William Weber have shown, however, the concept of the 'body of established classics' is itself an historical phenomenon: see, for example, William Weber, *The Rise of Musical Classics in Eighteenth-Century England* (Oxford: Clarendon, 1992).

[7] Nicholas Temperley, ed., *Music in Britain: The Romantic Age, 1800–1914*, Athlone History of Music in Britain 5 (London: Athlone, 1981), 4.

[8] Temperley, *Romantic Age*, 172. It would appear that Temperley's distinction between 'parish and non-conformist' and 'cathedral' music therefore has more to do with issues of class and institutional power, or perhaps even musical complexity, than with function.

The borders between church music and art are obviously not easily defined. The complexities of musical practice resist Temperley's taxonomy.

Such taxonomies, however, serve a powerful evaluative function. Lydia Goehr spells out just what is at stake in her influential book, *The Imaginary Museum of Musical Works*:[9]

> since 1800, serious music has come to be known as classical music and to be packaged in terms of works. The easy connection thus provides a pre-scription: to be a serious musician one creates or performs works. [...] The result is that serious, classical, and 'work' music have come to be equated and, together, have come to be accorded the highest status possible [...] in European musical culture.[10]

Elsewhere, in a discussion of the impact of institutionalisation and aestheticisation upon classical music, she wrestles with the terminological dilemma of how to describe the precise sphere of musical activity that is the subject of her discussion; she defines 'classical music' as 'what we nowadays include under opus, concert hall, or "serious" music'.[11] By the twentieth century the concert hall and the recording studio had become the primary loci of serious musical activity.[12] Yet at the same time that composition for the church was increasingly being excluded from the realm of serious music, the sacred music of earlier eras was being rediscovered as a result of the twentieth-century early music movement:[13] it could not simply be ignored. In order to be taken seriously, the sacred music upon which the history of the Western European Classical Tradition is built had to be distanced from its liturgical function and approached as an autonomous musical work.

The process whereby the aesthetic function came to dominate all others in the practice of serious music is at the heart of *The Imaginary Museum of Musical Works*. Goehr's 'central claim' is that, sometime around 1800, the concept of the musical

---

9 Lydia Goehr, *The Imaginary Museum of Musical Works* (Oxford: Clarendon, 1992).

10 Goehr, *Imaginary Museum*, 121.

11 Lydia Goehr, 'Writing Music History', *History and Theory* 31 (1992): 191, n. 18. For a thoughtful discussion of the use of the term 'serious music' to described music 'worthy of consideration as an essential part of human cultivation', see James Garratt's review of David Gramit's *Cultivating Music* in *Music & Letters* 85 (2004): 441–2.

12 J. Peter Burkholder argues that the primary role of recordings and broadcast is to 'extend the public concert to a wider and ever more privatized audience' ('Museum Pieces: The Historicist Mainstream in Music of the Last Hundred Years', *Journal of Musicology* 2 (1983): 116, n. 1).

13 The Tallis Scholars, for example, perform only sacred music (for details of their recordings, see <http://www.gimell.com/>).

work assumed a regulative role in musical practice, and that those involved in the production and discussion of music began to treat 'the activity of producing music as one primarily involving the composition and performance of works'.[14] These works are enduring products, comparable to other works of fine art, the value of which is not dependent upon any extra-musical function but upon purely musical criteria.

Goehr's work-concept is an open concept, that is, it is not defined by 'exact and complete' definitions,[15] but is characterised by what Goehr terms 'paradigm examples',[16] Beethoven's Fifth Symphony being the paradigm example *par excellence*.[17] Even though we may not be able to define exactly what we mean by a musical work, there is a collective agreement that a Beethoven symphony is a good example of one. Almost by definition, this allows for the existence of non-paradigmatic or derivative examples: examples that do not typify the concept, or that have less 'conceptual proximity' with work music, but may still be 'brought to fall under a concept by a user of that concept'.[18] For derivative examples, therefore, work-status is not an essential quality of a piece of music, but rather something that it acquires through practice. Just as quantum physics has shown that electrons or photons can be seen as either particles or waves, depending upon the questions asked of them by an observer, so the work-status of non-paradigmatic music is contingent upon the way in which it is approached. Hence the question is not so much 'Does this piece of music have features that qualify it for the status of work?', but rather 'Was it perceived (or perhaps packaged), at a certain point in time or in a particular context, as a work?' As the title of Goehr's book suggests, the creation of an 'imaginary museum of musical works'[19] was an essential part of the process of packaging music as works. In such a museum, by 'estranging the work of art from its original external function so that its artness would now be found within itself', it was stripped of 'local, historical and worldly origins', so that only 'its aesthetic properties' would remain.[20] Peter Phillips's comments function in

[14] Goehr, *Imaginary Museum*, 113.

[15] Goehr, *Imaginary Museum*, 92.

[16] Goehr, *Imaginary Museum*, 96. Elsewhere she substitutes the term 'original' example (254, esp. n. 23).

[17] See Lydia Goehr, '"On the Problems of Dating" or "Looking Backward and Forward with Strohm"', *The Musical Work: Reality or Invention*, ed. Michael Talbot, Liverpool Music Symposium 1 (Liverpool: Liverpool University Press, 2000), 243.

[18] Goehr, *Imaginary Museum*, 255–6.

[19] The idea of the 'imaginary museum of art' comes from Carl Dahlhaus, *Foundations of Music History*, trans. J. B. Robinson (Cambridge: Cambridge University Press, 1983), 25.

[20] Goehr, *Imaginary Museum*, 173.

exactly this way: the sacred music of the Renaissance has been framed and hung in the imaginary museum of the modern concert hall. Temperley attempts to make the same distinction – that in order for music to be art, it must be divorced from function – but his tangled taxonomy suggests that in the nineteenth century, the transition from the church (or perhaps the cathedral) to the concert hall was not yet complete, and it is this transition that is the subject of this study.

Hans Robert Jauss has observed that:

> The development of a theory not infrequently has an unrecognised or essentially unreflected dependency on the kind and the limitations of the object through which the theory is to be exemplified or to which it is applied.[21]

The dependency of Goehr's theory on the identification of the symphonies of Beethoven as paradigmatic of 'the contemporary practice of concert-hall music' is neither unreflected nor unrecognised,[22] but her choice of example has, nonetheless, been the subject of criticism.[23] Willem Erauw, for example, argues that despite Goehr's 'discontent with conceptual imperialism', her preoccupation with symphonic music and neglect of opera show signs of the very imperialism she is attempting to critique.[24]

---

[21] Hans Robert Jauss, 'Theory of Genres of Medieval Literature', *Toward an Aesthetic of Reception*, trans. Timothy Bahti, intro. Paul de Man, Theory and History of Literature 2 (Minneapolis: University of Minnesota Press, 1982), 76. Leo Treitler also discusses the importance of the choice of examples in discussions of the ontology of the musical work, and examines several pieces by Chopin that fall within 'the tradition of Western art music during the period of common practice' yet form 'exceptions to the rules operating under the 19th-century work concept' ('History and Ontology of the Musical Work', *Journal of Aesthetics and Art Criticism* 51 (1993): 484–6).

[22] Goehr discusses the reasons for this choice at some length in 'Problems of Dating', 242–3.

[23] Much of the criticism of Goehr's work has revolved around the question of whether Bach did or did not compose works (see, for example, Harry White, '"If It's Baroque, Don't Fix It": Reflections on Lydia Goehr's "Work-Concept" and the Historical Integrity of Musical Composition', *Acta Musicologica* 69 (1997): 94–104). Goehr identifies Dahlhaus's discussion of the late eighteenth-century emergence of the work-concept as a stimulus to her thinking ('Problems of Dating', 234), but whereas Goehr takes the symphonies of Beethoven as her paradigm, Dahlhaus repeatedly assigns this role to Bach (see, for example, *Foundations of Music History*, 10 and 28, *Nineteenth-Century Music*, trans. J. Bradford Robinson (Berkeley: University of California Press, 1989), 31). The different choice of examples results in a subtly different theoretical position, and it is interesting that this is the exact area that is the locus of criticism of Goehr's work.

[24] Willem Erauw, 'Canon Formation: Some More Reflections on Lydia Goehr's Imaginary Museum of Musical Works', *Acta Musicologica* 70 (1998): 111.

In this book I wish to explore questions of autonomy, function, historiography and reception similar to those raised by Goehr, but via the study of music that lies at a considerable conceptual distance from the 'Beethoven paradigm' – the music of Thomas Tallis.[25] Tallis occupied a position of power and privilege at the centre of English musical culture at a time that has long been regarded as a golden age, and his music is still highly regarded, as evidenced by the very name of the Tallis Scholars.[26] Yet if the Beethoven symphony is seen as the epitome of serious work music – that is secular, instrumental, autonomous, German – Tallis's music could hardly be more different. It consists almost entirely of sacred choral music, clearly intended for church use: his keyboard music played almost no part in his reception prior to the twentieth century; the few secular choral works were comprehensively ignored; the consort music was almost completely unknown.

William Byrd, whose music in now held in particularly high esteem, may seem a more obvious choice of subject, but the very reasons for this esteem render him less suitable for my purposes. Byrd left a substantial body of less overtly functional music, including consort music and secular partsongs; Burney included *The Carman's Whistle* as an example of his keyboard music in his *General History*.[27] Furthermore, Byrd's persistence in composing music for the Roman rite with no obvious opportunities for performance appeals to the romantic ideal of the composer, true to his own artistic values in the face of external opposition. Tallis's very adaptability, his ability to weather the constant changes in religious and political climate, suggests a more workman-like approach that places him at a greater distance from the Beethoven ideal. And while Byrd may have been the subject of a certain amount of antiquarian interest in the nineteenth century, no portion of his music ever achieved the close identity with the rites of the Church of England enjoyed by Tallis's Responses during the nineteenth century.[28]

[25] The choice of Tallis as the subject of this study is not, however, meant to imply that his music was a particularly prominent part of the nineteenth-century musical landscape, even in the Church of England.

[26] The ideological implications of the use of the term 'English' rather than 'British' have been the subject of a great deal of recent discussion; see, for example, Krishan Kumar, *The Making of English National Identity* (Cambridge: Cambridge University Press, 2003), 1–17. This study rarely ventures beyond the geographical boundaries of modern England, and makes no claim to examine the broader British perspective, so the term 'English' is used throughout.

[27] Charles Burney, *A General History of Music: From the Earliest Ages to the Present Period (1776–89)*, ed. Frank Mercer, 2 vols. (London, 1935; repr. New York: Dover, 1957), 2:78–9.

[28] The Musical Antiquarian Society, for example, published editions of Byrd's five-part mass (1841), the first book of his *Cantiones Sacrae* (1842) and *Parthenia* (1848), but no music by Tallis (Richard Turbet, 'The Musical Antiquarian Society, 1840–1848',

Carl Dahlhaus has identified a 'deep gulf' that lies between 'general music histories, which habitually ignore such topics as the church hymn, the liturgy, and
the restoration of choral music, and the specialist, hermetic, historical studies
of church music';[29] my study attempts to bridge this gulf by recognising church
music as an integral part of nineteenth-century musical life. Many, although not
all, of the performances discussed in this book took place at sites of institutional
authority, such as Westminster Abbey and St Paul's Cathedral; musicians like
Henry Aldrich, William Crotch and A. H. Mann, who promoted and disseminated
Tallis's music, held positions of power and authority. By examining perceptions of
Tallis and his music in a variety of contexts, sacred and secular, public and private,
I hope to show the importance of religious and sectarian issues in shaping our
attitudes towards music that is now generally presented as 'just very good music'.

This study will therefore focus on the reception of Tallis and his music to examine perceptions of early choral music during the transitional period of the nineteenth century,[30] when the work-concept increasingly regulated musical practice,
but before the annexation of early sacred music by the 'imaginary museum' was
complete. It will focus predominantly on the half-century following the 'revival' of
musical activity in England in the 1830s and 40s identified by Temperley, Rainbow
and others,[31] but the period under examination begins somewhere around the
publication of Boyce's *Cathedral Music* in 1760 and Burney and Hawkins's *General
Histories* in the 1770s and 80s (and occasionally extends back to the early seventeenth century), and continues until the publication of Tallis's Latin polyphony
in the Tudor Church Music series in 1928. While the nineteenth century of this
project is, therefore, a long one, the earlier and later periods function more as a
prelude and postlude to the central period.

As a reception history, concerned with the 'aesthetics of reception and influence' rather than 'production and representation',[32] this study is predicated upon
the belief that, in the words of Hans Robert Jauss:

Brio 29 (1992): 17–18). For more information on the nineteenth-century reception
of Byrd's music, see my article, 'Who is the Father? Changing Perceptions of Tallis
and Byrd in Late Nineteenth-Century England', *Music & Letters* (forthcoming).

[29] Dahlhaus, *Nineteenth-Century Music*, 179.

[30] Goehr, *Imaginary Museum*, 206.

[31] Temperley, *Romantic Age*, 5, and Bernarr Rainbow, *The Choral Revival in the Anglican Church (1839–1872)* (London: Barrie & Jenkins, 1970).

[32] Hans Robert Jauss, 'Literary History as a Challenge to Literary Theory', in *Toward
an Aesthetic of Reception*, 20. Jauss's work has been identified by Mark Everist as a
'fundamental point of contact between music history and reception theory' (Everist, 'Reception Theories, Canonic Discourse, and Musical Value', in Cook and
Everist, *Rethinking Music*, 382).

A literary [musical] work is not an object that stands by itself and offers the same view to each reader [listener, performer] in each period. It is not a monument that monologically reveals its timeless essence.[33]

Jan Mukařovský, who together with Felix Vodička was a significant influence on both Jauss and Dahlhaus, provides a fuller explanation of the causes of this instability:[34]

First of all, the work of art itself is not a constant. Every shift in time, space, or social surroundings alters the existing artistic tradition through whose prism the art work is observed, and as a result of such shifts that aesthetic object also changes which in the awareness of a member of a particular collective corresponds to the material artifact – an artistic product. And even, for example, when a certain work in two chronologically separate periods is evaluated affirmatively and equally, the aesthetic object being evaluated is a different one in each case, and hence, in some sense, is a different work.[35]

This instability leads to Vodička's concept of the 'concretization' of the work, related to but distinct from Roman Ingarden's use of the same term. For Ingarden, the term refers to an individual experience of a musical work. Not only will two different performances give rise to different concretizations, but even the same performance, heard differently, whether from different positions in a concert hall by different individuals each with a unique combination of education, interest and 'emotional attitude', or even by one individual listening repeatedly to a recording, will be subject to multiple concretizations.[36] Vodička, however, in his 'The History of the Echo of Literary Works', uses the term in a more collective sense to refer

---

[33] Jauss, 'Literary History', 21.

[34] Robert C. Holub, *Reception Theory: A Critical Introduction* (New York: Methuen, 1984), 29–52, and James Hepokoski, 'The Dahlhaus Project and its Extra-Musicological Sources', *19th Century Music* 14 (1991): 231.

[35] Jan Mukařovský, *Aesthetic Function, Norm and Value as Social Facts*, trans. Mark E. Suino, Michigan Slavic Contributions (Ann Arbor: University of Michigan, 1970), 60–1. Also quoted, in a different translation, in Felix Vodička, 'The Concretization of the Literary Work: Problems in the Reception of Neruda's Works', *The Prague School: Selected Writings, 1929–1946*, ed. Peter Steiner, trans. John Burbank (Austin: University of Texas Press, 1982), 108. To one sensitised to the 'baggage' carried by the work-concept, and hence the term 'work' itself, the language used by Jauss and Mukařovský is problematic. I cannot see, however, that there is anything to suggest that music that falls outside Goehr's 'work-concept' would not be subject to this same instability.

[36] Roman Ingarden, *The Work of Music and the Problem of its Identity*, trans. Adam Czerniawski, ed. Jean G. Harrell (Berkeley: University of California Press, 1986), 12–13.

to the 'shape' of the work as an aesthetic object 'from the standpoint of the literary and esthetic perception of the period.'[37] Rather than the isolated perceptions of an individual, it is those concretizations that 'reflect the encounters between the structure of the work and the structure of the literary [musical] norms of a period' that are of interest.[38] A study of changes in concretization can therefore reveal information not only about perceptions of the work, but also about the artistic norms that formed the background of such perceptions, and is, according to Vodička, the primary task of literary (or music) history.[39] In this study I wish to examine not only the changes in shape of Tallis's works, as 'aesthetic objects', but also the degree to which the aesthetic function dominated, the degree to which this music was perceived in purely aesthetic terms.

Furthermore, it is not only the structure of the individual work that is subject to such concretization, but also larger structures, such as the author or composer.[40] Vodička differentiates two distinct aspects of the composer: the 'metonymical' composer, that is 'the unity comprised of the works of a particular author', and the psychophysical being, the flesh-and-blood person. Bruno Nettl makes essentially the same distinction between these two aspects of the composer in his 'Ethnomusicological Study of Western Culture'; he observes that, in the musical and academic culture of the West in the late twentieth century, the term 'Mozart', for example, refers primarily to 'a group of pieces'; the composer 'as a person' is a 'relatively minor form of Mozart'.[41]

Vodička justifies his ideas about the concretization of the author by observing that the 'tendency to perceive an author's works as a whole can be verified by ordinary experience.'[42] He then goes on to describe the 'spontaneous' comparison of a new work by an author with other works with which the reader is already acquainted, and claims that even a single work is sufficient to construct the author as 'a literary fact'. The importance of the composer in our current (post-1800)

---

[37] Vodička, 'The History of the Echo of Literary Works', *A Prague School Reader on Esthetics, Literary Structure, and Style*, ed. and trans. Paul L. Garvin (Washington DC: Georgetown University Press, 1964), 74.

[38] Vodička, 'Concretizations', 118.

[39] Vodička, 'History of the Echo', 79.

[40] Vodička, 'Concretizations', 123. For a further discussion of the author as structure, see Jan Mukařovský, 'On Structuralism', *Structure, Sign, and Function*, trans. and ed. John Burbank and Peter Steiner (New Haven, CT: Yale University Press, 1978), 3–16.

[41] Bruno Nettl, 'Mozart and the Ethnomusicological Study of Western Culture: An Essay in Four Movements', *Disciplining Music*, ed. Katherine Bergeron and Philip V. Bohlman (Chicago: University of Chicago Press, 1992), 140.

[42] Vodička, 'Concretizations', 124.

engagement with music has been discussed by a number of scholars: Michael Talbot, for example, notes the tendency to assimilate music 'within a frame of reference defined first and foremost by the composer'.[43] Talbot, along with Dahlhaus, Samson and others, has, however, pointed out that the role of the composer in musical practice is itself a function of history, and that it is only in the 'ordinary experience' of the last 200 years, and within the Western European Classical tradition, that music has been approached primarily in this way.[44]

My decision to approach this study via the composer therefore reflects my own position at the beginning of the twenty-first century; the degree to which the composer acted as a category of reception in the nineteenth century is one of the subjects of this study. This decision to track attitudes to a single composer over an extended period of time, rather than taking a synchronic view of a broader category such as early Anglican church composers, also allows a fresh perspective, highlighting points of generational change or unexpected stability, and bringing into clearer focus the mutual interdependence of perceptions of the composer and of the music.[45]

The significance of approaching music via the composer is to a degree masked by its commonness, but most 'composer-centred' studies are of production rather than reception. The composer is inherently implicated in production in a way that is not true of reception. I have, therefore, devoted the first two chapters to examining perceptions of the composer and their role in the reception of Tallis's music. The first chapter, which is devoted to Vodička's metonymical composer, serves the dual purpose of providing a brief overview of Tallis reception prior to the nineteenth century, and of examining the nineteenth-century reception of the portion of Tallis's music that is not discussed in detail in later chapters.

This chapter is expressly founded upon Vodička's belief that the author, or composer, is subject to concretization. The concretization of the composer is doubly unstable: at different periods, or even in different cultural contexts,[46] different

---

[43] Talbot, 'Composer-Centredness', in Talbot, *Musical Work*, 180.

[44] This constitutes the 'central claim' of Talbot's article, 'Composer-Centredness'; see also Dahlhaus, *Foundations*, 20–2; Samson, 'Musical Work', 11–12.

[45] At the beginning of this study, after looking up Tallis in the index of innumerable books to find a passing reference to 'composers such as Tallis, Byrd and Gibbons', I had assumed that the stories told about these composers were all much the same. As I progressed, however, it became apparent that a distinct and separate mythology surrounded each of these composers, and that an examination of the reception of either Gibbons or Byrd would be substantially different from this study of Tallis.

[46] Vodička notes that different concretizations can coexist at the same time, 'run[ning] parallel to one another in the literature of a given moment' ('Concretizations', 111).

works will be seen as representative of the composer's output, but the works them-selves are also unstable and subject to change. In this chapter, for example, I will show that although the Short Service – later known as the Dorian Service – played an important role in Tallis reception until well into the twentieth century, its aes-thetic 'shape' and the nature of its contribution changed substantially during the Victorian era. I will argue, however, that the concretization of Tallis as the 'Father of English Church Music', who set the standard for the music of the English lit-urgy, also influenced which works were attributed to him.

In the second chapter I examine perceptions of the psychophysical composer, that is, the composer as a flesh and blood human being. Vodička explicitly excludes this from his discussion of the concretization of the author, yet I believe that, at least for a long-dead and poorly documented individual such as Tallis, it displays a similar instability. Research may uncover new details of the composer's life,[47] leading to a restructuring of the biography, but the weight assigned to various bio-graphical details in different historical contexts and the importance of the figure of the composer in the reception of the music will also be subject to change.[48] Although Nettl considers this aspect of the composer to be secondary, he shows that myths or stories about the composer-as-a-person nevertheless influence per-ceptions of their music and can provide insight into the 'values of our musical culture'.[49]

The next two chapters are devoted to a closer examination of the reception of individual pieces of music: *Spem in alium* and the Preces and Responses. These two works form an almost perfect set of opposites, not only in terms of size, func-tion and complexity, but also in terms of the theoretical issues raised by their reception. They were not, however, chosen because of their conceptual symmetry, but because they emerge from the nineteenth-century sources as the primary sites around which interest in Tallis and his music was configured.

Spem in alium, of all Tallis's music, would seem to have the most 'conceptual proximity' to work music. Its immense size and obscure text taken from a pre-Reformation Matins responsory,[50] with no obvious relevance to the liturgies of the Victorian Church, render it the most autonomous of Tallis's works, and yet

---

47 For example, Tallis's association with Waltham Abbey was first published in 1876 (William H. Cummings, 'Tallis – Waltham Abbey', *Musical Times* 17 (1876): 649–50).

48 Dahlhaus, for example, argues that during the eighteenth and nineteenth centu-ries, the 'artistic persona' of the composer was the underlying 'aesthetic premise' of music history (*Foundations of Music History*, 20ff).

49 Nettl, 'Ethnomusicological Study', 141, 145.

50 See Denis Stevens, 'A Songe of Fortie Partes, Made by Mr. Tallys', *Early Music* 10 (1982): 178.

nineteenth-century critics harboured serious doubts about its status as a 'work of interest or entertainment'. The doubts about the aesthetic validity of *Spem in alium* were such that for roughly 200 years it appears not to have been performed at all, raising questions about whether, during this period, it can be considered to have had anything other than an 'historical existence'.[51] The fourth chapter examines the performance history of this work, from the earliest recorded performance in 1610 to its revival in the mid-nineteenth century. It also looks at the manuscript copies made over the same period, and their relationship – or lack thereof – with the known performances. The reception history of this exceptional work raises questions about the connections between scores, performances and works.[52]

The Responses, which are comprised of a few fragments of harmonised plain-song, are in contrast inherently and essentially functional, and as such are very poor candidates for workhood. Yet they were held in exceptionally high esteem in the nineteenth century, and were praised in terms strongly suggestive of work-status. A large number of editions of the Responses were published in the nineteenth century, and these editions, along with examples of the high critical esteem in which they were held, are the subject of the fourth chapter. The Responses were often described as timeless and immutable, yet a multiplicity of different versions are found in the nineteenth-century editions, and the disjunction between the reception of this music and the lack of unanimity in the sources raises a number of questions.

In the final chapter I will attempt to provide at least a partial answer as to why this relatively insubstantial music was so popular by examining the meanings that were attached to Tallis's liturgical music, particularly the Litany and Responses, and the stories that were told about it. I begin by tracing some of the music-historical narratives that were mapped onto the Responses, and then examine the tropes of purity and corruption that surrounded the music of Tallis, and of Elizabethan music in general. I finish with a brief examination of new narratives of the history of English church that began to emerge around the turn of the twentieth century, and their relationship to the rediscovery of the music of the pre-Reformation English church.

---

[51] This question was raised explicitly in reviews of a performance in 1845: see *Spectator*, 7 Jun 1845, 546, and 'Exeter Hall', *The Times*, 5 Jun 1845, 6.

[52] The relationship between scores and performances features prominently in discussions of the ontology of the musical work. Roman Ingarden, for example, dedicates chapters of *The Work of Music* to 'the Musical Work and Its Performance' and 'The Musical Work and Its Score'.

CHAPTER 1

'It is here that we must look for Tallis': Tallis's music

IN the course of this book I will examine many different pieces of music: music that ranges from simple harmonisations of plainsong to the pinnacle of technical complexity; that was performed by farm labourers and 'country boys in frocks',[1] and in the Chapel Royal and at the creations of Princes; that was published in elaborately bound volumes selling for many pounds and in single sheets costing only pennies; that was attributed to Tallis, written by Tallis, and written about Tallis. The one thing that unifies these disparate musical phenomena into an entity that could be considered a valid subject for investigation is the over-arching figure of the composer. To someone immersed in the musical and academic culture of the West in the early twenty-first century (characterised by Bruno Nettl as a 'denizen of the Music Building'), this may seem to be an unremarkable way of approaching music, but as Nettl points out in his 'Ethnomusicological Study of Western Culture', the current musicological primacy of the composer is neither universal nor self-evident.[2] Michael Talbot has argued that the change in status of the composer is one of the most important that took place in the musical practice of Western Europe around the turn of the nineteenth century, giving rise, in response to Lydia Goehr, to his own 'central claim':

> between 1780 and 1820, approximately, a genre-centred and performer-centred practice became a composer-centred one. Ordinary music-lovers in their mass […] began to 'sort' music in their minds primarily according to composer, and not, as previously, according to genre […] or performer.[3]

[1] A review of a performance of *If ye love me* at a lecture on Church Music at Maidstone, given by a Mr Dawson, argued that 'if compositions such as these can be sung with taste and precision by country boys in frocks, we ought in all reason to hear no more of the *impossibility* of a reform' (William Dawson, 'Church Music in Kent', *Parish Choir* 1 (1847): 124) [all emphases are original, unless stated otherwise]. Bernarr Rainbow also describes Frederick Helmore teaching Tallis to 'about a dozen hearty looking men in round [smock] frocks, and half a dozen boys' at East Farleigh (*Choral Revival*, 118–19).

[2] Nettl, 'Ethnomusicological Study', 142. Also implicit within this approach is the privileging of works over practice in the study of music (see Samson, 'Musical Work', 24).

[3] Talbot, 'Composer-Centredness', 172. Talbot states that his 'central claim' is complementary, rather than antagonistic to Goehr's.

In such a composer-centred practice, individual works become 'one piece of the jigsaw that we assemble in our minds as part of our quest to arrive at the fullest possible picture of [...] the composer of genius'. If each work is a piece of the jigsaw puzzle, Talbot argues, then the 'completed jigsaw represents a composer's œuvre.'[4] This is similar to Vodička's theory of the concretization of the composer, but Talbot implies that there is, in the way of jigsaw puzzles, a fixed number of unchanging pieces that always come together to form a single, unchanging 'picture' of the composer.[5] Vodička's theory of concretisations, however, leads to an ever-changing series of pictures (becoming, as Thomas Sipe has observed, something like a motion picture),[6] each constructed from a different set of pieces whose shapes are also subject to change. The metaphor of the collage or the mosaic would be more appropriate here: the pieces from which the picture is composed, the size, prominence and arrangement of the pieces in relation to each other, will change with every new concretization.

The first half of this chapter will explore, in the very broadest terms, the changing concretizations of the 'metonymical' Tallis from the seventeenth to the nineteenth centuries. This will serve as a brief overview of the reception history of his music prior to the late eighteenth century, to fill us in, so to speak, on the 'story so far'. I will do little more than identify the pieces (in both sense of the term) that were considered representative of Tallis at different times. This overview provides little sense of the 'shape' of any of these individual pieces, partly due to lack of evidence, but also because this chapter is primarily an attempt to look at the reception history of Tallis through the lens of nineteenth-century attitudes to him. Particular attention will therefore be paid to events and opinions that were significant to the nineteenth-century understanding of Tallis. No doubt a different picture of these earlier concretizations of Tallis would result if they were the primary focus of the study.[7] I do not wish to suggest that this music was necessarily 'sorted' by

---

4 Talbot, 'Composer-Centredness', 180–1.

5 The suggestions that there is one 'correct' result that is implied by the metaphor of the jigsaw puzzle can itself be seen as part of the culture of Nettl's 'Music Building'. Even leaving aside the possibility of the discovery of new pieces, such as Janice B. Stockigt's recent unearthing of a previously unknown *Dixit Dominus* by Vivaldi (see Janice B. Stockigt and Michael Talbot, 'Two More New Vivaldi Finds in Dresden', *Eighteenth-Century Music* 3 (2006): 35–61), the weight assigned to individual works changes over time.

6 Thomas Sipe, 'Interpreting Beethoven: History, Aesthetics, and Critical Reception', PhD diss., University of Pennsylvania, 1992, 2.

7 The selective nature of this study of the pre-nineteenth-century reception at least partially attempts to meet Dahlhaus's criterion of selecting documents based on their role 'in the creation of what was later to be accepted and dutifully handed down as the verdict of "History"' (*Foundations of Music History*, 161).

composer in the way that I have done here; this represents a clear case of the impo-
sition of my composer-centred perspective onto the historical subject.[8]

The second half of the chapter will examine in rather more detail the dominant nineteenth-century concretization of Tallis as the 'Father of English Church
Music', paying particular attention to the music that is not discussed in more detail
in later chapters, but also introducing many works, people and events that will.

❧ Tallis's Music before the Nineteenth Century

RELATIVELY few documents of reception survive from the sixteenth and
seventeenth centuries. The eighteenth century saw a gradual increase in published essays and histories, and in the nineteenth century, records of performances
became reasonably widely available with the rise of journals such as the *Musical Times* and the *Parish Choir*, but before this the main documents of reception
are the surviving copies of the music. The bulk of the following discussion will,
therefore, be based upon musical sources, primarily those listed in Hofman and
Morehen's *Latin Music in British Sources, c. 1485–1610* and Daniel and Le Huray's
The Sources of English Church Music, 1549–1660,[9] although this methodology is
not without its problems. These lists provide an invaluable starting point, but were
prepared with the editor rather than the reception historian in mind. Priority is
therefore given to early or unique sources, and their coverage of later sources is
far from complete. Furthermore, the surviving copies of church music have been
described as 'only the tip of a fairly large iceberg, much of which has, alas, melted
away during the last three centuries',[10] and we should assume that the copies that
survive represent only a relatively small proportion of those made, particularly
before the iconoclastic ravages of the mid-seventeenth century.

Unless each individual source is scrutinised with a thoroughness beyond the
scope of the present study, it is also difficult or impossible to distinguish the different types of sources: those held in private hands, those associated with choral
foundations, copies intended for regular performance or those made by the collector. John Milsom undertakes just such an examination of late sixteenth- and early
seventeenth-century British sources of Latin liturgical music in his 'Sacred Songs

---

[8] See Samson, 'Musical Work', 12–13.

[9] May Hofman and John Morehen, *Latin Music in British Sources, c. 1485–1610*
(London: Stainer & Bell, 1987); Ralph T. Daniel and Peter le Huray, *The Sources of
English Church Music, 1549–1660*, Early English Church Music Sup. vols. 1/1 and 1/2
(London: Stainer & Bell, 1972).

[10] Clifford Mould, *The Musical Manuscripts of St George's Chapel, Windsor Castle:
A Descriptive Catalogue* (Windsor: Oxley, 1973), v, cited in Percy M. Young, 'Music
in English Cathedral Libraries', *Fontes Artis Musicae* 36 (1989): 252.

Table 1 Motets by Tallis published in the *Cantiones sacrae* of 1575

Title	Voices	English versions (with earliest source of adaptation)
Salvator mundi I	5	Arise, O Lord and hear (mid-17th C; GB-DRc MS A3)
		With all our hearts (late 16th C; GB-Lbl Add. 30480–4)
Absterge domine	5	Wipe away my sins (1570; GB-Ckc MS 316)
		Discomfit them, O Lord (1580; GB-Lbl Add. 22597)
		O God, be merciful (1635; GB-Cp MS 35–44)
		Forgive me, Lord, my sin (1650; GB-Lbl Harl. 4142);
		I look for the Lord (recomposed Aldrich: all in GB-Och Mus. 16.)
		I will magnify thee (Aldrich recomposed)
In manus tuas domine	5	O pray for the peace of Jerusalem (recomposed Aldrich)
Mihi autem nimis	5	Blessed be thy name (1590)
		Great and marvellous (1843; Motet Society)
O nata lux de lumine	5	O pray for the peace of Jerusalem (recomposed Aldrich)
O sacrum convivium	5	I Call and Cry (late 16th C; GB-CF MS D/DP.z6/2)
		O sacred and holy banquet (1616; GB-Lbl Add. 29372)
Derelinquat impius	5	
(Dum transisset) Sabbatum	5	
(Honor) virtus et potestas	5	
(Sermone blando) Illae dum pergunt concitae	5	
(Te lucis) Procul recedant somnia (2 parts)	5	
Salvator mundi II	5	When Jesus went (late 16th C; GB-Lbl Add. 30480–4)
Candidi facti sunt	5	
In ieiunio et fletu	5	
Suscipe quaeso domine (2 parts)	7	
Miserere nostri	7	

of the Chamber', and the richness and depth of his study highlight the dangers of drawing overly simplistic conclusions from undifferentiated sources.[11] I am not, however, attempting a source study, but rather to identify those works which were seen as representative of Tallis at a particular time, or whose 'echo' was significant to subsequent generations, and I believe that such broad goals may be achieved by a careful analysis of even incomplete lists of sources.

As will be discussed in the following chapter, we know relatively little about Tallis's biography, but one of the few recorded events in his life had a substantial effect upon the subsequent reception of his music: the publication, with Byrd, of the *Cantiones quae ab argumento sacrae vocantur* (generally known as *Cantiones sacrae*) in 1575. The granting of the Elizabethan printing monopoly to Byrd and Tallis features prominently in almost all biographies of Tallis; the *Cantiones sacrae* was the first publication produced under the monopoly, and the letters-patent were reproduced at the end of the volume.[12] The *Cantiones sacrae* comprised seventeen works each by Tallis and Byrd (although some of these works are really subsections of larger works): see Table 1 for the works composed by Tallis, in the order in which they appear in the publication.

The act of publication at this early date lent weight to the music contained within it, but this publication was particularly heavy with markers of authority and royal privilege. The music was preceded by an ornate title page; a verse on English music (*De Anglorum musica*); a dedication to the Queen; the printer Vautrollier's crest; and two 'commendatory verses',[13] one by Richard Mulcaster and the other by Ferdinand Richardson, all in Latin.[14] Milsom argues:

[11] John Milsom, 'Sacred Songs in the Chamber', *English Choral Practice, 1400–1650*, ed. John Morehen, Cambridge Studies in Performance Practice 5 (Cambridge: Cambridge University Press, 1995), 161–79.

[12] For a detailed discussion of the patent and its commercial implications, see Iain Fenlon and John Milsom, '"Ruled Paper Imprinted": Music Paper and Patents in Sixteenth-Century England', *Journal of the American Musicological Society* 107 (1984): 139–63. For a discussion of differences between the surviving print copies of this publication, see John Milsom, 'Incorrected Copy' (appendix to the article). Milsom's minute discussion of the differences between the surviving copies, while appearing to fall squarely within the category of the positivistic source study, manages to evoke a clear sense of the flesh and blood Tallis, scrupulously overseeing his publication. This invocation of the composer is ironically reinforced by the device of beginning the article with reference to Batt's 'portrait' of Byrd in the *Oxford Companion to Music* (p. 348); the role of portraits in constructing the figure of the composer will be examined further in the next chapter.

[13] Hawkins, *A General History of the Science and Practice of Music (1776)*, intro. Charles Cudworth, 2 vols. (1853; repr. Dover: New York, 1963), 456.

[14] *Cantiones quae ab argumento sacrae vocantur (1575)*, 6 vols. (Leeds: Boethius Press, 1976). The sexta part has an additional prefatory page with a Latin motto.

The proud, sometimes even defiantly belligerent tone of its prefatory material suggests that it was published not only to the glory of Tallis and Byrd
but also to the glory of English music, even to the glory of Elizabeth herself,
through whose patronage publication of the book was made possible [...][15]

In this additional material, Tallis and Byrd not only reinforce their privileged position as recipients of Elizabeth's royal favour, but also establish their claim, which
became extremely important in their reception by later generations, to be the pro-
genitors of English music.[16] Metaphorical references to parenthood and childbirth
run right through the prefatory material.

The composers are referred to as the offspring of 'Our England';[17] they in turn
call the music in the collection their 'offspring', and ask the Queen to protect it.[18]
This procreative metaphor is developed, somewhat unexpectedly, in the brief verse
that follows the last motet:

> THE AUTHORS OF THE SONGS TO THE READER
>
> Like the woman still weak from childbirth who entrusts her infant to the
> care of the faithful wetnurse, we thus commend these firstborn [songs] to
> you, friendly reader, for your esteem will be their milk. Supported by this
> they will dare to promise a great harvest; if unfruitful, they will fall by an
> honourable sickle.[19]

For translations and a detailed discussion of the prefaces, see Craig Monson's
introduction to the *Cantiones Sacrae (1575)*, Byrd Edition, vol. 1 (London: Stainer
& Bell, 1977).

[15] Milsom, 'Incorrected Copy', 359–60.

[16] The title frequently bestowed upon Tallis of 'Father of English Church Music' will
be discussed further below. Byrd was described, after his death, as a 'ffather of
musick' (Andrew Ashbee and John Harley, trans. and ed., *The Cheque Books of the
Chapel Royal: With Additional Material from the Manuscripts of William Lovegrove
and Marmaduke Alford*, vol. 1 (Aldershot: Ashgate, 2000), 30); this title was used
by William Barclay Squire for a series of articles about Byrd ('A Father of Music',
Musical Review 1 (1883): 299–300, 317–18, 331–2).

[17] 'Tallisium, Birdumq[ue], duces iam nacta lubenter, Quae peperit, patitur pignora
luce frui ...' Translated as 'But now, gladly having found leaders in Tallis and
Byrd whom she bore, she permits her offspring to enjoy the light ...' in Monson,
Cantiones Sacrae, xxvi.

[18] 'quae prolem hanc nostram [...] tueare'. Translation in Monson, *Cantiones Sacrae*,
xxv.

[19] 'AUTORES CANTIONUM AD LECTOREM./ Has tibi primitias sic commendamus,
amice/ Lector, ut infantem depositura suum/ Nutricis fidei vix firma puerpera
credit,/ Queis pro lacte tuae gratia frontis erit./ Hac etenim fretae, magnam
promittere messem./ Audebunt, cassae, falcis honore cadent.' Translation in
Monson, *Cantiones Sacrae*, xxvii.

The verse 'De Anglorum Musica' concludes with the claim that British music has declared Tallis and Byrd to be her parents [*parentes*].[20] The title of this publication, 'Songs which from their argument are called sacred', as Monson, Milsom and others have noted, indicates that the music was not intended primarily for liturgical use, and that the known holders of this publication were individuals and collectors, rather than choral foundations.[21] Tallis and Byrd were not, therefore, describing themselves as the Fathers of English church music in quite the way of subsequent generations, but they were presenting themselves as the fathers (or even mothers) of both the particular works contained within it, and of English music in general.

This publication appears to have been put together as a 'showpiece' by Tallis and Byrd[22] – Milsom describes the painstaking care and expense that the composers poured into it[23] – and there is a sense in which they used it to construct an image of themselves and their music to present to the world. Its echoes reverberated through the reception of their music for at least 200 years.

An early reference to the *Cantiones sacrae* is found in 1636, in Charles Butler's treatise, *The Principles of Musik*.[24] As Hawkins notes:

> Charles Butler, of Oxford, a man of great learning, and known to the world by his attempts to reform the English orthography, commends 'Absterge Domine', the second of the Cantiones Sacrae of Tallis, in the highest terms, and makes use of the authority of it for several purposes.[25]

Butler not only draws on the authority of *Absterge*, but of the whole collection. In his discussion of the 'Setting of the Song', *Absterge* is used as an example of counterpoint where each voice enters separately on the same point of imitation (a music example is also provided),[26] as opposed to all entering together, as in the '8th Motet of Mr Tallis', which would appear to be *Dum transisset Sabbatum*, the eighth motet by Tallis in the *Cantiones sacrae*. *Absterge Domine* is also described at length in the section 'Of Formaliti'.[27] Butler's identification of the motets in terms of their position in the 1575 publication suggests that he was physically referring

[20] 'Tallisium, Birdumque suos testata parentes/ Audacter quo non ore canenda venit.' Translation in Monson, *Cantiones Sacrae*, xxv.

[21] Milsom, 'Sacred Songs', 177, and Monson, *Cantiones Sacrae*, vii.

[22] Milsom, 'Sacred Songs', 176.

[23] Milsom, 'Incorrected Copy', 358–9.

[24] Charles Butler, *The Principles of Musik* (1636; repr. Amsterdam: Da Capo, 1970).

[25] Hawkins, *General History*, 456.

[26] Butler, *Principles of Musik*, 91–2.

[27] Butler, *Principles of Musik*, 85.

to the partbooks in the preparation of his treatise, as does his reference to 'Tallises and Bird's *Cantiones Sacrae*' for examples of motets, 'specially of the Lydian mood' with more than four parts.[28] It also suggests that he expected his readers to be familiar with the contents of this publication. Cristle Collins Judd has identified the tendency of sixteenth-century Continental writers and theorists to select musical examples from printed sources, and Butler appears to be using the *Cantiones sacrae* in a similar manner.[29]

Tallis's music continued to be copied, collected and performed in the half-century after his death, and many manuscript sources of both the Latin and English works survive from the period between his death and the Civil Wars in the mid-seventeenth century.[30] The number of Latin sources tends to undermine the assumption of later writers that there were no opportunities for the performance of music with Latin texts after the Reformation. While some of the sources containing Latin motets, such as Tenbury St Michael's MSS 341–4 (now held in the Bodleian Library) and British Library Add. MSS 41156–8, are associated with prominent Catholics such as Edward Paston, Milsom notes that some non-Catholics also acted as 'diligent protectors of threatened Catholic repertories'.[31] Although the motets from the *Cantiones sacrae* continued to be transmitted in Latin and performed in domestic settings, English versions of several of these motets became increasingly common and completely replaced the Latin versions in sources associated with church choirs.[32] As the seventeenth century progressed the number of Latin sources dwindled, but prior to the cataclysmic events of the 1640s a wide range of Tallis's music survived in manuscript form.

In 1641 a second publication that was to have a profound impact upon Tallis's later reception was produced: John Barnard's *The First Book of Selected Church Musick*.[33] This collection comprised services and anthems with English texts by composers such as Byrd, Gibbons, Parsons and Mundy, beginning with Tallis's

---

[28] Butler, *Principles of Musik*, 40–1. He mentions particularly Tallis's seven-part *Miserere* and Byrd's *Deliges Dominum* in eight parts.

[29] Cristle Collins Judd, *Reading Renaissance Music Theory* (Cambridge: Cambridge University Press, 2000), 31. One of the reasons for using printed sources was that the reader was more likely to have a copy at hand which could be consulted while reading the treatise (see quote from Pietro Aron's *Toscanello* on p. 37).

[30] The relative longevity of polyphonic church music in England, and Europe generally, is discussed by Weber, *Rise of Musical Classics*, 23–6.

[31] Milsom, 'Sacred Songs', 173–4.

[32] Milsom, 'Sacred Songs', 177.

[33] John Barnard, *Selected Church Musick ... (1641)*, 10 vols. (Farnborough: Gregg, 1972). Barnard, a minor canon at St Paul's Cathedral, London, was one of the few people involved in the early reception of Tallis who was not associated with Oxford.

Table 2 Works by Tallis contained in Barnard's *Selected Church Musick*

Title	Latin version	Cantiones sacrae
Short (Dorian) Service		
Preces, Responses, Litany and Psalms		
Blessed be thy name	*Mihi autem nimis*	✓
O Lord, give thy Holy Spirit		
I call and cry	*O sacrum convivium*	✓
Wipe away my sins	*Absterge Domine*	✓
With all our hearts	*Salvator mundi I*	✓

Short Service. The title page shows that Barnard's collection was intended primarily for liturgical use:

> The First Book of Selected Church Musick, Consisting of Services and Anthems, such as are now used in the Cathedrall, and Collegiat Churches of this Kingdome [...] Whereby such Bookes as were heretofore with much difficulty and charges, transcribed for the use of the Quire, are now to the saving of much Labour and expence, publisht for the generall good of all such as shall desire them either for publick or private exercise.

The publication was dedicated to Charles I, a bold political statement at the time. The anthems by Tallis (see Table 2) were all English adaptations of works from the *Cantiones sacrae*, with the exception of *O Lord, give thy Holy Spirit*. These adaptations all date from the mid- to late sixteenth century – some may have been originally composed in English[34] – and had been copied frequently in the decades preceding Barnard's publication. While there is no evidence to attribute their popularity directly to the 1575 publication, the correspondence is suggestive. It was from these few anthems and the Dorian Service that the 'metonymical' Tallis was constructed for at least the next century and a half.

Barnard's dedication explains that the purpose of the collection, 'a safe bundle of perpetual memory consecrated to your Majestie's glorious patronage', was to protect 'the choycest Master-pieces left us in Hymnes, Anthems, and Services' from 'the danger of perishing, or corrupting in erroneous and manuscript obscurity'. 1641 was indeed a dangerous time for the publication of church music, and Barnard's *Church Musick* appears not to have been distributed until the Restoration. Weber claims that even then 'only a small number of copies remained in use,

---

34 See, for example, John Milsom, 'A Tallis Fantasia', *Musical Times* 126 (1985): 658–62.

many of them incomplete',[35] but the disruption of the choral establishments in the mid-seventeenth century was dramatic, and the Restoration cathedral repertory relied heavily on old works, many of which appear to have been taken from Barnard's collection.[36] Ian Spink argues that the conservative repertoire of Barnard's collection 'provided a core round which new repertoires could be built',[37] and this claim is supported by the sources.

Henry Purcell's scorebook, Cambridge, Fitzwilliam Museum MS 88, for example, includes Tallis's *I call and cry*, one of nine full anthems copied from Barnard.[38] Robert Shay and Robert Thompson suggest that Purcell transcribed these anthems for the Chapel Royal library, some time around 1678.[39] Fitzwilliam MS 117, which Ian Spink argues recorded the repertoire of the Chapel Royal at around the same time, included the Short Service, *I call and cry*, *Wipe away my sins*, *With all our hearts* and *Blessed be thy name*.[40] A Durham Cathedral service sheet surviving from June 1680 lists performances of the Service, *I call and cry*, *Blessed be thy name* and *Arise O Lord* (a contrafactum of *Salvator mundi 1* from the *Cantiones sacrae* that appears to have been local to Durham).[41] Although Weber warns against exaggerating the impact of Barnard's publication,[42] these few works continued to be the most copied portions of Tallis's music until the end of the eighteenth century, and Barnard's goal of protecting them from obscurity appears to have been well and truly realised.

Oxford had been something of a haven for church musicians, particularly from the Chapel Royal, during the civil unrest, and the earliest and most important attempts after the Restoration to re-establish the choral tradition came from that city.[43] Henry Aldrich, who matriculated at Christ Church, Oxford, in 1662, became a canon of the cathedral in 1681 and was dean from 1689 until his death in 1710,

---

35 Weber, *Musical Classics*, 26. See also Young, 'Music in English Cathedral Libraries', 255.

36 Weber, *Musical Classics*, 26.

37 Ian Spink, *Restoration Cathedral Music, 1660–1774* (Oxford: Clarendon, 1995), 76.

38 Robert Shay has shown that Barnard was probably the direct source of Purcell's copies ('Purcell as Collector of "Ancient" Music: Fitzwilliam MS 88', in *Purcell Studies*, ed. Curtis Price (Cambridge: Cambridge University Press, 1995), 44).

39 Robert Shay and Robert Thompson, *Purcell Manuscripts: The Principal Musical Sources* (Cambridge: Cambridge University Press, 2000), 40.

40 Spink, *Restoration Cathedral Music*, 81.

41 Brian Crosby, 'A Service Sheet from June 1680', *Musical Times* 121 (1980): 399–401.

42 Weber, *Musical Classics*, 25.

43 On the importance of Oxford as 'political and intellectual stronghold' for Tories and high-church Anglicans, and Aldrich's position 'as one of the most important of Oxford's high Tories', see Weber, *Musical Classics*, 32–6.

played a pivotal role in what Weber has termed 'the learned tradition of ancient music'. Aldrich was actively involved in the music at Christ Church throughout his life, and was remembered with a great deal of respect and affection well into the nineteenth century, as a composer, musical antiquarian, collector, and, first and foremost, an arranger. The cathedral had a very large collection of early music by both English and continental composers, and Aldrich made a number of adaptations, arrangements and translations of works by composers such as Palestrina and Carissimi, which were performed well into the nineteenth century.[44] These arrangements were held in particularly high esteem: in *An Apology for Cathedral Service* (1839), to cite just one example, John Peace specifically exempts Aldrich's adaptations from his general condemnation of the use of translations of Continental music in the liturgy.[45]

Aldrich's reputation as an arranger seems to have reached quasi-mythical status by the late eighteenth century: he was also credited with many of the popular English arrangements of motets from the *Cantiones Sacrae*. Hawkins attributed the English adaptation of *O sacrum convivium* to Aldrich,[46] despite noting elsewhere that it had been published in Barnard in 1641 (seven years before Aldrich's birth), and Burney claims that 'most of these excellent compositions [the works in the *Cantiones sacrae*], of which the words were originally in Latin, were afterwards adjusted to English words by Dr. Aldrich, and others, for use of our cathedrals.'[47] William Mason, who also attributed the adaptation of *I call and cry* to Aldrich, argued that the Dean had improved upon Tallis's original, and should be commended on his taste 'in finding words more suited to the original strain than those to which they were set'.[48]

The library at Christ Church held two copies of the *Cantiones sacrae*,[49] and

---

[44] See Robert Shay, '"Naturalizing" Palestrina and Carissimi in Late Seventeenth-Century Oxford: Henry Aldrich and his Recompositions', *Music & Letters* 77 (1996): 368–400. For a discussion of Aldrich's activities as a collector, see Weber, *Musical Classics*, 34.

[45] [John Peace], *An Apology for Cathedral Service* (London: John Bohn, 1839), 11.

[46] A copy of *I call and cry* is found in the Christ Church library (*GB-Och* Mus. 1220–4).

[47] Burney, *General History*, 2:66. As recently as 1982 Craig Monson made a similar error, suggesting that Aldrich was responsible for the English adaptation of Byrd's *Ne irascaris, O Lord turn thy wrath*, which was also published by Barnard ('Authenticity and Chronology in Byrd's Church Anthems', *Journal of the American Musicological Society* 35 (1982): 303, n. 46).

[48] William Mason, 'Essays on English Church Music', *Musical Standard* 7 (1867): 207. Originally published as *Essays Historical and Critical, on English Church Music* (York, 1795).

[49] Milsom, 'Incorrected Copy', 366.

Aldrich did produce what Robert Shay has termed 'recompositions' of several works by Tallis, including two based on *Absterge Domine* (*I look for the Lord* and *I will magnify thee*), and *O pray for the peace of Jerusalem* (based on *In manus tuas* and *O nata lux*).[50] These 'recompositions', however, appear to have been little known outside Oxford.[51] Christ Church Mus. 16 also includes two versions of *All people that on earth do dwell* in Aldrich's hand: as we shall see, this anthem was one of the more popular anthems attributed to Tallis in the nineteenth century, although it is now believed to be either an original composition by Aldrich, or a reworking of an earlier model. These copies, together with a four-part arrangement for men's voices of Tallis's Litany and Responses, played an important role in Tallis's reception in the nineteenth century.[52]

Aldrich's respect for Tallis need not, however, be simply inferred from his manuscripts. Both Burney and Hawkins record that Aldrich had repaired the stone in St Alfege, Greenwich, upon which Tallis's epitaph was engraved,[53] and William Hayes, in his *Remarks on Mr Avison's Essay on Musical Expression* (1751), records

> the great Veneration which the Dean had for those [old] Masters, and their Compositions; particularly TALLIS: For he has often been heard to say, that should the World be so unfortunate to lose all the CHURCH-MUSIC, except his Anthem *I call and cry*, that alone would be sufficient to convey a just Idea of the true *Church-Style*, and would furnish future Composers with Matter and Method enough, to enable them to excel in it [...][54]

Weber claims that Aldrich built a 'corps of practitioners around a taste for old music that was to have a powerful influence in the course of the eighteenth

---

[50] Shay, '"Naturalizing" Palestrina', 389, 392.

[51] The only source apart from Aldrich's own manuscripts is *GB-Lbl* Add. 17842, in the hand of the eighteenth-century Oxford copyist William Walond.

[52] *GB-Och* Mus. 9 and 48. The various versions of the Litany and Responses will be discussed further in Chapter 4.

[53] Burney, *General History*, 2:68, and Hawkins, *General History*, 458. The stone was destroyed when the church collapsed in 1711 and was not rebuilt (*Thomas Tallis: English Sacred Music: 1 Anthems*, ed. Leonard Ellinwood, rev. Paul Doe, Early English Church Music 12, rev. ed. (London: Stainer & Bell, 1973), x).

[54] [William Hayes], *Remarks on Mr Avison's Essay on Musical Expression* (London: 1753), 106. Hayes, who was Professor of Music at Oxford from 1741, and organist at Magdalen College and the University Church, was too young to have known Aldrich personally – his source is an unnamed student of Aldrich's – so we (in the twenty-first century) are looking at the account by Hayes (in the eighteenth) of the views of Aldrich (in the seventeenth) of the music of Tallis (composed in the sixteenth).

Table 3 Works by Tallis in Tudway's collection

Title	Latin text	Barnard
Short Service, Litany and Responses		✓
I call and cry	O sacrum convivium	✓
Wipe away my sins	Absterge Domine	✓
O Lord, give thy Holy Spirit		✓
With all our hearts	Salvator mundi 1	✓
Discomfit them, O Lord	Absterge Domine	

century',[55] one of whom was Edward, Lord Harley, who had 'become devoted to' Aldrich while at Christ Church between 1707 and 1713. From 1714 to 1720 Thomas Tudway, Professor of Music and organist at King's and Pembroke Colleges, Cambridge, compiled a six-volume collection of services and anthems for his patron, Lord Harley.[56] This collection is arguably the earliest attempt at an historical survey of English music, and was known to both Burney and Hawkins.[57] Weber argues that the enthusiasm for 'ancient music' generated by Aldrich – whom Tudway referred to as the 'most ingenious, & incomparable Dr Henry Aldrich' – can be seen in this collection.[58]

The first volume begins with Tallis's Service, Litany, *I call and cry*, *Wipe away my sins*, *With all our hearts* and *O Lord, give thy Holy Spirit* – the same works that had been published by Barnard – after which is inscribed 'Here ends all ye works of Mr Tho: Tallis' (see Table 3). Later in the volume, however, a second adaptation of *Absterge Domine*, *Discomfit them*, which Tudway claimed had been performed 'On ye occasion of ye Spanish invasion in 1588', was also added. This may have come into Tudway's possession later in the process of compilation, possibly explaining the inclusion of two different adaptations of the same motet.

The historical orientation of this collection is made explicit in the extensive introductions to the volumes. Tallis is presented not just as the first composer of English church music, but as having established a standard for those who followed:

---

[55] Weber, *Musical Classics*, 34. For an analysis of Aldrich's political and music influence and his role in the Christ Church Music collection, see Weber, 33–6.

[56] *GB-Lbl* Harl. 7337–42.

[57] Weber, *Musical Classics*, 46.

[58] Quoted in Spink, *Restoration Cathedral Music*, 438; Weber, *Musical Classics*, 39–41.

The Pious Reformers of our Church, from the Errors of Popery, having
settl'd the Doctrines thereof, thought it very necessary, & advisable allso, to
appoint a standard of Church Musick which might adorn the dayly Service
of God, by such a solemn performance, as might best stir up devotion, &
Kindle in mens hearts, a warmth for devine worship.

I dare affirm my Lord, that there cou'd never have been any thing better
devis'd, than what was compos'd first of that Kind, by Mr Tallis, & Mr Bird.
[…] They were both Servants, & Organists, to her Majesty Queen Elizabeth, […] & though both of them Papists, have sett an inimitable pattern of
solemn Church musick, which no one since, has been able to come up to, &
remains to this day, a demonstration of their exalted Genius […][59]

After establishing Tallis and Byrd as the first and foremost exponents of the
'standard of Church Musick', he then goes on to identify its opposite in 'all vibra-
tive, & operose Musick; things perfectly secular'.[60] In the Preface to the second
volume he again refers to the 'Standard of Church Music, begun by Mr Tallis &
Mr Bird' and argues that most churches would have done better to have 'kept
close to the old, Grave, & solemn way' rather than attempting, unsuccessfully
due to lack of resources, to imitate the 'light, and Airy Compositions' of Charles
II.[61] Whereas Barnard was trying to preserve a repertory – Weber warns that
Barnard's use of 'the term "master-peeces" had a more literal and less ideological sense than it does today'[62] – Tudway, at least in his introductions, appears to
be moving towards defining a canon. These works are not being reproduced for
ease of performance, but are being 'authorized […] for contemplation, admiration,
interpretation, and the determination of value'.[63] Until around this time, we have
been able to do little more than identify the pieces of the jigsaw that formed the
metonymical Tallis; Tudway's introduction gives us the first glimpses of the picture
of the composer that they formed, a picture that became clearer as the century
progressed.

In 1752 John Alcock, organist at Lichfield Cathedral, advertised a proposed
publication of the 'choicest antient and modern Services', beginning with the

59 Reproduced in Christopher Hogwood, 'Thomas Tudway's History of Music',
    Music in Eighteenth-Century England: Essays in Memory of Charles Cudworth, ed.
    Christopher Hogwood and Richard Luckett (Cambridge: Cambridge University
    Press, 1983), 23.

60 Hogwood, 'Thomas Tudway's History of Music', 24.

61 Hogwood, 'Thomas Tudway's History of Music', 26.

62 Weber, *Musical Classics*, 25.

63 Joseph Kerman, 'A Few Canonic Variations', *Critical Inquiry* 10 (1983): 107. For
    more on the distinction between repertory and canon, see Kerman, 114.

'famous Mr Tallis's'.[64] The orientation of Alcock's proposal was entirely towards the performer: he claims to have decided upon publication 'Having observed how incorrect the Services, &c. are at Cathedrals' and he hoped that 'all Members of Cathedrals, and others, will encourage so useful an Undertaking.' One of the ways in which Alcock hoped to avoid the inaccuracies of the older copies was by publishing his volumes in score, a relatively novel approach at the time.[65] Alcock abandoned his plan upon hearing of a similar proposal by Maurice Greene, and sent Greene his copy of the services of Tallis, Byrd and Gibbons as a gesture of good will.[66] Greene was not to complete the project either: he died in 1755 with the collection still unpublished. He did, however, collect, copy and edit a substantial amount of music, which can be found in several manuscripts, particularly British Library Add. MS 31443. Once again, four of the five anthems published by Barnard over a century earlier can be found in this source: only *I call and cry* is omitted.[67]

Greene bequeathed his extensive library to William Boyce, who finally brought the project to fruition in 1760 with the publication of the first volume of his *Cathedral Music*. As originally proposed by Alcock, it once again begins with Tallis's Service (including the Responses and Litany), continuing the tradition established by Barnard and Tudway, but includes only one other work by Tallis, the ubiquitous *I call and cry*.

Boyce's collection was primarily practical in focus, providing what he claimed (rather optimistically) to be accurate and reliable resources for performing choirs. The title, describing it as 'A Collection in Score of the Most Valuable & Useful Compositions for [the cathedral] Service', suggests that it is merely concerned with repertoire, but in the foreword Boyce also claims that he hopes to provide some 'reputable models' of 'what has hitherto been considered as the true style and standard of such compositions'.[68]

Greene's original plan was that the publication would be produced 'at his own Expence' and would be presented to every cathedral in England.[69] In the end, Boyce's volumes were published by subscription, and the response was

---

64 The full text of the advertisement in the *London Evening-Post*, along with a comprehensive discussion of the collections of Alcock and Greene, can be found in H. Diack Johnstone's 'The Genesis of Boyce's "Cathedral Music"', *Music & Letters* 56 (1975): 29.

65 See Johnstone, 'Boyce's "Cathedral Music"', 28.

66 *GB-Lbl* Add. 23624. Johnstone, 'Boyce's "Cathedral Music"', 30.

67 Johnstone, 'Boyce's "Cathedral Music"', 34.

68 William Boyce, *Cathedral Music being a Collection in Score of the Most Valuable & Useful Compositions for that Service by the Several English Masters (1760)*, 2nd ed. (1789; London: Kraus Reprint, 1975), iii.

69 Johnstone, 'Boyce's "Cathedral Music"', 29.

disappointing; although several cathedrals subscribed to at least a few copies, it did not reach anything like all of them. The second edition published in 1788 was more successful, however, and, as the discussion of the Responses in Chapter 4 will show, the influence of Boyce's collection continued to be felt throughout the nineteenth century.

Opinions about the merits of Tallis's polyphonic anthems became increasingly polarised in the second half of the eighteenth century, in line with the broader debate between what could be termed the ancients and the moderns.[70] The anthems originally published in Barnard – and in particular *I call and cry*, which survives in a large number of seventeenth-century manuscript sources, and was published in about 1730 in William Pearson's *Divine Companion* as well as Boyce's *Cathedral Music*[71] – continued to be popular with self-consciously learned musicians such as William Hayes. Hayes, in his *Remarks on Avison's Essay on Music Expression*, not only reported Aldrich's 'great Veneration' for *I call and cry*, but also used it to defend 'ancient' music – defined as music from the 'Time of Palestrina to the Introduction of the modern Operas' – against charges of being overly attached to 'Harmony' at the expense of 'Air':

> I have been told that GEMINIANI, has been quite enraptured with the subject of *I call and cry*, an Anthem of TALLIS's; insomuch that in the utmost Extacy, he has said the Author was certainly inspired when he invented it.[72]

Hayes was an avid Handelian, and he took particular exception to Avison's claim that Geminiani (with whom Avison had studied) and Marcello were better composers than Handel.[73] In calling upon Geminiani, therefore, Hayes is drawing upon an authority respected by his opponent Avison, and suggesting that Tallis's anthem was popular even among the modern school.

Despite Hayes's efforts, however, Tallis's counterpoint did not find favour with the moderns. William Mason, identified by Howard Irving as the quintessential 'partisan for modern music and its values',[74] used *I call and cry* as an example of the inadequacies of 'ancient' music. He argued that the 'primary use of music is to

---

[70] For more on the quarrel between the advocates of ancient and modern music, see Howard Irving, *Ancients and Moderns: William Crotch and the Development of Classical Music* (Aldershot: Ashgate, 1999), esp. 3–9.

[71] *The Second Book of the Divine Companion; or, David's Harp New Tun'd* ... (London: William Pearson, 1730). See Percy Lovell, '"Ancient" Music in Eighteenth-Century England', *Music & Letters* 60 (1979): 404–6.

[72] [Hayes], *Remarks*, 45.

[73] Norris L. Stevens, 'Avison, Charles: (2) Writings', *Grove Music Online*, accessed 7 Aug 2004.

[74] Irving, *Ancients and Moderns*, 18.

please the ear, and of vocal [sic] to convey the words it is joined to in a pleasing and intelligible strain; the secondary, and yet much more essential use, is to convey sentiment and to affect the passions'. 'The old masters', he claims, 'were deficient in both these points', and Tallis would have done better to have set the text *O sacrum convivium* to 'a movement of devout exultation and thanksgiving'.[75] He concedes that the English version, which he attributes to Aldrich, is better than the original, but argues that the text is still 'almost entirely unintelligible' to the listener unless he 'peruses the words which he hears sung'. A sermon by a William Hughes published in 1763 makes a similar point considerably more strongly: Tallis, he claims, has 'sacrificed the whole Sense and meaning of the Te Deum for the Sake of his Favorite Counter-Point', which, in the interest of 'Simplicity and easy Execution', should be 'Exploded out of all Choirs'.[76]

In 1790 Samuel Arnold produced a three-volume collection intended as a supplement to Boyce, which also included Tallis's *Hear the voice and prayer* and one of the versions of *All people that on earth do dwell* found in Aldrich's manuscript, spuriously attributed to Tallis.[77] These two anthems are considerably simpler than *I call and cry* – they are only in four parts, and are shorter and largely homophonic – and as such were more suitable for the parish choir that was to become so important in the nineteenth century. Arnold's decision to include these homophonic anthems, rather than the same few five-parts anthems that had been published by Barnard, may well have reflected the new desire for 'Simplicity and easy Execution', and was a sign of things to come.

While the moderns were calling for the 'explosion' of polyphony from the choir stalls, however, the supporters of ancient music were beginning to show a new interest in the Latin music of the sixteenth and seventeenth centuries. The manuscript which Alcock passed on to Greene, British Library Add. MS 23624, contained not only the services of Tallis, Byrd and Gibbons, but also copies in score of most of the motets from the *Cantiones sacrae* in their original Latin.[78] This was one of a number of sources containing Latin works by Tallis copied around the

75 Mason, 'Essays on Church Music', 206.

76 William Hughes, *Remarks Upon Church Musick, to which are added Several Observations upon some of Mr. Handel's Oratorios and other Parts of his Works*, cited Irving, *Ancients and Moderns*, 164–5, and Christopher Dearnley, *English Church Music, 1650–1750, in Royal Chapel, Cathedral and Parish Church* (London: Barrie & Jenkins, 1970), 91.

77 Samuel Arnold, *Cathedral Music; being a Collection of Score, of the most valuable & useful Compositions for that Service by the Several English Masters of the last Two Hundred Years.* (London: 1790).

78 *GB-Lbl* Add. 23624. See Johnstone, 'Boyce's "Cathedral Music"', 28. Oddly enough, Alcock's manuscript does not contain *Absterge Domine* or *Salvator mundi 1*, but does include *O salutaris hostia*, which was not in the original publication.

mid-eighteenth century, the first to be made (or, more accurately, to survive) since the disruption of the Civil War.[79] John Awbery (a fellow of New College, Oxford, and friend of William Hayes) also scored the *Cantiones sacrae*,[80] and two other eighteenth-century manuscript copies are held in the Royal Music collection at the British Library.[81] While the motets from the 1575 publication were the most popular, other less well-known Latin works were also copied, such as *Domine quis habitabit* and *Laudate Dominum* in the collection of antiquarian Henry Needler.[82] British Library R.M.24.h.11 also contains several Latin works that had not been published in the *Cantiones sacrae*, such as *Salve intemerata virgo* and *Ave Dei patris filia*, although in many of these works only the sections in three parts were copied,[83] and three copies of the forty-part *Spem in alium* also survive from around this time.[84] Many of these eighteenth-century manuscripts were score copies of music that had previously only been available in partbooks, suggesting a type of 'translation' of the original notation to allow private study.[85]

This new scholarly interest in the less well-known portions of Tallis's output and in the original Latin versions of the music rather than the English adaptations was just one of many signs of a growing historical interest in the music of the past.

---

[79] No sources of works by Tallis with Latin texts dating from the period between the mid-seventeenth and the mid-eighteenth centuries are listed in Hofman and Morehen, *Latin Music in British Sources*.

[80] *GB-Ob* Mus. d.101. Peter Ward Jones, music librarian at the Bodleian library, has identified the scribe as Awbery (private communication, 19 April 2002), although Simon Heighes erroneously attributes it to William Hayes (*The Lives and Works of William and Philip Hayes* (New York: Garland, 1995), 19). Lovell ('"Ancient" Music', 404) claims that Henry Needler also copied the *Cantiones Sacrae*, but while *GB-Lbl* Add. 5054 and 5059 contain some of these motets, he does not appear to have copied the entire collection.

[81] *GB-Lbl* R.M.24.g.22 in score and partbooks R.M.24.f.10–5.

[82] *GB-Lbl* Add. 5058 and 5059. Needler was a talented amateur violinist and member of the Academy of Ancient Music, famous for his performances of the Corelli concertos.

[83] Milsom discusses the practice of copying only the 'verse' sections of larger works, presumably for a group with a limited number of performers, for domestic use in the early seventeenth century ('Sacred Songs in the Chamber', 172). It is hard to imagine that these fragments of relatively obscure Latin works would have been copied for the same reason in the mid-eighteenth century. It is possible that this later source may have been a copy of an earlier selection.

[84] *GB-Lbl* R.M.4.g.1; Mad.Soc.H.100; and *GB-Ob* Tenbury 1270.

[85] Judd argues that we should not underestimate the ability of early musicians accustomed to working from partbooks to 'read' a polyphonic composition from partbooks (*Reading Renaissance Music Theory*, 15). It would appear from these copies that this skill was on the decline by the middle of the eighteenth century.

Table 4 Examples by Tallis in Burney and Hawkins's *General Histories*

Hawkins	*Absterge Domine*	*Cantiones sacrae*
	Miserere nostri	*Cantiones sacrae*
	Like as the dolefull dove (App)	
Burney	*Hear the voice and prayer*	John Day, *Certaine Notes …* (London, 1560)
	Salvator mundi 1	*Cantiones sacrae*
	Derelinquit impius	*Cantiones sacrae*

The histories of Burney and Hawkins are the most obvious manifestations of this nascent historicism, and their musical examples illustrate the new perspective (see Table 4). The examples in both histories are biased towards the Latin polyphony: this is a quite different Tallis from the Tallis of Barnard and Tudway. Although the Latin examples are all taken from the *Cantiones sacrae*, *Absterge Domine* and *Salvator mundi* were known only in their English adaptations, and both *Derelinquat* and the seven-part *Miserere* would have been almost completely unknown.

This new antiquarian interest in the music of the sixteenth and seventeenth centuries was also manifest in the formation of societies for the cultivation and performance of old music, such as the Academy of Ancient Music (founded as the Academy of Vocal Music in 1726), the Concert of Ancient Music (from 1776) and the Madrigal Society (founded 1741).[86] Weber has shown that while madrigals by composers such as Byrd and Wilbye were performed at the Concerts of Ancient Music, no sixteenth-century sacred music was included in their programmes.[87] There is, however, evidence that both the Academy of Ancient Music and the Madrigal Society occasionally performed pieces by Tallis, although information about their programmes is limited. The 1768 edition of *The Words of Such Pieces, as are Most Usually Performed by the Academy of Ancient Music*, for example, includes the words of *I call and cry* and of the Lamentations, *Incipit lamentatio*, although no music by Tallis is included in the 1761 volume, nor in any of the sixteen programmes

---

[86] Philip Olleson and Fiona M. Palmer provide a very useful overview of eighteenth and early nineteenth-century interest in the music of the past in 'Publishing Music from the Fitzwilliam Museum, Cambridge: The Work of Vincent Novello and Samuel Wesley in the 1820s', *Journal of the Royal Musical Association* 130 (2005): 38–73, esp. 41–4. For more on the Academy of Ancient Music, see Weber, *Musical Classics*, 56–73, and on the Madrigal Society see Reginald Nettel, 'The Oldest Surviving English Musical Club', *Musical Quarterly* 34 (1948): 97–108, and J. G. Craufurd, 'The Madrigal Society', *Proceedings of the Royal Musical Association* 83 (1955–6): 34–46.

[87] Weber, *Musical Classics*, 178, 184: see also Table 12 (p. 257) for details of madrigal performances.

ranging from 1733 to 1791 held in the Leeds Central Library.[88] Needler's copies may have been made for the Academy as, according to Hawkins, he spent his leisure time making copies of old music 'to improve himself and enrich the stores of the Academy'.[89] The Madrigal Society library also contains several important Tallis sources, including the most complete source of the *Missa Puer natus est*.[90]

For almost two centuries the group of pieces by Tallis that was known, copied and discussed – that is, the handful of works published in Barnard's *Selected Church Musick* of 1641 – had been particularly stable. Towards the end of the eighteenth century, however, this began to change. At the same time that a small group of scholars was exploring an expanding range of previously unknown music, the five-part anthems published by Barnard were increasingly portrayed by church musicians as unnecessarily difficult and inaccessible, concerned more with the technical tricks of composition than with their proper function of pleasing the ear and conveying the spirit and meaning of the words: Tallis's counterpoint was, at least for a time, largely exploded from the choirs. For most of the nineteenth century the music that was considered most representative of Tallis – and indeed the only music that was published or performed with any regularity – was a small group of simple homophonic anthems and the English service music.

[88] *The Words of Such Pieces, as are Most Usually Performed by the Academy of Ancient Music*, 2nd ed. (London, 1768), 7, 73. The collection in the Leeds Central Library is described as 'the most important' by Weber, who also lists the location of the other surviving programmes. He also suggests that *The Words of Such Pieces* may represent 'the Academy's library more than its actual repertoire' (*Musical Classics*, 63).

[89] Hawkins, *General History*, 806. For more on Needler, see Owen Rees, 'Adventures of Portuguese "Ancient Music" in Oxford, London, and Paris: Duarte Lobo's "Liber Missarum" and Musical Antiquarianism, 1650–1850', *Music & Letters* 86 (2005): 46–7.

[90] See Joseph Kerman, 'The Missa "Puer natus est nobis" by Tallis', in *Sundry Sorts of Music Books: Essays on the British Library Collections: Presented to O. W. Neighbour on his 70th Birthday*, ed. Chris Banks, Arthur Searle, Malcolm Turner (London: British Library, 1993), 41–2. Olleson and Palmer have noted that although the Madrigal Society performed sacred Latin music occasionally, it is difficult to identify from their records exactly which works were performed ('Publishing Music', 59).

🪶 The Nineteenth Century

CHURCH music, and particularly cathedral music, was at a low ebb in the early nineteenth century:[91] discipline was lax, and absenteeism, particularly among the choir men, was rife. By the early 1840s, however, this situation had become the focus of increasingly vocal complaint. A series of articles in the short-lived *Musical Journal*, established in 1840 by Edward Francis Rimbault and George Alexander Macfarren, bemoaning the low standards of cathedral music was typical.[92] An article on 'The Cathedral Choirs' describes the emaciated state of the choirs of Westminster Abbey and the Chapel Royal: only one singer per part is rostered for the men's parts at the evening service, and if one of these singers is absent 'the service is gone through without them.' Not only were the standards of performance poor, but 'our finest church music is but seldom heard [...]. The anthems of Tallis, Bird, Gibbons, &c. &c. are banished from the chapel.'[93] Another article in the same journal claimed that the musical service of the English church 'has long been felt and acknowledged to be a disgrace to England'.[94]

The early 1840s also saw the publication of several books addressing the question of church music. The most influential was the Rev. John Jebb's *The Choral Service of the United Church of England and Ireland* (1843), but others included *An Apology for Cathedral Service* (1839) and William Burge's *On the Choral Service of the Anglo-Catholic Church* (1844).[95] In 1844 Edward Taylor, Gresham Professor of Music, member of the Madrigal Society and music critic for the *Spectator* from 1829 to 1843, reviewed these publications in the *British and Foreign Review*.[96]

---

[91] For general accounts of the 'slovenly' performance of Anglican services in the 1830s and 40s, see, for example, Philip Barrett, 'English Cathedral Choirs in the Nineteenth Century', *Journal of Ecclesiastical History* 25 (1974): 15–37, Temperley, 'Cathedral Music', 171, and Rainbow, *Choral Revival*, 6–8.

[92] The *Musical Journal* ran for forty-seven weekly issues ('Periodicals, §3: List: Europe: Great Britain (GB)', *Grove Music Online*, accessed 24 Jun 2004).

[93] 'The Cathedral Choirs', *Musical Journal* 1 (1840): 120–1.

[94] 'Church Music and Choirs', *Musical Journal* 1 (1840): 310.

[95] Rev. John Jebb, *The Choral Service of the United Church of England and Ireland* (London: W. Parker, 1843); *An Apology for Cathedral Service* (London: John Bohn, 1839); W[illiam] B[urge], *On the Choral Service of the Anglo-Catholic Church* (London: G. Bell, 1844).

[96] Leanne Langley, 'Taylor, Edward', *Grove Music Online*, accessed 21 Mar 2003. The review is unsigned, but Langley identifies Taylor as the author in 'The Musical Press in Nineteenth-Century England', *Notes* 2nd series 46 (1990): 583–92. Many passages in this review are identical to passages in Taylor's *The English Cathedral Service, Its Glory, – Its Decline, and Its Designed Extinction* (London: Simpkin, Marshal & Co., 1845).

In this review Taylor claims that English cathedral music 'seems destined to be quietly thrust aside as a thing of nought, and amidst all the din with which the Church of England now resounds, to be suffered to fade, and droop and die.'[97]

Given this general neglect, it is not surprising that there is little evidence of interest in Tallis or his music in the early years of the nineteenth century. Around the turn of the century the Heather Professor of Oxford, William Crotch, had set Tallis's epitaph to music, and published a Latin edition of Tallis's Litany together with a setting of the *Veni Creator Spiritus* spuriously attributed to Tallis:[98] these will all be discussed further below. Crotch also included the 'Gloria Patri' from the Nunc Dimittis in his *Specimens of Various Styles of Music*.[99] The only other publications of Tallis's music from between 1800 and 1840 held by the British Library are two piano arrangements of the 'Evening Hymn'. In the 1820s Samuel Wesley began work on an edition of Byrd's Latin music, although the project was never brought to fruition, but there is nothing to suggest that he, or indeed anybody else, had any particular interest in Tallis's music in the first third of the nineteenth century.[100]

The books and articles published in the early 1840s lamenting the sad state of cathedral service music were, however, also among the first indicators of change: as well as documenting the inadequacies of the choirs, the *Musical Journal* noted that 'a reformation of some sort is evidently approaching, and the signs of it are obvious.'[101] One of the earliest manifestations of this revival was the formation of societies for the dissemination and publication of early music. In 1840, the same year as the foundation of the *Musical Journal*, the Musical Antiquarian Society was established by the antiquarian William Chappell for the publication of the music of 'early English Composers [...] and of works illustrating the history and progress of music'; Rimbault, Macfarren and Taylor were all members.[102] The following year the Scottish-born William Dyce, best known as the painter of the Arthurian

---

97 [Edward Taylor], review of *The Choral Service*, etc., *British and Foreign Review* 17 (1844): 84.

98 William Crotch, *Tallis's Litany, Adapted to the Latin Words with Additions by Dr Aldrich ...* (Oxford, 1803). This edition of the Litany appears to be based on one of Aldrich's manuscripts, now held at *B-Bc* MS 27,919.

99 William Crotch, *Specimens of Various Styles of Music: Referred to in a Course of Lectures, Read at Oxford & London*, vol. 2 (London: Royal Harmonic Institution, 1808–10).

100 See Olleson and Palmer, 'Publishing Music', 53–60. In the third of his series of lectures given at the Bristol Institution in 1830, Wesley praises the 'immortal compositions for the Church' of Purcell, Gibbons, Blow, Croft and Greene, but he does not mention Tallis in these lectures (*GB-Lbl* Add. 35104).

101 'Church Music and the Choirs', *Musical Journal* 1 (1840): 323.

102 For more on the society, see Turbet, 'Musical Antiquarian Society', 13.

frescos in the Robing Room of Pugin's Houses of Parliament,[103] founded the Motett Society 'for the study and practice of church music of the sixteenth and seventeenth centuries, and for re-printing selections of standard Church Music'.[104] Rimbault was the musical editor of the Motett Society publications; Dyce was a member of the Musical Antiquarian Society.

This renewed interest in church music, and particularly the music of the six-teenth and seventeenth centuries, was part of a general fascination with the past that manifested itself in many areas in the early years of Victoria's reign: Edward Taylor identifies the activities of the Musical Antiquarian Society with the 'grow-ing desire to preserve and perpetuate whatever is most venerable and beautiful in English art'. The Prospectus of the Musical Antiquarian Society explicitly linked its endeavours to the work of the Camden and Percy Societies, established to publish and promote early English literature.[105]

Taylor draws a direct parallel between music and architecture, comparing the neglect of early English music with that suffered by the Gothic cathedrals at Ely, Norwich and Llandaff.[106] The Cambridge Camden Society (as distinct from the Camden Society), founded in 1839 and later known as the Ecclesiological Soci-ety, was very active in the promotion of Gothic Revival architecture in the Angli-can Church. Dale Adelmann has shown that the Society's activities, with which Dyce was also involved, soon extended to music and other aspects of worship, and played a substantial role in improving standards of church music and in promot-ing the music of the sixteenth and seventeenth centuries.[107] In 1852 the Motett

---

[103] For more on Dyce, and the Arthurian frescoes, see Marion Pointon, *William Dyce, 1806–1864: A Critical Biography* (Oxford: Clarendon, 1979). The immense popu-larity in Victorian Britain of the Arthurian legends, together with the legend of Robin Hood, is examined in Stephanie L. Barczewski, *Myth and National Iden-tity in Nineteenth-Century Britain: The Legends of King Arthur and Robin Hood* (Oxford: Oxford University Press, 2000). Macfarren went on to write operas on a number of historical subjects, including Robin Hood (1860).

[104] Quoted from a manuscript account by James Stirling Dyce of his father, William's, activities in Richard Turbet, 'William Dyce and the Motett Society', *Aberdeen Uni-versity Review* 56 (1996): 443.

[105] [Edward Taylor], 'Works Printed for the Members of the Musical Antiquarian Society', *British and Foreign Review* 16 (1844): 399. Rimbault was also secretary of the Percy Society ('Dr. Rimbault', *Musical Times* 17 (1876): 651).

[106] Taylor, 'Musical Antiquarian Society', 397–8.

[107] Dale Adelmann, *The Contribution of Cambridge Ecclesiologists to the Revival of Anglican Choral Worship, 1839–62* (Aldershot: Ashgate, 1997). See particularly pp. 5–11 for a general discussion of the contribution of the sight-singing move-ment, Gothic revival architecture and medievalism to the ecclesiologists' views on early church music. For more on the relationship between Dyce, the Motett Society and the Cambridge Ecclesiologists, see pp. 31–3, 140–2.

Society officially amalgamated with the Ecclesiological Society.[108] The Cambridge Camden Society can be seen as part of a broader process of religious reform usually considered to have been initiated by the Oxford Movement. James F. White has, however, observed that the Tractarians (so called after the series of *Tracts for the Times* published by members of the movement) were not primarily concerned with aesthetics, and Adelmann argues that 'the Oxford Movement has far too sweepingly been identified with the impetus for the revival of choral worship which began to take shape in the 1840s.'[109] Nicholas Temperley similarly claims that the Oxford Movement had less impact on the state of church music than is often believed and argues that the Dean and Chapter Act of 1840, which ended some of the most 'flagrant financial abuses' that had been draining funds intended for choirs and music, played a more significant role in this 'reformation'.[110] This view is supported by Taylor's review of the *Choral Service*, which includes an extensive discussion of the statutes relating to the financial provisions for choirs.

The Musical Antiquarian Society published nearly twenty volumes of early music between 1840 and 1848, beginning with Byrd's *Mass for Five Voices*, and including Byrd's first book of *Cantiones sacrae* of 1589, but did not publish any of Tallis's music.[111] A proposed edition by William Crotch of the joint *Cantiones sacrae* of 1575 never appeared, although the annotations in a copy of the *Cantiones* now housed at Brussels (*B-Br* Fétis MS 1753) indicate that it was consulted by Crotch as well as by Chappell, Taylor and Joseph Warren,[112] and Rimbault claimed to have a copy in his own library.[113] No other editions of Tallis's Latin music were published until the turn of the twentieth century, nor to my knowledge was any of it performed, apart from *Spem in alium*, which was revived by the Madrigal Society in 1836.[114] With the exception of this one extraordinary work, discussed at length

[108] Turbet, 'Motett Society', 445, and Adelmann, *Cambridge Ecclesiologists*, 77–8.

[109] James F. White, *The Cambridge Movement: The Ecclesiologist and the Gothic Revival* (Cambridge: Cambridge University Press, 1962), 20; Adelmann, *Cambridge Ecclesiologists*, xii. Philip Barrett has argued that the Tractarians were an important impetus to the Choral Revival, but all the examples cited refer only to Gregorian chant ('The Tractarians and Church Music', *Musical Times* 113 (1972): 301–2, 398–9).

[110] Temperley, 'Cathedral Music', 173.

[111] For a list of the volumes published, see Turbet, 'Musical Antiquarian Society', 17–18.

[112] Milsom, 'Incorrected Copy', 366.

[113] Edward F. Rimbault, ed., *Order of the Daily Service of the United Church of England and Ireland, as Arranged for Choirs by Thomas Tallis* (London: D'Almaine, [1846]), v.

[114] It is again possible that other Latin works by Tallis were performed in private by organisations such as the Madrigal Society in the nineteenth century, but if such performances did take place they were not widely reported in the press.

in Chapter 3, Tallis's Latin polyphony does not appear to have been the subject of much antiquarian interest in the nineteenth century, and did not play a substantial role in general perceptions of Tallis until the end of the century.

Despite the common membership, the goals of these two societies were quite distinct. The Musical Antiquarian Society published both sacred and secular music and was devoted to preserving 'scarce and valuable musical works [which …] are unattainable by those who may wish to possess them.'[115] The Motett Society was more interested in the active promotion of good church music. It was devoted exclusively to 'the study and practice of the ancient Choral Music of the Church', and membership was limited to 'Members of the English Church'. The Motett Society did not, however, limit its publications to English music: most of the works published were English adaptations of works by continental (predominantly Italian) composers. Once again, the 'Services of Tallis, Gibbons, and others' were listed in the original proposal, but a Sanctus and Gloria by Blow were the only pieces of English service music that were actually published. Several anthems by English composers, including Gibbons, Byrd, Farrant and Tallis were, however, published between 1841 and 1842.[116]

While Tallis did not feature particularly prominently in the publications of the Motett and Musical Antiquarian Societies, these volumes were just a small and relatively specialised part of a general boom in music publishing that took place in England in the 1840s.[117] A flood of editions of Tallis's English service music, including the Litany and Responses, was published in the 1840s and 50s, and writers such as Jebb held up Tallis's music, and particularly his Service, as a model for all students of sacred music. In 1843 Jebb gave a series of three public lectures in Leeds at the request of the vicar, Dr. W. F. Hook, in which he extolled the virtues of Tallis's Service:

> As to the intrinsic excellence of this Service itself, I would observe, what every musician will acknowledge, that its harmonies are perfect models for sublimity, fullness, and exquisite judgement. […] I must claim for the services of this eminent composer a character of sublime expression eminently befitting the worship of the Church of England.[118]

Similarly, in his *Choral Service* he argued that:

[115] From the Prospectus of the Society, cited in Taylor, 'Musical Antiquarian Society', 399.

[116] Turbet, 'William Dyce', 444–5. The anthems by Tallis are listed in Table 5.

[117] See D. W. Krummel, 'Music Publishing', in Temperley, *Romantic Age*, 49. The number of music copyrights increased roughly tenfold between 1835 and 1845.

[118] John Jebb, *Three Lectures on the Cathedral Service of the Church of England*, 2nd ed. (Leeds: T. N. Green, 1845), 137–8.

The Service of the celebrated TALLIS is the earliest of those which have been published, or practically known in our Choirs. Those persons must have peculiar ideas indeed as to the requirements of solemn devotional music, who can object to the Service of this admirable composer. The resources of his most religious harmonies are unrivalled: there is a chastened gravity throughout, the effect of which not the most dead and careless perform-ance can altogether destroy: and there is the most evident recognition of the devotional spirit of antiquity.[119]

S. S. Wesley was amongst those who objected to this music; he dismissed Tallis's 'claims to peculiar merit', arguing that

> a portion of [his] writings, [...] tends to bring anything but good will to the musical offices; being destitute, it really must be said, of almost every kind of merit, and constituting one interminable monotony which no one can, or ought to, put up with.

He observes in a footnote, however, that 'this does not apply to his fine Responses.'[120] Jebb counters this criticism by arguing that that such comments were brought about by the 'dead and monotonous manner of its general performance', and that this situation could be remedied by the 'varied mode of performance which is amply lavished upon the thin and showy compositions of more modern times.'[121]

Another sign of particular interest in Tallis in the early 1840s was the series of 'Tallis Days' instituted at Westminster Abbey by James Turle, the Abbey organist and another of the founding members of the Musical Antiquarian Society, at the urging of his friend and President of the Madrigal Society, Sir John Leman Rogers, bart. These Tallis Days were celebrated annually at Westminster Abbey on or about the Feast of St Simon and St Jude (28 October) and were reported in the press. In his book on the English Cathedral Service, Taylor claimed that these celebrations were immensely popular, although not as popular as similar 'Purcell Days', and Westminster Abbey was 'thronged with hearers';[122] the *Musical World* reported

---

[119] Jebb, *Choral Service*, 337.

[120] S. S. Wesley, *A Few Words on Cathedral Music (1849)* (London: Hinrichsen, 1965), 45–6. In the Preface to *A Morning and Evening Service* (London, 1845) he mentions the '*sublime* qualities of certain portions of TALLIS'S SERVICE (omitting the Canticles)', by which he presumably means the Responses.

[121] Jebb, *Choral Service*, 338.

[122] Taylor, *English Cathedral Service*, 32. Similarities between this publication and a review first published in the *Spectator*, reprinted in *Musical World* 16 (1841): 269, particularly anxiety as to whether any clergy will be musically capable of intoning the service after a certain Mr Lupton is 'gathered to his fathers', make it clear that Taylor is the author of both. William Burge also mentions these Tallis Days (*Choral Service*, xxxiv).

that the congregation in 1841 'must have exceeded a thousand persons'.[123] The main attraction of these Tallis Days was the performance of Tallis's 'Service in D'. The first of these events appears to have taken place on 28 October 1840: a notice in the *Musical Journal* claims that the Service in D had not been performed in London in its entirety, with the Litany – described as 'an interesting relic of the solemnities of the ancient church' – since 1827. It continued:

> We hope, on this interesting occasion, to see the church (more particularly the choir) well filled, and we trust that those vocalists whose engagements will permit of their so doing will attend at Westminster without waiting for the ceremony of an invitation; those who possess the first volume of Boyce's Cathedral Music taking it with them, that their services may not be lost for the want of copies.[124]

A review of the 1841 event records that the choir was 'augmented, by the voluntary assistance of the eminent professors, to the number of forty, a force which is absolutely necessary to the due performance of the duty'.[125] A choir of this size would have been particularly impressive when compared with the customary offerings described above.

An account of the 1841 'Tallis Day' celebration lists the qualities of Tallis's 'grand old gothic service', and draws explicit parallels between the musical and architectural revivals:

> The characteristics of Tallis's work [...] are vastness, gloomy grandeur, and ponderous solemnity, achieved by the most elaborate combinations and harmonies – features which to us continually associate it with the gothic in architecture, its groinings and tracery; and listened to in this most sacred of all holy places, the performance presents as near an approach to the sublime, as to minds in general is comprehensible.[126]

In 1841 Thomas Oliphant published his *Full Cathedral Service*, one of the first of the many nineteenth-century editions of Tallis's Short Service.[127] The *Musical World* review of the 1841 Tallis Day commended Oliphant's industry, suggesting

---

[123] 'Musical Intelligence: Metropolitan: Westminster Abbey', *Musical World* 16 (1841): 232.

[124] 'Tallis', *Musical Journal* 2 (1840): 250.

[125] 'Musical Intelligence: Metropolitan: Westminster Abbey', *Musical World* 16 (1841): 232, and 'Tallis', *Musical Journal* 2 (1840): 250.

[126] 'Westminster Abbey', *Musical World* 16 (1841): 232.

[127] Thomas Oliphant, ed., *The Full Cathedral Service as Used on the Festivals and Saints' Days of the Church of England, Composed by Thomas Tallis ...* (London: C. Lonsdale, 1841).

that these Tallis Days were a direct stimulus to its publication.[128] Oliphant's musical interests were wide ranging – he produced English translations of *Fidelio* and *Lohengrin*, for example[129] – but he was chiefly known as the secretary of the Madrigal Society, a position he held for forty years from 1832, and as a champion of early music.[130] His tireless activities as a scribe, translator and editor brought many 'lost' works to performance and gave voice to music that had been silent for centuries, including Tallis's *Spem in alium*. The *Morning Post* review of the 1835 Annual Festival of the Madrigal Society records Oliphant's wish 'that the shades of the old masters would arise […] to hear their works after a lapse of 250 years'.[131]

While the service music continued to be the most highly valued portion of Tallis's output, several of his anthems were also published and performed in the 1840s, both by the Motett Society and as supplements to journals such as the *Musical Times* (1844–), the *Musical World* (1836–91) and the relatively short-lived *Parish Choir* (1846–51)[132] that were established at this time. (A summary of nineteenth-century publications of anthems attributed to Tallis is given in Table 5.) These periodicals also provided a forum for reviews and reports of concerts, church services, lectures and publications (see Table 6 for a list of press reports of performances of anthems by Tallis), which allow us to construct a much clearer sense of how Tallis and his music were perceived at this time.

The lists of publications in Table 5 shows a dramatic shift away from the five-part anthems published by Barnard towards relatively short, homophonic anthems in four parts. The only five-part anthems were two adaptations of works from the *Cantiones sacrae* published by the Motett Society; the previously popular *I call and cry* was not published at all, except in reprints of Boyce. Reports of performances of Tallis anthems (see Table 6) show an even more limited reliance upon a few simple four-part works than that suggested by the list of publications.

The trends observed in these press reports are supported by cathedral music lists. The library and surviving music lists at Worcester Cathedral provide just one example. A volume of 'Anthems collected […] and arranged for the use of Worcester Cathedral' compiled in 1835 by the Precentor, Rev. Allen Wheeler, included *All people, Hear the voice and prayer, I call and cry* and *O Lord, give thy Holy Spirit*.

[128] 'Westminster Abbey', *Musical World* 16 (1841): 232.

[129] W.H.C., 'Oliphant, Thomas', *Dictionary of National Biography*, ed. Sidney Lee (London: Smith, Elder & Co., 1895).

[130] Craufurd, 'Madrigal Society', 46.

[131] *Morning Post*, 16 Jan 1835, 3.

[132] For more on the *Parish Choir*, see Adelmann, *Cambridge Ecclesiologists*, 43–6, and Rainbow, *Choral Revival* 95–114.

Table 5 Nineteenth-century publications of anthems attributed to Tallis

Title	Previous publication	Source of publication	Date
All people that on earth	Arnold	Motett Society, Div 3	1841–2
		Musical Times 1 (1845): 127–30	1845
Blessed are those		Motett Society, Div 3	1841–2
Come, Holy Ghost (Veni Creator Spiritus)	Lowe*	Crotch, *Tallis's Litany, adapted to the Latin words with additions by Dr Aldrich* …	1803
		Supplement to *Parish Choir*	1846
		Havergal, *The Preces and Litany set … for four voices*	1847
		Musical Times 5 (1853): 183–5	1853
Great and marvellous	[Cantiones sacrae]	Motett Society, Div 3	1841–2
Hear the voice and prayer	Day	Motett Society, Div 3	1841–2
		Burns, *Anthems and Services for Church Choirs*	1847
		Novello	1850
If ye love me	Day	Motett Society, Div 1	1841–2
		Parish Choir 2 (1847): 69–72	1847
		Musical Times 10 (1862): 243–5	1862
		Supplement to *The Choir*	1864
		Novello (Tonic Sol-fa series No. 513)	1886
O Lord, give thy Holy Spirit	Barnard	Warren's edition of Boyce's *Cathedral Music*, app. to Vol. 2	1849
		Supplement to *The Choir*	1864
		Music Publishing Association: London, ed. Basil Harwood	1899, 1907

Note: Although these lists are unlikely to be complete, I am unaware of any evidence to suggest that any other music by Tallis, apart from the hymn tunes and psalm tones, and *Spem in alium*, which is discussed at length in Chapter 4, were either published or performed during the nineteenth century.

* See p. 48.

Table 6 Press reports of nineteenth-century performances
of anthems attributed to Tallis

Title	Place or Occasion	Date	Source
All people that on earth do dwell	York Minster	Jul 1875	Concordia 10 Jul 1875
Come, Holy Ghost	Consecration of Colonial Bishops	Jun 1847	Times 30 Jun 1847
	Chichester Cathedral	May 1875	Concordia 22 May 1875
Hear the voice and prayer	Consecration of St Barnabas Pimlico	1 Jun 1848	Parish Choir 3 (1848): 117
	Canterbury Cathedral	Oct 1875	Concordia 24 Oct 1875
	Tallis Tercentenary, St Alfege, Greenwich	23 Nov 1885	Musical Times 26 (1885): 722–3
I call and cry	'Tallis Day', Westminster Abbey	9 Sep 1841	Musical World 19 (1841): 232
If ye love me	Lecture on Church Music at Maidstone, by Mr Dawson	7 Jan 1847	Parish Choir 1 (1847): 124
	Public lecture, Rev J. W. Twist, 'Anthem music of the church' at the 'Hampstead Sacred Choral Institution'	9 Mar 1849	Parish Choir 2 (1849): 183
	Evensong of dedication feast for St John, Withyham	30 Jul 1849	Parish Choir 3 (1849): 24
	Evening service on Whitsunday, St Mark's, St John's Wood	31 May 1857	Rainbow, Choral Revival: 341
	Lecture at Church Congress, J. B. Dykes	7 Oct 1865	The Times 7 Oct 1865
	Canterbury Cathedral	Jan 1876	Concordia 16 Jan 1875
	Chichester Cathedral	Jan 1876	Concordia 30 Jan 1875
	Canterbury Cathedral	Apr 1876	Concordia 2 Apr 1876
	Tallis Tercentenary, St Alfege, Greenwich	23 Nov 1885	Musical Times 26 (1885): 722–3

A catalogue of the choir library compiled in about 1880 by James Smith, a lay clerk and Librarian of the Choir Music, lists *All people*, *If ye love me*, and *I call and cry*, and an 1890 Novello publication, *Anthems for Use at Worcester Cathedral*, includes the same works as the 1835 collection with the addition of *Come, Holy Ghost*. Yet the surviving service lists from the 1890s show that *If ye love me* was again the only anthem by Tallis performed, usually on the Saturday before Whitsunday, although the Responses and the Benedictus from the Dorian Service were given quite regularly.[133] Music lists from St Paul's Cathedral, London, for the period 1876–91 similarly only record performances of two anthems by Tallis: *If ye love me* (twenty-three performances) and *All people* (twenty-four performances).[134] Adelmann's summary of the works performed by the Ecclesiological Motett Choir between 1853 and 1862 shows one performance each of *All people* and *Hear the voice and prayer* and three of *If ye love me*.[135]

The handful of anthems that were published and performed during the nineteenth century represents a complete break with previous concretizations of the composer. Of the five anthems mentioned in the press and in the cathedral music lists, only *I call and cry* had enjoyed any previous popularity, and while it was performed at the Tallis Days in the early 1840s, and was favourably mentioned in publications such as Burge's *On the Choral Service of the Anglo-Catholic Church*,[136] it was performed rarely, if ever, in the second half of the century. *If ye love me*, by far the most popular of Tallis's anthems during the nineteenth and early twentieth centuries, had been virtually unknown prior to its publication by the Motett Society in 1847: although it had been published by John Day in his *Certaine Notes* and a number of pre-Commonwealth copies survive, only two post-Restoration sources are listed by Hofman and Morehen.[137]

The novelty of this music was recognised at the time. In 1847 the *Parish Choir* carried a report of a lecture given by a William Dawson on the 'History and Present State of Church Music', at Maidstone in Kent. The musical examples, including anthems by Tye, Farrant, Byrd and Gibbons, and Tallis's *If ye love me*, were referred to explicitly as the '"new music"(!) of Tallis, Byrd, Gibbons, &c.'[138]

---

133 Private communication from Vernon Butcher, on behalf of the Dean and Chapter, Worcester Cathedral, 17 Sep 1996.

134 'St Paul's Cathedral Music Bills inscribed by John S. Bumpus 3 Apr 1876 to 9 Sep 1891', British Library shelf-mark Cup.1247.s.1.2.

135 Adelmann, *Cambridge Ecclesiologists*, 219. Adelmann also notes that by the 1850s *If ye love me* had 'become a great favourite at parish choir festivals' (p. 208).

136 Burge, *Choral Service*, xxxii.

137 *GB-DRc* C17 and C19, and *GB-Lbl* Add. 30478–9.

138 William Dawson, 'Church Music in Kent', *Parish Choir* 1 (1847): 123 (exclamation mark in original). The examples were provided by a choir 'of about thirty *villagers*',

While *If ye love me* and *Hear the voice and prayer* were enjoying an unprecedented popularity, two of the anthems that were published and performed in the nineteenth century were more literally 'new': neither *All people that on earth do dwell* nor *Come, Holy Ghost* was actually by Tallis, nor were they generally attributed to him before the nineteenth century. These two spurious anthems, however, played an important role in shaping the image of Tallis, and an examination of the history of the early sources of these anthems and of their co-option into the Tallis canon provides valuable insights into nineteenth-century perceptions of Tallis and his music.

ALL PEOPLE THAT ON EARTH DO DWELL

All the earliest sources of *All people that on earth do dwell* are found in manuscripts in the library of Christ Church, Oxford, which contain several distinct versions in a variety of hands. Robert Shay has argued that, despite appearing twice in Mus. 16, a manuscript devoted almost exclusively to Dean Henry Aldrich's 'recompositions' of the works of other composers, this anthem is an original composition by Aldrich;[139] it is hard not to agree with Anthony Greening's assessment that 'On stylistic grounds alone the ascription [to Tallis] seems dubious.'[140]

The version that was most widely copied and that became the standard in the nineteenth century is in four parts, and consists of a series of short, homophonic 'verse' sections, alternating between the three upper and three lower parts, interspersed with 'full' sections and finishing with a contrapuntal Amen. The text is the metrical version of Psalm 100 usually attributed to Kethe; the sections correspond to the verses of the metrical text. The style is superficially similar to parts of the Dorian Service, with a regular crotchet rhythm, and a number of short sections alternating with little or no break in between. The alternation between full and verse sections is not, however, typical of Tallis's anthems, which rarely drop below four voices; the stark transitions between polyphonic and homophonic sections are also inconsistent with Tallis's style.

This version is found in Aldrich's hand in Mus. 16: 1–2 and 11: 15, and in other hands in several sources, including the organ books Mus. 1230: 15 and Mus. 1235: 95. It is only attributed to Tallis in the hand of the original scribe in the two organ books. The tenor and bass parts of this version are also found in

trained by Frederick Helmore, who were reported to have sung with 'taste and precision'.

[139] Shay, '"Naturalizing" Palestrina', 389.

[140] Anthony Greening, ed., 'All people that on earth do dwell', *Anthems for Choirs 1: 50 Anthems for Mixed Voices*, ed. Francis Jackson (Oxford: Oxford University Press, 1973), 23.

Figure 1. *All people that on earth do dwell*, GB-Och Mus. 16: 1, bars 1–6

Mus. 1220–4,[141] also possibly in Aldrich's hand, although the tenor parts do not include music for the first half of the 'verse' sections.[142] This, together with the change in clefs that occurs in Aldrich's score copies at the beginning of the ATB section (see Figure 1) suggests that the opening bars may have been intended to be sung SSA.[143] This theory is supported by the inclusion of both the upper voices in these sections of the organ part in Mus. 1229.

[141] *GB-Och* Mus. 1221, 200; 1222, 190; 1223, 188; 1224, 186.

[142] The treble part books are missing from this set, but it is unclear why this version is not included in the alto partbook Mus. 1220.

[143] A similar division of verse sections (from ATB to SSA) in a predominantly four-part texture is found in other works from the same period, such as the Magnificats from Purcell's Service in B flat and Evening Service in G minor.

A second version is found on pages 46–7 of Mus. 16, also in Aldrich's autograph. This differs from the 'standard' version in two main respects. The third verse is not, as in the other copies, a direct repeat of the first, but is a completely new setting that does not appear in any other source. It is in a triple metre, and is effectively in three parts, with the lower part alternating between the bass and tenor staves, and with a great deal of crossing between the upper parts. This version also differs from the others in that the seventh note of the melody of the first verse is an E rather than the C of the 'standard' version, and the alto part is slightly different to accommodate the changed treble line.

The version published in the *Musical Times* is essentially that found in Mus. 16: 1–2, except that this variant is reproduced in the first verse. Even though in all other respects the third verse is a repeat of the first, the third verse gives the C rather than the E. This inconsistency is also found in the mid-eighteenth-century copy in Tenbury MS 836.

A third substantially different version is also found in the Christ Church partbooks Mus. 1220–4,[144] possibly in the hand of Edward Lowe, with an original attribution to Tallis at the bottom of each page.[145] Anthony Greening, in his editorial comments in *Anthems for Choirs*, dismisses this version as incomplete.[146] It begins with the first 'full' section (bar 3 in Figure 1) from the standard version, although with the words of the first verse. There are some differences in the alto and tenor parts, but the bass line is unchanged.

It then moves straight to the words and music of the next full section, verse 4, again with some variations in the upper parts. Although several verses of the text have been omitted, the first and last verses function quite well as a free-standing text. The fourth verse is repeated and the final Amen omitted. This version is full throughout, with an ABB structure similar to anthems such as *If ye love me* and *Purge me, O Lord*, and is therefore much closer in style to Tallis's smaller English anthems than the 'standard' version. Arkwright, in his 1915 *Catalogue of Music in the Library of Christ Church Oxford*, lists this version alone as being by Tallis; all of the others he considers to be Aldrich's adaptations of this 'original'.[147] It seems likely that the attribution to Tallis stems from this copy; it is not impossible that,

[144] *GB-Och* Mus. 1220, 184; 1221, 179; 1222, 173; 1223, 173; 1224, 168.

[145] On Mus. 1224: 168 a later hand has added the words 'The Music by' before the attribution to 'Mr Thomas Tallis' and 'The Words by the celebrated Sternhold and Hopkins' on the following line. A cross-reference to p. 186 has also been added.

[146] Jackson, *Anthems for Choirs*, 23.

[147] G. E. P. Arkwright, *Catalogue of Music in the Library of Christ Church Oxford: Part 1. Works of Ascertained Authorship* (1915; [Wakefield, Yorkshire]: S.R. Publishers, 1971), 1, 111.

rather than being an incomplete version of Aldrich's setting, this was the original upon which Aldrich's versions were based.[148]

Several eighteenth-century manuscript copies of the anthem survive, including a copy, attributed to Tallis, in the material Greene collected for publication;[149] it was published by W. Thomson in his *Symphonia Angelica* of roughly 1780, in Arnold's *Cathedral Music* of 1790, in the *Musical Times* in 1845 and in the Motett Society's 1841–2 *Collection of Ancient Church Music: Miscellaneous Anthems* (see Table 5).

Doubts about the attribution to Tallis had begun to surface by the beginning of the twentieth century – it was termed '*opus dubium*' in an edition published in 1909[150] – but for most of the nineteenth century Tallis's authorship was unquestioned. The net of spurious attribution seems to have been cast still wider, however: the hymn tune the 'Old 100th', associated since its publication in the Geneva Psalter in 1560 with the metrical text of Psalm 100,[151] was also occasionally attributed to Tallis.

In 1885 a service was held at St Alfege's, Greenwich, to commemorate the tercentenary of Tallis's death.[152] The programme comprised the hymn 'The Son of God goes forth to war', the Litany, *Hear the voice and prayer*, *If ye love me*, *All people that on earth* and the Te Deum from the Dorian Service. An event such as this, dedicated to commemorating a single composer, will almost inevitably encapsulate the dominant conception of the composer. It was not, however, Aldrich's anthem that was performed, but the hymn the 'Old Hundredth', which was explicitly attributed to Tallis in the program. A review of the service in the *Musical Times* disputes the attribution, but notes that it was common.[153] It is, for example, attributed to Tallis in the table of contents of a set of partbooks from the 1840s at St George's Chapel,

---

[148] Robert Shay agrees that this is a plausible explanation, and would be consistent with Aldrich's general use of this manuscript for his reworkings of older models (private communication, 5 Mar 2004).

[149] Johnstone, 'Boyce's "Cathedral Music"', 37. It is also found, with the Tallis attribution, in the eighteenth-century *Lbl* Add. MS 17842, along with many other arrangements by Aldrich, including his Tallis recompositions, *I look for the Lord* and *I will magnifie thee*, and *I call and cry* and *With all our hearts*.

[150] Ed. J. West, *All people that on earth do dwell* (London: Bayley & Ferguson, 1909). The anthem heads the Oxford University Press collection *Anthems for Choirs* (1973), where it is described as 'Attributed to Thomas Tallis', but is still unquestioningly attributed to Tallis on a number of websites such <http://www.handlo.com>, accessed 7 Aug 2003.

[151] *Four Score and Seven Psalms* (Geneva, 1560). It was also published in a number of later metrical psalters, such as *Psalms of David* (London, 1561).

[152] This commemoration service will be discussed further in the next chapter.

[153] 'Tallis Commemoration Service', *Musical Times* 26 (1885): 722.

Windsor, although the ascription is in a later hand, and is not found in the body of the manuscript.[154] In 1925 W. H. Grattan Flood noted that Sir Richard Runciman Terry had repeated an 'oft-quoted' statement that Tallis had written the hymn 'for Anglican use'. Flood pointed out that the tune was of 'pre-Reformation origin [...] and is an adaptation of an old French air of the 15th century'; he seems content, however, to accept that Tallis was responsible for the adaptation.[155]

VENI CREATOR

A similarly complicated story of dubious attributions and confusion between different settings of similar metrical texts lies behind the *Veni Creator* or *Come, Holy Ghost*.

While exiled in Geneva during the reign of Queen Mary, Matthew Parker, later to become Archbishop of Canterbury, wrote *The Whole Psalter Translated into English Metre* ..., which was printed with nine hymn tunes by Tallis in about 1567.[156] Eight of the tunes, including the tune now known as 'Tallis Canon', were set to the eight church modes – their characters are described in verse in the preface – and marks in the text indicated which psalms were to be sung to which tunes. The ninth tune was for use with the *Veni Creator* from the rite of Ordination and is therefore known as 'Tallis's Ordinal'.

In 1661, in an attempt to facilitate the performance of the sung service after a break of almost two decades (particularly catastrophic in a system based upon boy trebles), Edward Lowe published a little volume entitled *A Short Direction for the Performance of Cathedral Service*.[157] Lowe was another important Oxford musician: he had been organist at Christ Church, Oxford, in the 1640s, and at the Restoration became one of the organists at the Chapel Royal, and was, from 1661 until his death in 1682, professor of music at Oxford.[158] The subtitle of the *Short Direction* explains that it was 'Published for the Information of such, as may be called to Officiate in Cathedrall or Collegiate Churches, where it hath formerly been in use.' The *Short Direction* makes no explicit reference to Tallis, but it contains, unattributed, a four-part arrangement of Tallis's Responses and Litany, which will be discussed further in Chapter 4. Three years later Lowe produced a revised and expanded edition,

---

[154] *GB-WRch* MS 45.

[155] W. H. Grattan Flood, 'New Light on Late Tudor Composers: XI. – Thomas Tallis', *Musical Times* 66 (1925): 801. By pointing out the earlier version of the tune, Flood is implying Catholic, rather than Anglican origins.

[156] See Leonard Ellinwood, 'Tallis' Tunes and Tudor Psalmody', *Musica Disciplina* 2 (1948): 192.

[157] Edward Lowe, *A Short Direction for the Performance of Cathedrall Service* ... (Oxford, 1661).

[158] Robert Thompson, 'Lowe, Edward', *Grove Music Online*, accessed 22 Mar 2002.

A Review of Some Short Directions, which incorporated the changes made in the 1662 revision to the Prayer Book.[159] Prior to 1662 the Ordination service included only one version of the text of the *Veni Creator*: a Common Metre text similar to Parker's version, 'Come, Holy Ghost, eternal God, Proceeding from above'. The tune provided by Lowe was not, however, 'Tallis's Ordinal', but a setting based on Ravenscroft's Psalms. The 1662 Book of Common Prayer added a Long Metre version of the text by Bishop Cosin, 'Come, Holy Ghost, our souls inspire, and lighten with celestial fire', and Lowe included this version of the text in his *Review* of 1664, with an unattributed four-part setting. Several manuscript copies of this setting are found in the library of Christ Church, including the organ book Mus. 1229 and the cathedral partbooks, Mus. 1220–4. None of the copies attributes the anthem to Tallis.[160] This setting was, however, attributed to Tallis by William Crotch in his 1803 publication of the Latin Litany.[161]

The anthem enjoyed a brief surge of popularity in the middle of the century, possibly due to its use at the 1847 Consecration at Westminster Abbey of the Bishops of the newly created dioceses of Cape Town, Newcastle, Adelaide and Melbourne.[162] It was published in the *Parish Choir* in 1847, according to Bumpus, 'in readiness for use at the memorable consecration of the four colonial Bishops';[163] Havergal included it, along with 'Tallis's Ordinal', in his 1847 edition of the Preces and Litany (discussed further in Chapter 4 below);[164] and it was published in the *Musical Times* in 1853. A manuscript copy, dated 1848, survives in the library of St George's Chapel, Windsor;[165] another copy, which differs substantially in the

---

[159] Edward Lowe, *A Review of Some Short Directions for Performance of Cathedral Service ...* (Oxford: 1664).

[160] E. H. Fellowes claims that Aldrich attributed the work to Tallis, but I have found no evidence of such an attribution (*English Cathedral Music* (London: Methuen, 1941), 49).

[161] Crotch, *Tallis's Litany*.

[162] 'Consecration of Colonial Bishops', *The Times*, 30 Jun 1847. The report erroneously locates Newcastle in South Australia. This event was significant, not only because multiple consecrations were uncommon, but also as an indicator of the colonial expansion of the Church of England. A further five new colonial bishops had been consecrated in 1842, and a report in *The Times* (25 Aug 1842) declared that 'Since this venerable pile has been dedicated to divine worship under the auspices of the Reformation no occasion has been presented in which the Protestant Church has had such reason to rejoice.'

[163] John S. Bumpus, *Cathedral Music* (London: T. Werner Laurie, 1908), 46.

[164] Henry E. Havergal, ed., *The Preces and Litany Set by Thomas Tallis for Four Voices ...* (Oxford, 1847).

[165] St George's, Windsor MS 45, 7–8. This manuscript also contains *If ye love me, This is my [commandment]*, *Hear the voice and prayer* and the Old 100th, attributed to Tallis in the table of contents.

second line from the others (although the bass part is the same), is found in British Library Add. MS 38541 with the attribution 'Melodie von T. Tallis AD 1550'.[166] It was reissued in 1908 by Novello, edited and 'corrected' by John E. West, and again, in a revised edition with a descant to the second verse by William H. Harris, in 1924.[167] Flood referred to it in 1925 as a 'fine English anthem'.[168]

A copy of Havergal's publication annotated by Vincent Novello survives in the British Library,[169] bearing the inscription: 'Kindly presented to me by Mr Havergal Dec.r 3 1847'; Novello is also listed as a subscriber. Havergal notes in the preface:

> The tunes of Veni Creator are to suit the two versions of the hymn in the Ordination service. The L.M. is attributed to Tallis by Dr Crotch, but he has not authorized his assertion. It was first printed without any compos-er's name in Low's [sic] 'Review of Some Short Directions for the Cathedral Service', 1663. The C.M. is taken from Archbishop Parker's 'Psalter' (1560).

Novello has indicated a number of 'harsh effects' and 'inartistic combinations' and parallel fifths (see Figure 2).[170] He concludes at the foot of the page: 'from the very harsh combinations in the harmonies and the very unskillful construction of the counterpoint, I strongly doubt that this "Veni Creator" was composed by Tallis'. Several of the 'errors' he has marked are, in fact, technically correct (the fifth marked in the third bar of the Doxology is not strictly consecutive, as it moves between a diminished and perfect fifth, and the fifth between the soprano and the tenor in the cadence of the verse is acceptable as the soprano note is an anticipation note), but the harmonisation is generally inelegant and stylistically unlike Tallis. Crotch published his version as a treble line and figured bass, which neatly circumvents the problems with the harmonisation, although he may have just reproduced the figured bass version found in Christ Church Mus. 1229. The version in the *Musical Times* has Lowe's harmonies in the voice parts, although the keyboard accompaniment smooths out many of the problems, and later versions, such as Harris's, use a substantially revised harmonisation.

The clumsiness of the harmonisation must inevitably have led to doubts such as Novello's about Tallis's authorship, and there is no evidence beyond Crotch's unsubstantiated attribution in 1803 to suggest that this piece was by Tallis, yet that

---

[166] This manuscript forms part of the collection, dating 1836–54, of Robert Lucas Pearsall, an English musical antiquarian who was a founding member of the Bristol Madrigal Society, but lived for many years in Europe.

[167] Harris's version is included, without the descant, as no. 153 in *The English Hymnal*, 2nd ed. (Oxford: Oxford University Press, 1933), where it is 'Attributed to T. Tallis'.

[168] Flood, 'Thomas Tallis', 801.

[169] Shelfmark F.1124.e.

[170] *Musical Times* 5 (1853): 183, 185.

Figure 2. *Veni, Creator Spiritus, Musical Times,* 1853: Verse 1 and Doxology

attribution survived. The reasons why Crotch ascribed the anthem as he did are unknown. It may have been that, as Lowe included an unattributed arrangement of Tallis's Litany and Responses in his publications, Crotch assumed that the other unattributed works in the publication were also by Tallis; perhaps, in the same way that Tallis had come to be associated with the text of Psalm 100, his setting of the Ordinal led to a general association of the text with Tallis; perhaps it was a combination of the two.

Although spurious, both *All people* and *Come Holy Ghost* were, therefore, firmly embedded in the traditions of the Church of England, and the strong association between Tallis and the English liturgy – the belief that Tallis had been 'raised up' by God to perfect the service of the English Church[171] – was one of the chief characteristics of his nineteenth-century reception. This led to a blurring of the boundaries between the liturgy and Tallis's music. A review of the Charity Children's Service at St Paul's Cathedral, for example, claimed that Tallis's Responses were regarded 'by universal consent [...] as inseparable from the cathedral service of the Church of England',[172] and firm rules, approaching the authority of rubric, governed the days on which Tallis's Responses – often referred to simply as *the Festal Responses*[173] – should be sung and when they should be accompanied by the organ. Jebb claims that the 'proper times' for the performance of the Litany and Responses were 'the Great Festivals, when [...] it is sung to the Organ.'[174] Vincent Novello's list of the appropriate occasion for their performance is more specific:

> Xmas Eve, Xmas Day, and on the *three* following days, Easter Eve, Easter Day, and on the *two* following days; Whitsun Eve, Whitsunday and on the *two* following days, Election Sunday and on the *two* following days.[175]

Other liturgical fragments, such as Anglican psalm chants,[176] and the chant for

---

[171] The article in which the Revd. J. Powell Metcalfe made this claim ('The Music of the Church of England, as Contemplated by the Reformers', *Musical Times* 12 (1865): 157–60) is examined further in Chapter 5.

[172] 'The Charity Children at St. Paul's', *Musical World* 40 (1862): 390.

[173] Tallis's Responses are still listed in the Royal School of Church Music 'Catalogue of Sacred Choral Music' (1997/8) as 'Preces and Responses (Festal)'.

[174] Jebb, *Choral Service*, 446.

[175] *GB-Lbl* Add. 33239. This manuscript, in Novello's hand, is described as having been taken from 'the ancient copy on Vellum, preserved in the Organ loft at Westminster Abbey'.

[176] A concert given by the Sacred Harmonic Society with 'specimens of the English cathedral writers, in progressive and chronological order' included, as its example of Tallis's composition, a psalm chant – 'a simple distribution of common chords, in a certain form, repeated over and over again, until the monotonous unchangeableness becomes absolutely tiresome. This was, nevertheless, finely

Example 1. Chant for the Athanasian Creed

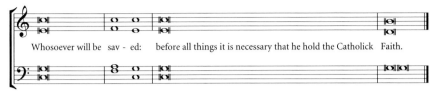

Whosoever will be sav - ed: before all things it is necessary that he hold the Catholick Faith.

Example 2. Doxology before the Gospel

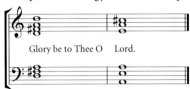

Glory be to Thee O   Lord.

the Athanasian Creed published in Boyce (see Example 1),[177] were also attributed to Tallis.[178] Robert Druitt, in his *Popular Tract on Church Music*, attributes a setting of what he terms the Doxology before the Gospel to Tallis, even though it is simply a plagal cadence (see Example 2).[179] Such fragments were taken quite seriously as significant components of Tallis's compositional output. William Burge, for example, wrote in 1844:

> All the chants composed by him [Tallis] partake of the character of his compositions. His sublime anthems 'I call and cry' and 'O Lord, give thy Holy Spirit,' are dear to all lovers of our early church music. His chant for the Athanasian Creed, when it is performed by those who have studied it carefully, and who give to it the expression of that devotional feeling which it breathes, in not surpassed by any human composition.[180]

executed by the choir, and loudly applauded' ('Cathedral Music at Exeter Hall', *Musical World* 21 (1846): 143).

[177] Boyce, *Cathedral Music*, 15–16.

[178] As several later writers pointed out, the chant for the Creed is not found in Barnard, but is the same as the 'Canterbury tune' published by Lowe, with the second alto transposed up an octave. See Rimbault, *Order of the Daily Service*, xiii, who accepts the attribution to Tallis and uses its absence to discredit Barnard, and John Bishop, *Order of the Daily Service of the United Church of England and Ireland as Arranged for Use 'In Quires and Places where they Sing'* (London: R. Cocks & Co., 1843), xxvi, who rejects it.

[179] Robert Druitt, *A Popular Tract on Church Music with Remarks on its Moral and Political Importance and a Practical Scheme for its Reformation* (London: Francis and John Rivington, 1845), 37. Stainer, in the article 'Response' in the first edition of Grove's *Dictionary* gives a similar version of this Doxology, without any reference to Tallis.

[180] Burge, *Choral Service*, xxxii.

In a similar, although less hyperbolic vein, Bernarr Rainbow describes Frederick Helmore beginning his first rehearsal with the newly established choir in East Farleigh with the 'three Amens as harmonised by Tallis'.[181] Assuming that this refers to the Amens after the collects at the end of the Responses, which are simple five-part, or possibly even four-part, cadences, it is hard to see how any authorship can be claimed for them, yet describing them as 'Tallis's Amens' gives them authority. Conversely, assigning authorship of a simple cadence or a harmonised Gregorian chant to Tallis also adds to his compositional gravitas. Similarly, the tunes Tallis wrote for Parker's Psalter – his association with Parker was seen as evidence of his suitability for the God-given task of setting the liturgy[182] – placed Tallis at the beginnings of the Protestant tradition of metrical psalmody. The power of these associations seems to have spread to other works with the same or similar texts.

Although *All people* and *Come, Holy Ghost* were in fact nineteenth-century additions to what was believed to be Tallis's œuvre, they were additions that paradoxically reinforced a belief in the continuity of the traditions of the Church and of Tallis's role in their establishment. They set texts that were an integral part of Anglican tradition, and gained authority from respected figures within that tradition. *All people* was believed to have been transmitted via Dean Aldrich, a figure held in high esteem, and the metrical text dates back to the Reformation. *Come, Holy Ghost* was authorised by Lowe's publication and also by a confused association with 'Tallis's Ordinal' and Archbishop Parker.

Furthermore, these anthems were simple, homophonic and within the reach of newly formed parish choirs, and of cathedral choirs struggling to re-establish themselves after centuries of neglect. Several genuine anthems by Tallis, however, such as *Purge me O Lord* and *Verily, verily*, would also have been suitable for these purposes, yet remained largely unknown until the twentieth century. They only survive in a few early manuscript sources, and it is possible that their lack of popularity can be attributed to ignorance rather than taste, although Rimbault lists them as 'rare inedited compositions' held in his own library.[183] Neither of them, however, carries the imprimatur of publication in earlier collections such as Barnard's or Day's; they were not adapted by Aldrich or Lowe; nor were their texts found in any of the metrical psalters. Works such as *All people* and *Come, Holy Ghost* not only met the need for simple, homophonic works that appealed to nineteenth-century taste and were within the reach of amateur choirs, but they were embedded within the traditions of the Church of England in a way that genuine

---

[181] Rainbow, *Choral Revival*, 119.

[182] Metcalfe, 'Music of the Church of England', 159.

[183] Rimbault, *Order of Daily Service*, viii.

works by Tallis such as *Purge me, O Lord* were not. The five-part anthems that had been seen as representative of Tallis for the previous two centuries were of little use or interest to the four-part choirs of the nineteenth century, yet Tallis's position as Father of English Church Music was too important for his music simply to be abandoned. Instead, a 'Tallis canon' was constructed that conformed to the aesthetic norms of the age, and which provided a sense of continuity with a suitable, if 'largely factitious', past.[184]

❧ *Tallis the Polyphonist*

THE dominant perception of Tallis throughout most the nineteenth century was, therefore, as the composer of English service music and of a few simple English anthems. While this image was not the same as the seventeenth- and eighteenth-century perspectives, the distinction was subtle. The last decades of the nineteenth century, however, saw the beginnings of a dramatically new image of Tallis, in which the English service music was largely replaced by the Latin polyphony. Like the revival of interest in early music in the 1840s, this was part of a more general reinvigoration of musical life. The late 1870s and early 1880s saw the formalisation of musical education in England and the surge in English composition generally, if imprecisely, referred to as the English Musical Renaissance.[185]

One of the major projects of this Renaissance was Grove's *Dictionary of Music and Musicians*, and one of the first signs of a re-evaluation of the relative merits of Tallis's Latin and English music is found in W. S. Rockstro's article

---

[184] Eric Hobsbawm has identified such a sense of continuity as the goal of 'invented traditions' (*The Invention of Tradition*, ed. Eric Hobsbawm and Terence Ranger (Cambridge: Cambridge University Press, 1983), 1–2).

[185] Meirion Hughes notes that the first use of the term 'Renaissance' to describe this period was in a review of Parry's Symphony no. 1, in 1882 (*The English Musical Renaissance and the Press, 1850–1914: Watchmen of Music* (Aldershot: Ashgate, 2002), 142). The most recent and comprehensive survey of this subject, Robert Stradling and Meirion Hughes, *The English Music Renaissance, 1840–1940: Constructing a National Music*, 2nd ed. (Manchester: Manchester University Press, 2001), has been subject of a great deal of criticism; see, for example, Alain Frogley, 'Rewriting the Renaissance: History, Imperialism, and British Music since 1840', *Music & Letters* 84 (2003): 241–57. The very brief mention of the role of early music in the Renaissance (pp. 211–12) is certainly flawed. In particular the implication that Ralph Vaughan Williams's *Fantasia on a Theme by Thomas Tallis* was influenced by the 'pioneer work of Edmund Fellowes in Tudor polyphony' is simply wrong: Fellowes did not begin work in this area until 1911 (see Watkins Shaw, 'Edmund H. Fellowes, 1870–1951', *Musical Times* 111 (1970): 1104–5), while the *Tallis Fantasia* was premièred in 1910 (not 1909 as Stradling and Hughes claim).

'Schools of Composition' in the third volume, first published in 1882, of Grove's *Dictionary*:[186]

> [Tallis] is, perhaps, better known, and more fairly judged, than any other English Composer of the time, though his most popular works are not in all cases his best. To speak to English Organists of his Responses, his Litany, or his Service in the Dorian Mode, would be superfluous. But, how many are equally well acquainted with his Motet, 'Salvator mundi', or his fearfully intricate Canon, 'Miserere nostri'? How many know that the original of 'I call and cry' is an 'O sacrum convivium' worthy of any Church Composer in the world short of Palestrina himself? How many have looked into the 'Cantiones Sacræ' [...] ? Yet it is here that we must look for Tallis, if we wish to form any idea of his true greatness.'[187]

This passage not only flags the change in concretization, but also articulates clearly the idea that the identity of the composer can be located within a particular body of work.

Henry Davey, in his 1895 *History of English Music*, reiterates Rockstro's argument:

> To say anything in praise of Tallis, whose Preces are daily heard in the Anglican choral service [...] may seem needless. Yet it is necessary to point out that he is generally underrated and misunderstood, because his simpler works are so very well known that they have obscured the more ambitious and elaborate. Tallis can only be fairly judged by his great contrapuntal works; the title of 'Father of English Cathedral Music' is not his most honourable title.[188]

By the end of the nineteenth century Tallis's Service was no longer performed at festivals, but had been relegated to mid-week services or penitential occasions.[189] It was frequently performed at Worcester Cathedral on Fridays, when the organ

---

[186] For a sophisticated examination of the production of Grove's *Dictionary*, see Leanne Langley, 'Roots of a Tradition: The First *Dictionary of Music and Musicians*', in *George Grove, Music and Victorian Culture*, ed. Michael Musgrave (London: Palgrave Macmillian, 2003), 168–215. The table of the original publication dates of the various fascicles on p. 190 is particularly useful.

[187] Rockstro, 'Schools of Composition', 273. Ernest Walker makes essentially the same point in *A History of Music in England* (Oxford: Clarendon Press, 1907), 44–5.

[188] Henry Davey, *History of English Music* (London: J. Curwen & Sons, 1895), 146–7.

[189] It remained in the repertoire, however. The Church Music Society's *Forty Years of Cathedral Music, 1898–1938* (London: SPCK, 1940), 11, lists Tallis's Service as a 'perennial', which was in the repertoire of twenty-two of the fifty cathedrals surveyed in 1898, and twenty-eight of thirty-seven cathedrals in 1938.

was not used,[190] and the St Paul's music bills showed that it was traditionally performed on Ash Wednesday and Good Friday. Edward Pine recalls that in his days at Westminster Abbey in the late nineteenth century the choirboys – perhaps not the most reliable judges – regarded Tallis and Gibbons as 'dreary old codgers':

> These composers were sung on Fridays, unaccompanied; and the boys considered that this must have some connection with the fact that Friday was a fastday, when one had to do without something good.[191]

Bumpus's comments in his *Cathedral Music* of 1907 are also typical of this new position:

> Compared with his magnificent contrapuntal mass and motetts, Tallis' setting of the Canticles and Communion Service in the Dorian Mode cannot be considered his *chef d'œuvre*, as many still appear to so consider it, and one is unable to share the unbounded admiration expressed for it by Dr. Jebb in his book on the Choral Service. [...] his music, being in the Dorian Mode with plain counterpoint in unbroken notes, and without points of imitation is heavy and lugubrious in its effect. [...] unless the pitch is raised a whole tone and marks of expression judiciously introduced, it becomes absolutely tiresome [...][192]

The change in perceptions of the Dorian Service extended beyond simple questions of value: its perceived aesthetic qualities also changed dramatically over the course of the nineteenth century. The difference between the Service as described in Sir Henry Hadow's 1931 *English Music* and the complex gothic 'groinings and tracery' of the Tallis Days a century earlier could hardly be greater:

> As a rule Tallis's music has little intricacy, little involution; it is strong, simple, dignified, caring more for solidity of structure than amenity of decoration [...] the common plan of his architecture is Norman – even Romanesque – rather than Gothic.[193]

As enthusiasm for the English service music waned, however, interest in Tallis's Latin polyphony grew. In the closing years of the nineteenth century Richard Terry (later Sir Richard) began his life-long work of reviving the lost heritage of English

---

[190] Personal communication, Vernon Butcher, 17 Sep 1996.

[191] Edward Pine, *The Westminster Abbey Singers* (London: Dennis Dobson, 1953), 227–8.

[192] Bumpus, *Cathedral Music*, 45.

[193] Sir W. H. Hadow, *English Music* (London: Longman, Green & Co, 1931), 57.

Latin polyphony.[194] In 1899 the choir of Downside Abbey, under Terry, performed Tallis's Mass for four voices.[195] They also performed a Latin adaptation of *If ye love me*, *Bone Pastor*, and a work listed as *O vos omnes*, also, presumably an adaptation of one of Tallis's English anthems.[196] The most popular work by Tallis that Terry revived, however, was the Lamentations.[197] Terry came across the Lamentations in about 1898 in the early seventeenth-century partbooks British Library Add. MSS 17792–6,[198] and performed them at the Benedictine Downside Abbey in Holy Week 1901; in November of the same year he took up the position of organist and director of music at Westminster Cathedral, where he also introduced the Lamentations, which rapidly became a regular feature of the Holy Week services. In 1910 an English arrangement of the Lamentations was introduced into the Holy Week liturgies at the Anglican Cathedral in Birmingham.[199] The English version was published in about 1914 in Royle Shore's Cathedral Series – Shore held the somewhat unusual positions of 'Diocesan Instructor in Plain-chant, Birmingham' and 'Lecturer in Ecclesiastical Music, Birmingham Cathedral' – and the Latin version in 1916 in an edition by H. B. Collins, organist at Birmingham Oratory.[200] There

---

[194] For discussions of Terry's influence during his time at Westminster Cathedral, see Elizabeth Roche, '"Great Learning, Fine Scholarship, Impeccable Taste": A Fiftieth Anniversary Tribute to Sir Richard Terry (1865–1938)', *Early Music* 16 (1988): 232, and Timothy Day, 'Sir Richard Terry and 16th-Century Polyphony', *Early Music* 22 (1994): 297–307.

[195] Terry published the Mass as *Missa sine titulo* (Leipzig: Breitkopf & Härtel, 1907).

[196] A list of Latin works by 'Old Composers' performed by Terry's choir was published in the *Downside Review* 18 (1899): 218, and reproduced in Hilda Andrews, *Westminster Retrospect: A Memoir of Sir Richard Terry* (London: Geoffrey Cumbelege; Oxford University Press, 1948), 49, but many of the items listed are actually Latin adaptations of English originals.

[197] The popularity of the Lamentations was not short-lived: in 1980 Doe claimed that they were possibly Tallis's best-known works (Paul Doe, 'Tallis, Thomas', *New Grove Dictionary of Music and Musicians*, ed. Stanley Sadie (London: Macmillan, 1980), 544).

[198] Richard Runciman Terry, 'Some Unpublished Tallis', *The Chord* No. 5 (1900): 65, reproduced in *A Forgotten Psalter and Other Essays* (London: Humphrey Milford; Oxford University Press, 1929) 84–92.

[199] This appears to be an early example of the adoption within the Anglican liturgy of early Latin music popularised within Roman Catholic services ('Ecclesiastical Intelligence', *The Times*, 22 Mar 1910, 4). Terry claimed that the Lamentations were first performed at Birmingham Cathedral on Friday 8 October 1909, presumably at that year's Birmingham Festival ('"The Church Times" and Dr. Terry', *Tablet*, 23 Dec 1911, 1018; see also 'Birmingham Cathedral', *Musical Times* 50 (1909): 721).

[200] Collins was organist at the Italian Church in Hatton Garden for many years before taking up the position in Birmingham in 1915.

was a degree of animosity between Terry and Collins and Shore,[201] and a letter from Terry suggests that this may partially have been due to Shore publishing 'as his own work' two pieces, quite possibly including the Lamentations, which had been loaned to him by Terry and Ramsbotham.[202]

These regular Holy Week performances were quickly reflected in contemporary music histories. In 1907 Ernest Walker included the opening bars of the 'truly noble' Lamentations as evidence that 'it is in contrapuntal work that the real Tallis is alone displayed'.[203] H. Orsmond Anderton cites it in 1914 as a 'fine work', and compares the poignancy of the false relations with the 'Lacrymosa' from Mozart's Requiem.[204] Jeffrey Pulver, in his 1927 *A Biographical Dictionary of Old English Music* asks:

> Great as were the writings of William Byrd and others, what works appeared in this country before the genius of Henry Purcell awakened England to a short Indian summer of renown that could compare with the 'Lamentation' [...], the examples printed by Hawkins and Burney, or the popular *O Sacrum Convivium* [...]? Great as Henry Purcell undoubtedly was, there were certain aspects in which Tallis was even greater.[205]

While anthems such as *Veni Creator* and *All people* were valued because they preserved a sense of continuity with an invented tradition, the revival of Tallis's Latin polyphony represented a genuine departure from the practice of the previous 300 years, and this is emphasised by Terry. In the introduction to the 1929 reprint of his 1900 article, 'Some Unpublished Tallis', Terry claimed that when he 'discovered' the Lamentations they were unknown to 'Grove's *Dictionary* or any

---

[201] For more on the ill-feeling between Shore, Collins and the editors of the Tudor Church Music series, particularly Terry, see Richard Turbet, 'An Affair of Honour: "Tudor Church Music", the Ousting of Richard Terry, and a Trust Vindicated', *Music & Letters* 79 (1995): 595. Percy Buck claimed that Shore was 'trying hard to stir up opposition to [...] Dr Terry' and 'has been written off by his enemies and friends alike as entirely a bore and more than half a charlatan.' He continues that 'One of his chief guns is a Mr Collins – a poor little Grub-street man quite without value.' Alick Ramsbotham later attributes the tension between Collins and Terry to Collins's editorial competence, and claims that Terry was 'blindly jealous' of Collins.

[202] Turbet, 'An Affair of Honour', 595.

[203] Walker, *Music in England*, 44.

[204] H. Orsmond Anderton, 'Thomas Tallys', *Musical Opinion and Music Trades Review* 34 (1914): 283. This article was reproduced in Anderton's *Early English Music* (London: Musical Opinion, 1920), 104–10.

[205] Jeffrey Pulver, *A Biographical Dictionary of Old English Music* (London: Kegan, 1927), 446.

musical histories'.[206] This claim is not strictly true; the first edition of Grove's *Dictionary* listed Henry Needler's British Library Add. MS 5059 as containing 'Incipit lamentatio (Aleph, Beth) à 5'.[207] The Lamentations are also found in another eighteenth-century manuscript, British Library Add. MS 34726, and in the mid-nineteenth-century British Library Add. MS 34070. Add. MS 34726, which was mostly in the hand of John Travers, had been in the possession of Philip Hayes (the son of William), Vincent Novello and the Musical Antiquarian Society, and, as previously mentioned, the Academy of Ancient Music had probably performed the Lamentations in the 1760s. The second edition of Grove's *Dictionary* in 1910 listed several other sources of the Lamentations, including manuscript copies in the Bodleian Library and at St Michael's, Tenbury. The Lamentations were, therefore, not unknown amongst earlier scholars and antiquarians, but Terry's claim of 'discovery' serves to emphasise the distance between this music and the established traditions.

Terry concluded his 1899 article with a plea for 'some addition to the meagre catalogue of [Tallis's] published works',[208] and the early decades of the twentieth century saw a modest number of publications of Tallis's Latin music. Terry published *Bone Pastor* and a new edition of *O sacrum convivium* in his series of 'Downside' Motets, and the Mass in F (*Missa sine titulo*); H. B. Collins published several of the Latin motets, including *Salvator mundi II, In jejunio et fletu* and *Dum transisset sabbatum*. In 1928 Tallis's complete Latin music was published in volume six of the Tudor Church Music series.[209] Yet despite these new publications, and the reordering of the structure of Tallis's œuvre in the history books, the older concretization, based largely upon the English service music, lingered on. The Latin music was not widely performed until well into the twentieth century.

The image of Tallis, the Father of English Cathedral Music, occupied a considerably larger place in the nineteenth century imagination than performances of his music would suggest. The very few recorded performances do not fully reflect the range of music available in print, which in itself only comprised a small and unrepresentative portion of his music. This disjunction between the image and the reality was not unrecognised at the time: Terry described Tallis as 'a composer whose name a churchgoing public honours in print, and whose music it systematically

[206] Terry, *A Forgotten Psalter*, 84.

[207] W[illiam] H[enry] H[usk], 'Tallys', *A Dictionary of Music and Musicians*, ed. Sir George Grove (London: Macmillan, 1889), 54.

[208] Terry, 'Some Unpublished Tallis', 91.

[209] *Thomas Tallis, c. 1505–1585*, ed. P. C. Buck, A. Ramsbotham, E. H. Fellowes and S. Townsend Warner, Tudor Church Music 6 (London: Oxford University Press, 1928). Hereafter, TCM 6.

neglects in practice.'[210] The preface to the Tudor Church Music edition of Tallis's Latin works begins with a similar observation:

> The name of Thomas Tallis has without doubt been the most widely and continuously known among those of the English sixteenth-century composers, not excepting even that of Thomas Morley. This is not a little strange, seeing that few musician to-day could claim to know much of his works beyond the 'Short' Service, two or three of his small anthems, such as 'If ye love me', his Preces, Responses, and Litany, and two of his 'Tunes' from Archbishop Parker's Psalter.[211]

The fact that a substantial number of the more popular works attributed to Tallis in the nineteenth century had dubious claims to his authorship points to this disparity between the symbolic significance of the composer and the relative lack of interest in his music, and suggests that the high esteem in which he was held was largely a result of his unique position in the history of English church music, rather than a genuine aesthetic response to his music. The image of Tallis as the 'Father of English Church Music' was not primarily built upon the music; rather a body of music was constructed that supported this view of the composer. Michael Talbot has argued that, as a result of the increased importance assigned to the composer around the turn of the nineteenth century, 'Our focus is no longer on the individual work that we credit to a given composer: it is on the individual composer to whom we ascribe given works.'[212] In the next chapter we shift our focus from the perceptions of the works to the images that were constructed of Tallis, the composer to whom they were ascribed.

---

[210] Terry, 'Some Unpublished Tallis', 91.

[211] TCM 6, xi.

[212] Talbot, 'Composer-Centredness', 180.

CHAPTER 2

'Such a man as Tallis': Tallis the man

I N November 1861 Prince Albert died, and discussions about the construction of
an appropriate memorial began almost immediately. By the mid-1860s sculp-
tor Henry Hugh Armstead had begun construction of his share (the Poets and
Musicians) of the 169 figures forming the Parnassus of the fine arts that surround
the four sides of Gilbert Scott's Victorian Gothic memorial.[1] The Parnassus was,
in the words of Stephen Bayley, 'encrusted with all mankind's eternal geniuses of
the fine arts, suggestive of the timeless basis upon which the arts in England pres-
ently flourished or, at least as they were supposed to'.[2] Tallis was one of twenty-
five musicians represented. Armstead went to a great deal of effort to ensure the
accuracy of likeness in these sculptures, drawing upon portraits, death masks and
personal acquaintances of the composers,[3] yet no such models were available for
Tallis. The well-known engraving of Tallis by G. van der Gucht (see Figure 3) is
believed to have been produced for an illustrated history of music roughly 150
years after Tallis's death, and there is no reason to believe that it is anything other
than an artist's fancy.[4] It is moreover unlikely that Armstead was familiar with this
portrait, which bears no resemblance to the Tallis of the Albert Memorial (see
Figure 4). Armstead had, literally, to invent the figure of the composer.

Recent discussions of the changes in musical practice that took place around
the turn of the nineteenth century, particularly in the context of the debate about
the work-concept generated by Lydia Goehr's *The Imaginary Museum of Musical
Works*, have identified the increasing importance placed upon the composer at
this time. Although the church music of Tallis lies a long way from the 'Beethoven

---

[1] The Albert Memorial is located in Kensington Gardens, one of the Royal Parks of
London.

[2] Stephen Bayley, *The Albert Memorial: The Monument in its Social and Architectural
Context* (London: Scolar Press, 1981), 67.

[3] Bayley, *Albert Memorial*, 67–70.

[4] This history, proposed by Nicola Haym, is discussed further below. Lowell E. Lindgren, in his edition of *Nicola Francesco Haym: Complete Sonatas, Part 1*, Recent
Researches in Music of the Baroque Era 116 (Middleton, WI: A-R Editions, 2002),
xii, points out that one of the other surviving 'heads' from Haym's history has an
identical frame, suggesting that the engravings were prepared specifically for that
project. Alistair Dixon, in the notes accompanying the first volume of the Chapelle
du Roi recording of the complete works of Tallis (Signum SIGCD001, 1997, 41)
claims that the style of dress in the portrait is Jacobean rather than Tudor, and a
new image was commissioned for this series of recordings.

Figure 3. Engraving of Tallis and Byrd (© The Trustees of The British Museum)

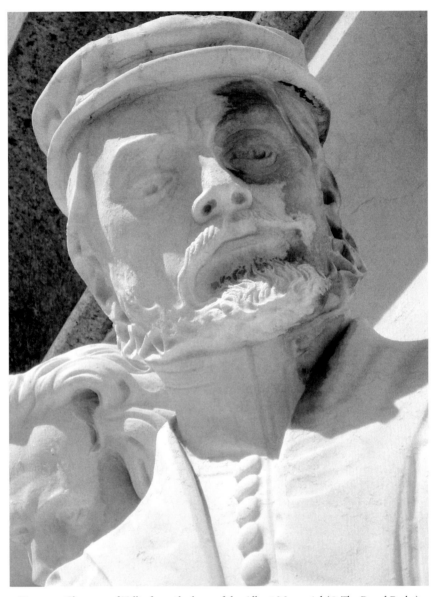

Figure 4. Close-up of Tallis from the base of the Albert Memorial (© The Royal Parks)

prototype'[5] that is the focus of such discussions, a similar increase in emphasis upon the composer can be observed in Tallis reception between the late eighteenth and early twentieth centuries. Even today very few details about Tallis's life are known;[6] in the early nineteenth century the biographical data were even fewer. In a genre or performance-based practice the absence of biographical detail or of a clear sense of the composer is not critical, but as composition came increasingly to be seen as 'reflect[ing] the state and course of a composer's inner life',[7] a stronger sense of the psychophysical composer, the person behind the music, was required. Whilst it may have been the most substantial, Armstead's was far from the only image of Tallis constructed in the nineteenth century. In this chapter I will examine the techniques whereby a number of monuments to Tallis, both literal and metaphorical, were constructed and the (very) bare bones of Tallis's biography were fleshed out to lend weight to the image of Thomas Tallis as an historical entity and as a member of a musical and ecclesiastical community stretching back to the Reformation. I will also trace what could be termed the changing concretizations of the psychophysical composer: the ways that shifts in biographical emphasis led to the construction of new and different images of Tallis.[8]

❧ *Epitaphs and Monuments*

MICHAEL Talbot argues that in Quantz's *On Playing the Flute*, 'Composers are introduced by name as examples of good practitioners within a genre, but only in the same spirit as one would cite Stradivarius as a good violin-maker or Chippendale as a good chair-maker.'[9] There is no suggestion that a well-constructed chair is an expression of the craftsman's inner life, and in the same way, the references to Tallis in the earliest sources as a good maker of church music say little or nothing about Tallis himself. Thus when Charles Butler cites examples from Tallis in his *Principles of Musik,* the biography of the composer is of as little interest as the life of Mr Chippendale is to the collector of antiques. Although Tudway holds up the 'excellent persons' Tallis and Byrd as the originators and standard-setters

---

[5] Goehr, 'The Problems of Dating', 243.

[6] Paul Doe's *Tallis* – still the only monograph on the composer – dispenses with the few known biographical facts in the three-page introduction (*Tallis* (1968; 2nd ed. London: Oxford University Press, 1976)).

[7] Talbot, 'Composer-Centredness', 180.

[8] These different concretizations are essentially similar to the different 'profiles' of Chopin identified by Jim Samson ('Chopin Reception: Theory, History, Analysis', *Chopin Studies 2*, ed. John Rink and Jim Samson (Cambridge: Cambridge University Press, 1994), 2).

[9] Talbot, 'Composer-Centredness', 174.

of church music, the brief details of their royal employment that he provides act rather as markers of authority than as insights into the personality or individuality of the composers. His admission that they were 'both of them Papists' is not seen as any impediment to their establishment of 'an inimitable Pattern of solemn Church Musik' as required by the 'Pious Reformers of our Church'.[10]

By the end of the eighteenth century, however, this situation was beginning to change. Boyce's *Church Music* of 1760 not only literally sorts the music by composer, but is prefaced by a 'Succinct Account of the Several Authors, whose Works are contained in this Volume'. These 'biographies' were indeed brief, but their presence draws attention to the composers behind the music and suggests an emerging musical historicism. The essentially modern use of the term 'works' also points to a change in the relationship between the composer and the musical product.[11]

Boyce's account of Tallis was the first of the Several Authors (see Figure 5), and adds little to Tudway's description of Tallis's royal employment, but this very brief biography is fleshed out by a transcription of the epitaph inscribed on Tallis's gravestone in the parish church of St Alfege in Greenwich.[12] The epitaph adds depth to the bald biographical data: it describes not only Tallis's musical achievements and, again, his service under 'Fower Soveregnes', but also his mild and virtuous disposition and his late, childless marriage. As well as providing additional information about Tallis's life, it also reminds the reader of his humanity.

Charles Burney's discussion of Tallis in his *General History* is considerably longer, taking up almost five pages (plus six pages of musical examples), but is mostly devoted to the description of works and sources. He claims that Tallis was 'born early in the reign of Henry VIII', disputes the exact nature of the much-discussed royal employment, and mentions that he was the 'master' of William Byrd, but no substantial biographical information is added to Boyce's Succinct Account. Burney's account of Tallis is surprisingly impersonal: Tallis himself is strangely absent. Burney's heavy reliance on the passive voice limits any sense of direct compositional agency, most notably in his discussion of *Spem in alium*, referred to as 'this wonderful effort of harmonical abilities'. Burney begins by calling it 'the most curious and extraordinary of all his [Tallis's] labours', but in the extended

---

[10] Hogwood, 'Thomas Tudway's History of Music', 23.

[11] Lydia Goehr discusses the use of the term 'work' at some length, although predominantly with reference to instrumental music. She argues that at the end of the eighteenth century 'the term "work" [...] came generically to signify any original and completed and whole composition of music, whether instrumental or vocal.' (Goehr, *Imaginary Museum*, 203). It is hard to tell exactly what Boyce meant by the term in this context, but it would seem to be something along these lines.

[12] Although the church was destroyed in 1711, the epitaph was recorded in Strype's continuation of Stow's *Survey of London* (London, 1720), app. 1, 92.

[vii]

A Succinct ACCOUNT of the

Several Authors, whose Works are contained in this Volume.

THOMAS TALLIS was Organiſt of the Royal Chapels to King *Henry* VIII, King *Edward* VI, Queen *Mary*, and Queen *Elizabeth*.

He was eſteem'd a moſt excellent Compoſer of Church Muſic, at leaſt equal to any Contemporary, either of his own Country or of Foreign Nations.

He, in conjunction with *William Bird*, a Muſician of great Eminence, who had been his Scholar, obtain'd of Queen *Elizabeth*, in the Year of our Lord 1575, Letters patent, by which they claim'd the excluſive Right of printing all Ruled Paper, as well as of all Muſic Books, for the Term of 21 Years.

He died *November* 23d, 1585, and was buried at *Greenwich* in *Kent*.

On his Grave-Stone is the following Inſcription:

Enterred here doth ly a worthy wyght,
    Who for long Tyme in muſick bore the bell:
His name to ſhew, was Thomas Tallis *hyght,*
    In honeſt vertuous Lyff he dyd excell.

He ſerv'd long Tyme in Chappel with grete Prayſe,
    Fower Sovereygnes Reygnes (a Thing not often ſeen)
I mean Kyng Henry & Prynce Edward's dayes,
    Queen Mary & Elizabeth our Quene.

He maryed was, though Children he had none,
    And lyv'd in Love full thre and thirty yeres
Wyth loyal ſpouſe, whoſe name yclyipt was Jone,
    Who here entomb'd, him Company now bears.

As he did lyve, ſo alſo did he dy,
    In myld & quyet ſort (O! happy man)
To God ful oft for mercy did he cry,
    Wherefore he lyves, let Death do what he can.

RICHARD FARRANT was Gentleman of the Royal Chapels to King *Edward* VI, and Queen *Elizabeth*, and in 1564 was appointed Organiſt of *St. George*'s Chapel, *Windſor*, and Maſter of the Choriſters there. In 1580 he reſign'd his Place in the Royal Chapels, and died in 1585.

His Compoſitions for the Church Service were peculiarly ſolemn, and well adapted for that Purpoſe.

b

THOMAS

Figure 5. Boyce's 'Succinct Account' of Tallis

description of 'this stupendous, though perhaps Gothic, specimen of human labour and intellect' that follows, he manages to avoid any direct reference to the composer. His justification for including two lengthy musical examples – to prove that at the time of Palestrina 'we had Choral Music of our own, which for gravity of style, purity of harmony, ingenuity of design, and clear and masterly contexture, was equal to the best productions of that truly venerable master'[13] – is couched in terms of national, rather than personal, achievement.

A passage at the end of Burney's description of Byrd, however, draws a more intimate picture of the two men:

> That he [Byrd] was pious, the words he selected, and the solemnity and grav-ity of style with which he set them, sufficiently evince. Of his moral character and natural disposition, there can perhaps be no testimonies more favour-able, or less subject to suspicion, than those of rival professors, with whom he appears to have lived during a long life with cordiality and friendship. And, of the goodness of his heart, it is to me, no trivial proof, that he loved and was beloved, by his master Tallis, and scholar, Morley; who, from their intimate connexion with him, must have seen him *en robe de chambre*, and been spectators of all the operations of temper, in the opposite situations of subjection and dominance.[14]

Burney concludes his Tallis entry with the epitaph.

Hawkins's description of Tallis is rather warmer than Burney's; his reference to Tallis as 'a diligent collector of musical antiquities, and a careful peruser of the works of other men' makes some attempt to attribute personal characteristics to the composer, as does his claim that Tallis 'laid the foundation of his studies in the works of the old cathedralists of this kingdom'.[15] He cites the joint publication of the *Cantiones sacrae* as evidence of Tallis's affection for Byrd, and speculates that in composing *Spem in alium*, Tallis 'had an emulation to excel' Okenheim's [Ockeghem's] thirty-six part canon; such human motivations manage to evoke a relatively vivid image of the composer. Hawkins's account again concludes with the epitaph.

Tallis's was not the only epitaph published in these collections: Boyce repro-duced the epitaphs of Child, Gibbons and Blow, and Burney and Hawkins included epitaphs in many of their biographical entries (see Table 7). Furthermore, those epitaphs that were written in verse were set to music in the late eighteenth cen-tury: Robert Hudson, master of the children at St Paul's Cathedral from 1773–93

---

[13] Burney, *General History*, 2:69.

[14] Burney, *General History*, 2:81.

[15] Hawkins, *General History*, 456.

Table 7 Late eighteenth-century publications and settings of composers' epitaphs

		Boyce	Burney	Hawkins	Musical setting/s
Tallis	verse	✓	✓	✓	Cooke
					Crotch
Gibbons	prose	✓	✓	✓	
Purcell	verse (Latin)	–	✓	–	Mary Hudson
					(Dryden's *Ode on the Death of*
					Mr Henry Purcell was set by Blow)
Child	verse	✓	✓	✓	Robert Hudson
Blow	prose	✓	–	✓	

composed a setting of Child's epitaph,[16] his daughter Mary, who was also an organist, set Purcell's epitaph,[17] and Tallis's epitaph was set to music by Dr Benjamin Cooke in about 1768 and by William Crotch in 1799.

This interest in composers' epitaphs can be seen not only as evidence of the changing status of the composer, but as part of a broader eighteenth-century fascination with epitaphs, elegies and other forms of literary mourning. Most anthologies of eighteenth-century poetry include epitaphs, elegies or sonnets in memory of the dead; Gray's *Elegy Written in a Country Churchyard* was, and remains, one of the most popular poems of the eighteenth century. Esther Schor, in her study of eighteenth-century literary mourning, *Bearing the Dead*, examines the use of symbols of mourning in historical literary anthologies such as Henry Headley's *Select Beauties of Ancient Poetry* (1787) and Bishop Percy's *Reliques* (1765):

> In these literary histories and anthologies, the inventors of the literary dead typically pose as mourners erecting monuments to a lost heritage. [...] Headley's ostentatious sympathy asks English readers to read these poems as the relics of their own predecessors, identifying readers, editor, and corpus as part of a single literary community.[18]

---

[16] Bumpus, *Cathedral Music*, 165.

[17] W[illiam] H[enry] H[usk], 'Hudson, Robert', *Dictionary of Music and Musicians*. Hudson, with Burney and Cooke, was a member of the 'Musical Graduates' Society' until he left, ostensibly because 'he was never accustomed to dine at his own table without the company of his wife and daughter' (Percy Scholes, *The Great Dr Burney*, vol. 2 (London: Oxford University Press, 1948), 121). Scholes interprets this as showing that Hudson was 'under petticoat government', but this evidence of Mary's compositional activities and interest in the composers of the past suggests an interpretation rather more creditable to both Hudson and the women of his household.

[18] Esther Schor, *Bearing the Dead* (Princeton: Princeton University Press, 1994), 55–6. Headley had no corpse: the 'corpus' or body or works which formed his

Although the cathedral music of the sixteenth century could hardly be seen as a 'lost heritage', nor did Burney, Boyce or Hawkins indulge in 'ostentatious sympathy', I believe that the publication of epitaphs in Burney and Hawkins's *General Histories* and Boyce's *Cathedral Music* served in a similar way to 'invent' the musical dead and to create a sense of these long-dead and largely absent composers as fellow members of a musical community.

The ideal attributes of a good epitaph were outlined in 1740 by Dr Samuel Johnson in his 'Essay upon Epitaphs', and by William Wordsworth, who published a further three essays on the subject in 1810. In his first essay, Wordsworth argues that an epitaph should act as 'a record to preserve the memory of the dead, as a tribute due to his individual worth, for the satisfaction to the sorrowing hearts of survivors, and for the common benefit of the living'.[19] Johnson expands upon the nature of the benefits to the living, claiming that

> the principal intention of epitaphs is to perpetuate the examples of virtue, that the tomb of a good man may supply the want of his presence, and veneration for his memory produce the same effect as the observation of his life. Those epitaphs are, therefore, the most perfect, which set virtue in the strongest light, and are best adapted to exalt the reader's ideas, and rouse his emulation.[20]

Tallis's epitaph meets Johnson and Wordsworth's requirements admirably: it briefly sketches Tallis's most notable achievements as a musician, goes on to describe his marital felicity (Johnson urges that 'the best subject for epitaphs is private virtue; virtue exerted in the same circumstances in which the bulk of mankind are placed, and which, therefore, may admit of many imitators'),[21] and concludes with what Wordsworth termed 'a humble expression of Christian confidence in immortality'.[22]

Whilst Tallis's epitaph was, according to the principles laid down by Johnson and Wordsworth, an excellent example of a tombstone epitaph, it could not be expected to function in quite the same way in a history of music or collection of cathedral music. Wordsworth had observed that 'It need scarcely be said that an

anthologies had to be constructed, Frankenstein-like. In the same way collections such as Boyce's defined, if not constructed, the 'corpus' of music interred in the historical monument.

[19] William Wordsworth, 'Essays upon Epitaphs', *Selected Prose*, ed. John O. Hayden (Harmondsworth: Penguin, 1988), 327.

[20] Samuel Johnson, 'An Essay on Epitaphs', in *Samuel Johnson*, ed. Donald Greene (Oxford: Oxford University Press, 1984), 97.

[21] Johnson, 'Essay on Epitaphs', 101.

[22] Wordsworth, 'Essays', 330.

Epitaph presupposes a Monument upon which it is to be engraven',[23] yet in 1711 St Alfege's church collapsed, and, although the church was rebuilt, the epitaph was not replaced. For over 150 years, there was no physical monument upon which Tallis's epitaph was engraved. Publications such as Burney's and Hawkins's *General Histories* and Boyce's *Cathedral Music*, however, acted as a different type of monument to the composers of earlier generations.[24] The role of these publications as monuments is reinforced by the reproduction of composers' epitaphs, and the musical setting of these epitaphs carried this 'invention' of the musical dead a step further.

The earlier of the two settings of Tallis's epitaph, by Dr Benjamin Cooke, was published in Thomas Warren's *Seventh Collection of Canons, Catches and Glees* in 1768; a manuscript copy of this work survives in the commonplace book of J. Philpott of Bath, dated 12 July 1796.[25] Cooke was the conductor of the Academy of Ancient Music from 1752 until 1789 and one of the musical directors of the 1784 Handel Commemoration; as a child he had studied with Christopher Pepusch, from whom, according to Bumpus, 'he caught that taste for collecting music and for antiquarian research which tinged his life, his character, and his labours.'[26]

Cooke's setting is quite a substantial piece in the style of the glee, falling into a number of sections, in contrasting style, tempo and number and range of voices. The first two verses are modelled upon Tallis, whereas the second half becomes progressively more Handelian.

The opening phrase is based upon the main theme of the Dorian Service (see Example 3). Cooke maintains the open fifth of the original on the first chord, but softens it by moving to the third in the tenor on the second beat. At bar 9 he begins a brief point of imitation;[27] a second imitative point at bar 15 is based on bars 34–40 of the Dorian Te Deum (see Example 4), although Tallis does not treat this motive polyphonically.

At bar 20 Cooke reduces the texture to the lower three parts, before a faster four-part polyphonic section. Verse 3 is set for two trebles and an alto, possibly reflecting the domestic tone of this verse. This lighter texture contrasts with the

---

[23] Wordsworth, 'Essays', 322. These later revivals of the epitaph also fulfill a different function from contemporary memorials such as Byrd's lament, *Ye sacred Muses* or the verse in honour of Tallis's death in *GB-Och* Mus. 988, fol. 20.

[24] Percy A. Scholes uses exactly these words when he refers to the publication of Boyce's volumes as 'the erection of a national monument' ('Boyce', *Oxford Companion to Music* (Oxford: Oxford University Press, 1938), 124).

[25] *GB-Lcm* MS 722. This manuscript, which also contains Tallis's *Like as the doleful dove* and *Hear the voice and prayer*, is the source of the examples that follow.

[26] Bumpus, *Cathedral Music*, 308.

[27] Bar numbers refer to *GB-Lcm* MS 722.

Example 3. Thematic comparison of Cooke's and Crotch's
epitaph settings and Dorian Service

full splendour of the last verse, which takes up 53 of the work's 118 bars. 'As he did live, so also did he die' is set in a contemplative triple time, before the texture reduces to the two inner parts for 'in mild and quiet sort'. The music then erupts into a jubilant triple-time, five-part 'O happy, happy man' (see Example 5). This section is strongly reminiscent of the contrast used by Handel in the chorus 'Since by man came death' in *Messiah*.

The tempo then slows, and the music modulates to F minor for a thoughtful triple metre exposition of the text 'to God full oft for mercy did he cry' (see Example 6). Again a model from *Messiah* springs to mind: the concluding 'And the Lord hath laid on him the iniquities of us all' section of the chorus 'All we like sheep'. The piece concludes with a triumphant, duple-time setting of 'Wherefore he lives, let death do what he can' (see Example 7), reminiscent of the 'God save the King' section from *Zadok the Priest*.

Philpott's copy bears the comment 'fine imitation', and the first two verses are quite a good imitation of Tallis's style as reflected in the handful of his works that were popular at the time: indeed a rather better imitation and of considerably greater musical interest than *All people that on earth do dwell*. The final verse of the text turns from the particular details of Tallis's life to the broader topic of 'the consciousness of a principle of immortality in the human soul', to which Wordsworth attributes the human 'desire to live in the remembrance of his fellows'.[28] At this point Cooke abandons his musical evocation of Tallis, and adopts a more recent

---

[28] Wordsworth, 'Essays', 323.

Example 4. Comparison of (a) Tallis's 'Te Deum', bars 34–7 (treble only);
(b) Cooke's Epitaph Setting, bars 14–19

style. Cooke's setting of Tallis's epitaph 'participates in the […] historical construction of the dead' on a number of levels: the text functions as a brief biography of
the man; the references to Tallis's music are an act of homage to the composer; and
the Handelian climax locates Tallis within an extended historical community of
English musicians.

   William Crotch's rather less sophisticated setting is found in a three-volume
manuscript containing the compositions of the Harmonic Society of Oxford,[29]
which Crotch founded in 1796, shortly before he was appointed Heather Professor
of Music at Oxford at the age of twenty-two. The society, which he established 'for

---

[29] *GB-Ob* Tenbury 599, 166–8.

Example 5. Cooke's epitaph setting, bars 70–5

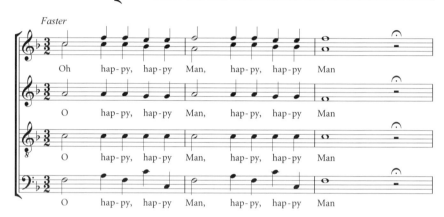

the encouragement and improvement of musical composition',[30] never actually met, as Crotch thought that this could lead to ill-feeling amongst members from different walks of life, as had happened at a similar society at Cambridge.[31] The books were, however, passed around the various members and honorary members, who each wrote in their compositions in turn. These were generally of an academic nature, with a preponderance of rounds, canons and glees. Only five works from the collection were published,[32] and it is unlikely that many were even performed, given the scattered nature of the society's membership.

Crotch's setting of Tallis's epitaph is dated September 1799. The memorial tone is maintained in the following work, a ten-part canon on the words 'Lord let me know mine end',[33] also by Crotch and dated September 1799, commemorating

---

[30] Inscribed on the title pages of volumes II and III.

[31] Jonathon Rennert, *William Crotch (1775–1847): Composer, Artist, Teacher* (Lavenham, Suffolk: T. Dalton, 1975), 37–8.

[32] Bumpus, *Cathedral Music*, 453.

[33] Psalm 39:5–6, as used in the Service of the Burial of the Dead in the Book of Common Prayer (1662).

Example 6. Cooke's epitaph setting, bars 88–102

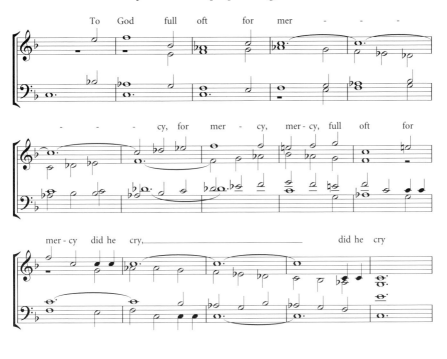

Example 7. Cooke's epitaph setting, bars 103–6

the death at the age of twenty-nine of Jacob Cubitt Pring, a fellow member of the Society.[34]

The setting of the epitaph, which is in four parts throughout, falls clearly into two contrasting sections. The first verse is a rather loose imitation of sixteenth-century polyphony (see Example 8), based upon the same motif from the Dorian Service used by Cooke (see Example 3). This may have been a deliberate reference to Cooke's setting; Cooke had taken an interest in Crotch's education as a child.[35]

[34] Jacob's brother Isaac died in October of the same year. The same manuscript volume contains works by William Horsley, an honorary member of the Society, commemorating the deaths of the brothers.

[35] Rennert, *William Crotch*, 31.

Example 8. Crotch's epitaph setting, bars 1–15

Example 9. Coda of Crotch's epitaph setting, bars 58–67

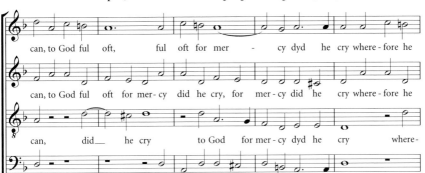

Despite its polyphonic style, this verse does not display the equality of voices typical of Tallis: the treble lines continues throughout, while the lower parts come in and out sporadically, and it is the only voice with the complete text. The spacing of the entries is irregular, and the text underlay in the lower parts is erratic. The altos, for example, begin half way through the first line of text at 'doth ly', and in bar 4 the tenor and bass entries coincide, obscuring the point of imitation in the bass. This verse is obviously intended to be an imitation of Tallis's polyphonic style, but these features point to a limited familiarity with it, and the effect is marred by the odd infelicity such as an exposed pair of consecutive fifths in bar 10.

The second section, which sets the last three verses, is largely homophonic. There is no break between verses 2 and 3 (bar 37), which are almost unreliev-edly chordal. The fourth verse, beginning at bar 48, begins in a similar style, but has a more polyphonic coda (see Example 9) repeating the last two lines of the text, somewhat reminiscent of the 'Amen' in *All people*. These verses consist of a series of regular phrases, all immediately repeated, but with the repeats shifted by half a bar, implying a *decani/cantoris* division. They bear a strong similar-ity to parts of the Dorian Service, particularly the Te Deum; a comparison of

Example 10. Crotch's Epitaph Setting, bars 27–37

Example 10 and Example 11 illustrates the parallels between the two works. Although Crotch's phrases are longer, the melodic shape, repeated at a higher pitch, and the rising scale passages in the lower parts suggest that the epitaph setting may have been directly modelled upon this section.

Despite these stylistic references, Crotch's setting is a fairly uninspired imitation of Tallis's original. Tallis used this style to set long prose texts, such as the Te Deum, which leads to a constantly shifting interplay of phrase lengths and accents. He rarely used direct repeats of more than two phrases in a row, and those phrases that were repeated often had accentual shifts in the repeated phrase – as in 'Hóly, Hóly, Hóly' and 'Lord Gód of Sábaóth' – leading to a greater sense of variety (see Example 12). Not only does Tallis intersperse his repeats with occasional unrepeated phrases, but the length of the repeated fragments changes constantly. Milsom observes that in his setting of *Like as the dolefull dove* Tallis manages, through the use of syncopation, to avoid a 'fatal sing-song'.[36] Crotch, however, is less successful, and the simple metrical structure of the text of the epitaph and rigid application of the compositional formula make his setting a rather wan reflection of Tallis's original.

---

[36] John Milsom, 'Songs, Carols and *Contrafacta* in the Early History of the Tudor Anthem', *Proceedings of the Royal Musical Association* 107 (1980–1): 42.

Example 11. Te Deum from Tallis's Dorian Service, bars 4–12

Example 12. Te Deum from Tallis's Dorian Service, bars 16–19

This setting does, however, confirm that at the turn of the nineteenth century, Tallis was primarily identified with the simple four-part textures of the Dorian Service, upon which this piece is modelled. The attempt at polyphony in the first section shows little familiarity with or understanding of Tallis's style, and such ignorance may explain, at least in part, the nineteenth-century readiness to accept the attribution to him of works such as *All people* and *Veni Creator*.

Despite these failings, however, these musical settings of Tallis's epitaph indicate an emerging interest in Tallis and his music, and contributed to the historicist construction of monuments to past composers begun by Burney, Hawkins and Boyce. Tallis's epitaph continued to be reproduced well into the nineteenth century: it was published in the Boston *Euterpeiad, or Musical Intelligencer* in 1820, at the end of Hawkins's account of Tallis in the *Harmonicon* in 1826,[37] and in the prefaces to many of the editions of his music that began to be published in the 1840s. But the importance of the epitaph waned in the nineteenth century as other types of monuments to Tallis were constructed.

---

37 *Euterpeiad, or Musical Intelligencer*, 22 Apr 1820, 16 and 'Memoir of Thomas Tallis', *Harmonicon* 4 (1826): 43–5.

❧ *Documenting the Biography*

O NE of the first of these was the series of 'Tallis Days' that were briefly popular in the early 1840s. Dedicating a 'Day' to a single composer – a clear example of 'sorting' music by composer, particularly in a liturgical context where composer-centredness is not the norm – served to personalise the event and to focus the attention on the composer. Despite Taylor's claims about the popularity of these Tallis Days, they appear to have been short lived: no further reports appear in the *Musical World* after 1842.[38] This did not, however, indicate a lessening of interest in Tallis or his music; rather the interest generated by these Days seems to have been channelled in new directions.

The 1840s and 50s saw the publication of an impressive number of editions of Tallis's music, particularly of the Dorian Service and the Litany and Responses. These editions, which were often physically imposing, printed in red and black with ornate borders and lengthy introductions, can in themselves been seen as a type of monument, and will be examined further in Chapter 4. The prefaces of these editions also provided an important forum for discussions of Tallis and his music. Rimbault's 1846 edition of *The Order of the Daily Service*, for example, was advertised as including 'a full and scientific account of Tallis's harmonies, and a new and curious biography of their celebrated author, written from 𝔒riginal 𝔇ocuments and compiled with great care.'[39] The few biographical details contained in the twenty-page preface are, however, swamped by a painstaking listing of manuscript sources and an extended discussion of the number of voices and placement of the plainchant in the Litany and Responses. Rimbault repeats the basic facts contained in Burney and Hawkins, but adds that Tallis was educated at the school of St Paul's Cathedral, under Thomas Mulliner. He cites no source, however, and this claim has since been discredited.

Rimbault was a little more successful in creating a coherent biography of Tallis in his 1872 edition of the *Old Cheque-Book of the Chapel Royal*, which contains a single reference to Tallis:

> 1585. Tho. Tallis died the 23rd of November, and Henry Eveseed sworne in his place the last of the same. Childe there.[40]

---

[38] Taylor does, however, refer to them as ongoing in his 1845 *English Cathedral Service*. It is, of course, possible that Taylor, who is responsible for most of our records of these events, inflated their popularity, but his desire for their success is in itself not without significance.

[39] Advertisement for the *Full Cathedral Service*, found at end of *Order of Daily Service*.

[40] Edward F. Rimbault, ed., *The Old Cheque-Book or Book of Remembrance of the Chapel Royal* (1872; repr. New York: Da Capo, 1966), 4.

In addition to his transcription of the entries in the *Cheque-Book*, Rimbault appended his own commentary. His note to the above entry is a brief biography of Tallis, including, yet again, the epitaph.[41] In addition to the biographical information contained in the *Order of Daily Service*, Rimbault claims that the phrase 'Childe there' implies that Tallis was a 'singing-boy' in the Chapel Royal. Once again, Rimbault seems to have jumped to conclusions on the basis of little evidence, and it is now generally accepted that the phrase applies to Eveseed.

Rimbault's note does, however, contain one significant new piece of information. He finishes his discussion of Tallis with a reference to van der Gucht's then little-known engraving of Tallis and Byrd, a copy of which was 'in the possession of the editor', a gift from 'his ever ready friend Mr. William Chappell.'[42] This engraving is thought to have been produced for a history of music proposed by Nicola Haym in 1726. Haym's publication, which is described at some length in Hawkins's *General History*, was to have been in five volumes, with the final volume comprising 'the lives of all eminent masters and professors of this art in all times, with their effigies', although it was never published, due to lack of interest.[43] Suzanne Aspden has argued that the early eighteenth century, when 'the idea of the incipient British nation both was shaped by and also in turn shaped the likenesses of its most famous sons', was characterised by a 'peculiarly physical' interest in image-making,[44] and Haym's proposed publication would appear to be a manifestation of this interest. The rediscovery of these portraits after 150 years of neglect can in turn be seen as indicative of a renewed interest in the images of early composers. This engraving is mentioned in the entry on Tallis in the first edition of Grove's *Dictionary*, and is reproduced in Bumpus's *Cathedral Music* of 1908. The publication and setting of epitaphs in the late eighteenth century can be seen as having constructed a monument to the composers of the past, and the performances and editions of the first half of the nineteenth century as having called up their 'shades'. The work of the late nineteenth century seems to have been the construction of a clearer picture of these old composers as individual human beings.

The most literally concrete image of Tallis can be found on the base of the Albert Memorial. Stephen Bayley, in his monograph on the memorial, argues that the Parnassus section upon which Prince Albert 'squats' constituted an 'attempt to classify and organise the past in a meaningful Whig manner so that the present

---

41 Rimbault, *Old Cheque-Book*, 192.

42 Rimbault, *Old Cheque-Book*, 193.

43 Hawkins, *General History of Music*, 821–2. See also Lindgren, *Nicola Francesco Haym*, xii.

44 Suzanne Aspden, '"Fam'd Handel Breathing, tho' Transformed to Stone": The Composer as Monument', *Journal of the American Musicological Society* 55 (2002): 43.

condition of the arts might be better accounted for', and as such was 'characteristic of European art at the time'.[45] In this classification, the arts are embodied in the persons of the authors, composers or creators; although Homer is depicted playing a lyre, there is little iconographic attempt to portray the particular arts that the figures represented. English composition is represented by Tallis, Lawes, Gibbons, Purcell, Arne, Boyce and Bishop. Continental composers include St Ambrose, Guido d'Arezzo, Palestrina, Monteverde [sic], Josquin, Carissimi, Bach, Handel, Lully, Rameau, Auber, Méhul, Grétry, Haydn, Mozart, Beethoven, Rossini and Mendelssohn. The German and English composers are on the right of Homer, the French and Italian on the left. The Painters were similarly arranged; Sculpture and Architecture, which were grouped around King Solomon, were considered 'more susceptible of chronological interpretation'.[46] J. L. Tupper describes Tallis as one of a 'spirited group' of three English musicians perusing a scroll (see Figure 6):

> What is in the scroll we do not know, for the sculptor will not condescend to the trick of writing on it; but it is grasped by Gibbons and held open by Lawes, while Tallis places an admonishing finger on it, and at the same time lays a gentle expostulating pressure on the hand of Gibbons that holds it. There is a living look in this action – which is wholly inexpressible.[47]

Tallis's posture clearly sets him apart from Beethoven, who stands to Tallis's left in, in Tupper's words, 'forlorn absorption'. The strong movement of Tallis's arms across his body in the direction of the later English composers can be seen to represent his position at the head of English music, pointing the way forward for his chronologically ordered successors.

The van der Gucht engraving of Tallis presents a mild and youthful figure, rather lacking in presence; Armstead's Tallis is considerably more impressive. He is dressed as a Tudor gentleman with a stiff neck ruff and tunic, in contrast to Gibbons, who is wearing a cassock. He appears older and more worldly than the earlier portrayal, altogether a man of substance. Armstead's work on the Albert Memorial predates Rimbault's *Cheque-Book* by almost a decade, and the lack of similarity between the two images suggests that he was unaware of the earlier engraving, and was forced, in the absence of a reliable model, to rely on his imagination in creating his image of Tallis. At around the same time, however, scholars and anti-

[45] Bayley, *Albert Memorial*, 67.
[46] Bayley, *Albert Memorial*, 69.
[47] John Lucas Tupper, 'Henry Hugh Armstead', *English Artists of the Present Day: Essays by J. Beavington Atkinson, Sidney Colvin, F. G. Stephens, Tom Taylor, and John L. Tupper* (London: Seeley, Jackson and Halliday, 1872), reproduced on *The Victorian Web*, accessed 21 Mar 2003, <http://65.107.211.206/victorian/sculpture/armstead/bio1.html>.

Figure 6. Detail from the Albert Memorial: Beethoven, Tallis, Gibbons and Lawes
(© The Royal Parks)

quarians uncovered several pieces of documentary evidence that allowed the construction of a more substantial and better-documented biographical picture of the
composer.

The first of these was published in the *Musical Times* in November 1876, by William H. Cummings. The article coincided with the reopening of Waltham Abbey,
which had been closed for three months for restoration. The occasion was celebrated with a 'series of special choral services', including works by Handel, Goss,
Elvey, Hopkins and Smart, and Tallis's 'Festal' Responses. After praising the 'noble
harmonies' of the Responses, which he claimed 'excite as much religious fervour

and admiration at this day as they did some three centuries since when they were first composed by the father of English Church Music', Cummings reveals his *coup*: 'doubtless it will be a great surprise to students of musical biography that Thomas Tallis was for some time organist at Waltham Abbey.'[48] Tallis's association with the abbey was documented in a list of payments made at its dissolution in 1540, discovered in the Public Records Office by a Mr W. Winters, 'a historian and antiquary at Waltham'.[49]

Not only does Cummings announce this substantial addition to the very small stock of biographical data, but he also manages to flesh out the few facts at his disposal to create a rather more human picture of Tallis. He wonders 'how long a period elapsed after the breaking of his voice before he became organist of Waltham Abbey' and observes that 'it is well known that King Henry VIII. was a frequent visitor to Waltham Abbey, and being a musician and composer himself, he would know how to value the worth of such a man as Tallis.' A more substantial sense of 'such a man as Tallis', complete with such human characteristics as a breaking voice, was beginning to form.

A similar mix of new documentary evidence combined with a physical evocation of the person of the composer is found in a letter to the *Musical Times* published two years later in 1878.[50] This letter, which will be discussed in greater detail in the next chapter, reproduces a manuscript account of Tallis rising to the challenge of an unnamed duke to prove that an English composition could rival an Italian song in thirty parts.[51] In this account, upon hearing the first performance of the forty-part *Spem in alium*, the duke 'tooke his chayne of Gold from his necke & putt yt about Tallice his necke and gave yt him'. The gold chain lends weight to a new image of Tallis, companion of dukes, motivated by a rather secular spirit of competition. The image of the composer conjured up by the tale seems to sit quite comfortably with Armstead's Tallis – it not difficult to imagine the Tallis of the Albert Memorial bearing the ducal chain – and can be seen as an early manifestation of the new image of Tallis that began to emerge towards the end of the century. The letter's author, a Rev. H. Fleetwood Shepherd, concluded his letter with the observation that:

---

[48] William H. Cummings, 'Tallis – Waltham Abbey', *Musical Times* 17 (1876): 649.

[49] 'Dotted Crotchet', 'The Abbey Church of Waltham Cross', *Musical Times* 47 (1906): 599. Although, according to Cummings, Winters was a 'painstaking and laborious antiquary', he did not record the reference to the document in the Public Records Office. Cummings finally tracked it down and published it in 1913 ('Tallis and Waltham Abbey', *Musical Times* 54 (1913): 789–91).

[50] H. Fleetwood Sheppard, 'Tallis and his Song of Forty Parts', *Musical Times* 19 (1878): 97.

[51] This account resonates with Hawkins's description of Tallis's 'emulation to excel'.

the picture of the greatest English musician of his time – the Master – in the heyday of his reputation conducting the performance of his own music […] and dignified with the ducal chain […] is a pleasing one to dwell upon, not only as illustrating the estimation in which musical talent was held three centuries ago, but as representing perhaps the sole incident preserved to us in the life of one, whose history we know so little of, whose genius we venerate so greatly, and whose name is so indissolubly bound up with English Church music.

As is to be expected, the known facts of Tallis's life were brought together in 1884 in William Henry Husk's 'Tallys' entry in the first edition of Grove's *Dictionary of Music and Musicians*.[52] The entry begins simply: 'Tallys, Thomas […] Father of English cathedral music'. The origins of this idea of Tallis's musical paternity can, as we saw in Chapter 1, be traced back to the *Cantiones Sacrae* of 1575, and similar references are scattered throughout history: Hawkins refers to Tallis as the 'father of the cathedral style',[53] for example, and an 1836 review of an early performance of *Spem in alium* dubs him the 'father of English Vocal Harmony'.[54] By the 1870s, however, this occasional usage had become ubiquitous, and in this *Grove* entry it hardens into definition. Husk's article is considerably briefer than those in Burney or Hawkins, but unlike these earlier writers, he attempts to construct a chronological biographical narrative not dissimilar to Rimbault's note to the *Cheque-Book*. Husk critically assesses the available evidence: he prefers the spelling 'Tallys' as found in the surviving specimens of Tallis's signature, and he questions both Rimbault's new 'facts', pointing out the conjectural nature of Tallis's association with St Paul's Cathedral and noting the ambiguity of the 'Childe there' reference. He reproduces Tallis's signature, as found in the Waltham Abbey manuscript, and mentions the van der Gucht engraving, somewhat sceptically, as 'a head, purporting to be his likeness'. Although Husk does not

[52] For more on Husk and his role in Grove's *Dictionary*, see Langley, 'Roots of a Tradition', 180 and 205, n. 6; the original date of publication of Part 19 is taken from Table 8.1 on p. 190. Percy Young claims that Grove wrote the Tallis entry himself (*George Grove, 1820–1900: A Biography* (London: Macmillan, 1980), 30), and the article is also attributed to Grove in the Index that was published in 1890. This confusion stems from the fact that Grove prepared the works list, and his initial, G, appears at the end of the entry, while the biographical article is separately attributed to Husk (W.H.H.).

[53] Hawkins, *General History*, 456. William Horsley challenged this title in 1842, arguing that while 'Tallis improved our "cathedral style," […] we cannot call him the Father of it, when we recollect what had been produced before him by White, Shepherd, Tye and others' (Richard Turbet, 'Horsley's 1842 Edition of Byrd and its Infamous Introduction', *British Music* 14 (1992): 45).

[54] 'The Madrigal Society', *Spectator*, 23 Jan 1836, 80.

reproduce the epitaph, he states that a copy had recently been placed in St Alfege's church.

In this detail, however, Husk was incorrect. In March 1874 the Rev. Walter Miller wrote to the *Musical Times*, on behalf of a 'small influential committee', soliciting funds for a 'Brass' to be placed near the altar rail of St Alfege's, Greenwich, 'as a memorial to the father of English church music.'[55] The initial response to the proposal was disappointing: Miller wrote again to the *Musical Times* in May of the same year, complaining that after sending out '200 circulars to members of the musical profession' only £6 had been raised and 'it was obvious that nothing worth doing can be done with so small a sum.'[56] He dismissed the possibility that this lack of interest could be due to 'any unwillingness to honour the memory of one to whom English music owes so much', and assured potential contributors that no sum would be considered too small. Some money must eventually have been forthcoming: in June 1876 a brief notice appeared in the *Musical Times*, stating 'that the Brass is now fixed by Messrs. Hart, on the East wall of Greenwich Parish Church, within a few feet of the altar rails where the father of English Church Music lies buried with his wife.'[57] No further details are given, but the rather prosaic inscription was reproduced in the service sheet accompanying the celebration of the tercentenary of Tallis's death in 1885:

> In Memory of Thomas Tallis, the Father of English Church Music. He died on the twenty-third day of November in the year of our Lord fifteen hundred and eighty-five aged sixty-five and with his wife lies buried in this church.[58]

Several contemporary sources confirm that the epitaph was not reproduced on the 1876 memorial brass, and it was not until 1936 that the epitaph was finally restored to St Alfege.[59]

The 1885 celebration of the tercentenary of Tallis's death at St Alfege's was also a modest affair. The programme, consisting entirely of music by Tallis, was performed by the combined choirs of St Stephen's and St Mark's Lewisham, All Saints' Blackheath and others, under the direction of the choirmaster of St Alfege's,

---

55 'Tallis Memorial', *Musical Times* 16 (1874): 426.

56 'Tallis Memorial Fund', *Musical Times* 16 (1874): 491.

57 'Tallis Memorial Fund', 504.

58 *Order of Service. 'Tallis' Commemoration Service Held in St. Alfege Church, Greenwich, November 23rd, 1885 ...* (Greenwich: H. Richardson, [1885]).

59 A tablet bearing the epitaph was presented to St Alfege, Greenwich, 'in the interest of Dr. E. H. Fellowes and Sir Sydney Nicholson', and was unveiled at a special service on Monday 22 Nov 1936, 351 years after the composer's death (*The Times*, 20 Nov 1936, 21).

Mr Charles E. Ellison.[60] The reviewer in the *Musical Times* agreed that it was right to hold the celebration at Greenwich, but would have 'preferred a festival on a more imposing scale than that which was held on the 23rd ult.'[61] He found that 'the singing was generally excellent, but the organ accompaniment was little better than a series of jerks and spasms, the staccato touch being absurdly out of character with the grave, dignified harmonies interpreted by the choir.' An entry fee of one shilling was charged, and an offertory was taken up during the singing of *If ye love me*, 'in aid of the Church Renovation Fund'. A further request for donations appeared at the end of the Order of Service:

> During the winter of 1882–1884, the above old Parish Church was renovated at the expense of £2,500. A debt of £270 still remains, towards the discharge of which donations are earnestly requested.

The reviewer observed wryly: 'the promoters of the festival did not therefore let the opportunity slip for doing a stroke of business, music being once more made the handmaid of charity.'

The Order of Service was prefaced by a brief, but generally accurate biographical introduction, which included the epitaph. The tercentenary celebration was held on the exact date of the anniversary of his death, and, like the 1876 memorial plaque, the service could be described as commemorative, rather than monumental.

❧ *The Man behind the Music*

B Y the late nineteenth century, therefore, the shade of Tallis had well and truly arisen and had been given physical form on the Albert Memorial and in the portrait that was beginning to circulate. Biographical details had been accumulated and the outlines of Tallis's identity established. Although there had been some shifts in the works considered most representative of his output (the concretization of the metonymical composer), throughout most of the eighteenth and nineteenth centuries the concretization of the psychophysical composer – as the Father of Church Music, devoted exclusively to the music of the English church – had remained relatively static. His position in the Chapel Royal at the time of the Reformation lent authority to his musical activities, and the Elizabethan patent was seen as evidence of favour by this beloved and Protestant monarch. His employment under four sovereigns was frequently mentioned, and appears to

---

[60] *'Tallis' Commemoration*. The programme is discussed in more detail the previous chapter.

[61] 'Tallis Commemoration Service', *Musical Times* 26 (1885): 722.

have been valued as a sign of continuity with earlier traditions, representative of the belief that the English church drew upon the best of the Roman traditions,[62] although little attention was paid to the pre-Elizabethan polyphony or to his relationships with the earlier monarchs. A review of Bishop's *Order of Daily Service*, for example, overtly skews Tallis's biography towards the later monarchs, claiming that he 'flourished in the reigns of Edward the Sixth, and Mary and Elizabeth, his successors; to all of whom he served as Gentleman of the Chapel Royal'.[63] His age is often underestimated, which serves to limit the importance of his work under the earlier sovereigns, and to shift the focus of compositional activities towards the Elizabethan period.[64]

Towards the end of the nineteenth century, however, we begin to see signs of a new image of the composer and of a nascent interest in Tallis's music as expressive of the 'inner life' of the composer. This can be attributed both to the change in attitude towards Tallis's music that was discussed in the previous chapter, and to a more psychologised approach to music biography in general, summed up some years later by W. R. Anderson. In response to a 1935 review of the *Lives of the Great Composers*, he argued for an approach to biography, based on 'modern research into mental processes', that would strive to know 'the man *in* the music' and to 'show us the influence upon the creative spirit of all the experiences, both open and hidden, that shape the inward life.'[65]

Given the dearth of factual information, writers hoping to catch a glimpse of Tallis's inner life were forced to draw heavily upon the evidence of the music. Looking for biographical clues in the music was not in itself new, but around the turn of the twentieth century such attempts took on a different, more psychological cast. A comparison between two passages from Hawkins and Bumpus, both

---

[62] See, for example, Metcalfe, 'Music of the Church of England'.

[63] *Musical World* 19 (1844): 62. Tudway states that Tallis 'began to appear eminent, in Henry ye 8th, & Edward ye 6^{ths} time; But ye greatest part of his compositions, were made in Queen Elizabeths time, & for ye use of her Chappell' (Hogwood, 'Thomas Tudway', 23).

[64] The age of sixty-five given on the memorial brass implied a birth date of around 1520; the service sheet accompanying the 1885 tercentenary celebration claimed he had been born in 1529, which would have made him 11 at the time of the dissolution of Waltham Abbey; the 1884 Grove article and Cummings's Waltham Abbey article suggests he was born in the second decade of the fifteenth century, as does Anderton; Flood dates his birth at around 1510, although Davey in 1895 suggested 1500–1510; the currently accepted date is around 1505.

[65] W. R. Anderson, 'The Man in the Music', *Musical Times* 76 (1935): 1084. This article was, however, written in response to a review by H.G., which argued that 'neither the persuasive Preface nor the biographies themselves convince this reviewer that a composer's life matters more than a toss-up in comparison with his work.'

addressing the predominantly sacred nature of Tallis's output, serves to highlight the difference. Hawkins argued that

> The studies of Tallis seem to have been wholly devoted to the service of the church, for his name is not to be found to any musical compositions of songs, ballads, madrigals, or any of those lighter kinds of music framed with a view to private recreation.[66]

Over a century later Bumpus made what, at first, appears to be a similar observation:

> Of the private enjoyments and extra-official recreations of such a man as Tallis it is difficult to form an idea, our associations with him being entirely coloured by the cloistral gravity of his music.[67]

Upon closer examination, however, it can be seen that Hawkins is making a relatively straightforward claim about Tallis's output: Tallis must have been dedicated to the service of the church, as he wrote no secular music. Bumpus, on the other hand, is trying to get a glimpse of the 'man behind the music', based not just upon the almost exclusively sacred nature of Tallis's composition, but upon Bumpus's subjective assessment of the 'cloistral gravity' of that music. Furthermore, he is interested not only in the official persona, but also in Tallis's 'private enjoyments and extra-official recreations'.

Neither writer is completely honest in his interpretation of the data, but their manipulations of the evidence pull in different directions. Hawkins's claim that Tallis wrote no secular music is demonstrably false: he includes the part song *Like as the dolefull dove* in the Appendix to his *History*.[68] It serves Hawkins's purpose, however, and is consistent with the dominant view of Tallis as Father of Church Music.

Bumpus also massages the facts, but with the opposite end in sight: he attempts to lighten up Tallis's image, and cites a passage from Hawkins that he argues 'enables us to see a smile on the solemn visage of Master Thomas Tallis'. It refers to a letter from Sir John Harrington in which mention is made of 'certain old monkish rhymes called "The Black Saunctus or Monkes Hymn to Saint Satan"'.[69] Bumpus paraphrases Hawkins, although the passage is presented as a direct quote. The version given by Bumpus suggests that Tallis taught the song in question to

---

[66] Hawkins, *General History*, 455.

[67] Bumpus, *Cathedral Music*, 37.

[68] Hawkins, *General History*, 926–7.

[69] Hawkins claims that the lines are 'singularly humorous'; one can only assume that something has been lost in the translation (*General History*, 922).

Harrington's father; in Hawkins's version it is clear that Harrington senior studied music under Tallis, but composed the song himself.[70] The image of Tallis presented by these two passages is subtly different: Hawkins manipulated the evidence to show Tallis as solely devoted to the church, while Bumpus works to undermine this image of 'cloistral gravity'.

The late nineteenth-century interest in Tallis's polyphony was also accompanied by a change in the way that Tallis the man was portrayed, and by an increasing interest in his personal reactions to the turbulent political times in which he lived. In place of the man raised up by God to complete the work of the Reformers in establishing the music for the Anglican liturgy, we begin to see a frustrated polyphonist, chafing against the restrictions of Protestant ideals.

Bumpus writes:

> There can be no doubt whatever that Tallis was much hampered by the regulations insisted upon by the Reformers in the composition of polyphonic music for the new Liturgy. He could not have felt at home, so to speak, in the new style, and it must have been with genuine satisfaction that he was enabled to return to that natural to him in the composition of the *Cantiones Sacrae*.[71]

A similar view can be found in Davey and Walker's histories of English music that were published at about this time. Davey argued in 1895 that Tallis should be

> ranked as a composer of the highest science, to whom all the difficulties of counterpoint were as child's play, and who produced motets and masses almost worthy to be ranked with Palestrina's; not as a man fettered by the regulations of the Reformed worship, and forcing himself to write a succession of solid heavy chords.[72]

Walker similarly claimed that it was only in the 'massive' polyphonic music 'that the real Tallis is displayed', although he observes that 'Tallis also could, when he so pleased, employ with equal success a tenderer and more expressively graceful style, as in the exquisite little work [...] "O Lord, give thy holy spirit".[73] Again, we see a more personal Tallis: tender and expressive, or fettered by regulations and oppressed by the weight of his own chords.

---

[70] Compare Bumpus, *Cathedral Music*, 37–8, with Hawkins, *General History*, 921. Johnstone has observed that 'for all his ardent antiquarianism, Bumpus, it must be confessed, was an indifferent scholar' ('Boyce's "Cathedral Music"', 27).

[71] Bumpus, *Cathedral Music*, 45–6.

[72] Davey, *English Music*, 147.

[73] Walker, *Music in England*, 44–5.

Around the turn of the twentieth century, at the same time that he began to revive the Latin music of Tallis, Byrd and their contemporaries, Richard Terry wrote several polemical articles deliberately challenging prevailing orthodoxies about the history of English church music. His 1899 essay 'Some Unpublished Tallis', in which he discusses the Lamentations and Tallis's Mass in F, is, despite the title, primarily concerned with promoting the music of Byrd, and is often damning in the faintness of his praise for Tallis and his music.[74] It concludes with the provocative statement that one of the advantages of a wider knowledge of Tallis's music would be the 'dissipation of the absurd yet generally accepted notion' that Tallis was superior in skill to Byrd.[75] Despite his personal ambivalence about Tallis, however, Terry's article still evokes a strong sense of Tallis's personal involvement in the compositional process absent from earlier writings. He attributes some of what he considers to be the more tedious passages to Tallis's lack of 'spiritual exaltation', concluding that 'Tallis was frankly human, and it is in the nature of purely human emotion to wear itself out by its very intensity'.[76] Although he claims that Tallis must have approached the Credo and Gloria of the Mass with 'a considerable sense of boredom',[77] elsewhere he praises his sincerity 'as an artist'.[78] Tallis's emotional engagement with his music is evoked particularly vividly in Terry's comparison of the Lamentations with Gounod's *Gallia*:

> No greater contrast to Gounod's cheap sentiment could be found than the pathetic dignity of Tallis's lament. In Gounod we have a feminine abandonment to the luxury of weeping; Tallis has tears in plenty, but they are the tears of a strong man who will not let them fall.[79]

In 1900 Terry also published an article in the *Downside Review*, 'Tallys, Byrde, and Some Popular Fictions', in which he challenged what he called the persistent myth that Tallis and Byrd were 'Anglican worthies', arguing that they had maintained a life-long allegiance to the Roman church.[80] He developed this

---

[74] Terry notes in several places in the 1929 reprint of this essay that his criticism had softened over the years with extended acquaintance with the music.

[75] Terry, 'Some Unpublished Tallis', 72.

[76] Terry, 'Some Unpublished Tallis', 66.

[77] Terry, 'Some Unpublished Tallis', 70.

[78] Terry, 'Some Unpublished Tallis', 67.

[79] Terry, 'Some Unpublished Tallis', 65. Gounod's *Gallia* sets essentially the same text as Tallis's *Lamentations*. The gendered nature of the comparison can be seen as part of a broader discourse of purity and corruption, which is discussed further in Chapter 5.

[80] Richard Terry, 'Tallys, Byrde, and Some Popular Fictions', *Downside Review* 19 (1900): 75–81.

theme further in an article on 'Anglican Church Music' that appeared in the same year in the *Chord*,[81] and in his 1907 *Catholic Church Music* he dismissed the title 'Father of English Church Music' as inaccurate: 'so far from Tallis being considered the founder of the Anglican School of Music, he would be more appropriately described as one of the last of the Catholic composers.'[82]

This new view of Tallis became increasingly common in the early decades of the twentieth century. A new edition by Granville Bantock of *I call and cry* was published in 1913, and in January of the following year a biographical review-article by H. Orsmond Anderton was published in the *Musical Opinion*.[83] The publication of the anthem is consistent with the renewed interest in the polyphonic works observed in the previous chapter, but the article largely follows the pattern laid down by Rimbault, Husk, Davey and Walker. The final paragraphs, however, point towards this new image of the composer. Anderton defends Tallis against the charge of pedantry:

> His name is sometimes greeted with a satirical smile, as of that of a mere pedant, largely owing to the forty-part motet, which (not being really known) suggests the mere ingenuity of a Chinese puzzle. He is in reality far removed from pedantry and was full of warm and true feeling, as an acquaintance with his work will convince any open minded student.[84]

The tension between the differing configurations of the composer can be seen: Tallis is now judged by the polyphony, which is neither well known nor understood, but Anderton assures us of his warmth and true feelings, neither of which were of much interest to the older way of thinking.

Anderton also overtly challenges Tallis's position as the 'Father of Church Music'; he credits Gibbons with the title 'Father of pure Anglican Music', whose music, he claims, had a 'more purely English sound than does that of Tallys, which suggests the older idiom of the Roman Church and the continental style that was prevalent wherever that church held its influence over the souls of men.' Furthermore, Anderton appears to be fully aware of the shift in perspective entailed by this reassessment, which he refers to as 'a difference in the angle of critical vision.'[85]

In 1925 W. H. Grattan Flood published another biographical article on Tallis

---

[81] R. R. Terry, 'Anglican Church Music', *The Chord*, no. 3 (1899): 17–25.

[82] Richard R. Terry, *Catholic Church Music* (London, Greening & Co., 1907), 187.

[83] Granville Bantock, ed., *I call and cry* (London: Curwen, 1913). Anderton, 'Thomas Tallys', 282–3. Anderton notes that the publication of the motet is 'the occasion of our present review' (p. 283).

[84] Anderton, 'Thomas Tallys', 283.

[85] Anderton, 'Thomas Tallys', 283.

in his 'New Light on Late Tudor Composers' series in the *Musical Times*.[86] Although he begins by noting that 'So much has been written of Tallis, and so ample are the biographical data, that it would appear superfluous to include him in the present series', this article does indeed shed a new light on Tallis when compared with similar articles from the previous century. Flood begins, in the traditional manner, with an estimate of the date of Tallis's birth (1510) and the record of his dismissal from Waltham Abbey in 1540 upon its dissolution. His next observation – that 'we are safe in dating some of Tallis's finest works to the years 1540–59' – marks not only a reassessment of the importance of Tallis's pre-Elizabethan composition, but is an early attempt at dating the works. He then mention several new pieces of biographical information linking Tallis with the earlier monarchs: the Marian lease of the manor at Thanet, his attendance at the funeral of Henry VIII and the coronations of Edward VI and Queen Mary. His first reference to the music is the statement that, 'had Tallis written nothing but his "Lamentations of Jeremias" […] he would deserve immortal praise.' He moves on to *Spem in alium* and the motets from the *Cantiones sacrae*; the English service music is left to the final paragraphs, after the secular songs and the instrumental music. He notes the 'preponderance of Tallis's Latin services over the few English examples', and quotes Terry's argument that Tallis was the last of the Catholic composers.

Three years later, in 1928, the sixth volume of the Carnegie Trust series of Tudor Church Music, devoted to the complete Latin church music of Tallis, was published. In many ways this can be seen as the culmination of the process of establishing the new concretization of Tallis, as Catholic composer of polyphonic music for the Roman rite.[87] The English music was relegated to a later volume, proposed but never published;[88] a scholarly collected edition of the Anglican music did not appear until the Early English Church Music volumes 12 and 13 in 1971–2. The Tudor Church Music volume is prefaced by a substantial biographical introduction, of considerably greater scope than any of the earlier biographies. It argues for the early date of 1505 for Tallis's birth, based upon a more thorough examination of the documentation of a 1577 petition to Queen Elizabeth, and reproduces several new documentary sources, including Tallis's will and that of his wife, Joan. The Tallis volume was reviewed by H. B. Collins in *Music & Letters* in 1929; his article displays, in addition to a strong critical engagement with the edition

---

[86] Flood, 'Thomas Tallis', 800–1.

[87] It also represents the increasing role of formal scholarship in the reception and dissemination of early music, but a closer examination of this is beyond the scope of the present study.

[88] H. B. Collins, 'Thomas Tallis', *Music & Letters* 10 (1929): 152.

and the music, a psychologically nuanced portrait of this new Tallis. The figure of Tallis that emerges from this review is very different from the mild and rather two-dimensional Tallis of the preceding century.

Unlike Terry, Collins's praise for the Lamentations is unqualified. Along with *Spem in alium*, he argues that they represent Tallis's 'crowning achievement', and must be classed among the outstanding musical works of the sixteenth century, not only in England, but in Europe. He attributes the 'main significance' of the Lamentations to their 'profound emotional appeal':

> The explanation of this is not far to seek. There is no reason to doubt that Tallis, like the mass of the older generation, remained Catholic at heart. To him these pathetic words must have sounded like an almost literal description of the ruin which had befallen the ancient Church, and which he witnessed with his own eyes.[89]

He finds a similar religious motivation for the composition of *Spem in alium*, suggesting that it was written in protest against the claim of the Reformers that England had, for the previous eight centuries of Catholicism, been 'drowned in abominable idolatry':

> Tallis knew the religion he had been taught as a child. It may well have occurred to him to utter his protest against these shameful calumnies in the only way, perhaps, that he could, and in a form which should not perish, but should survive to a late posterity. And he would answer, not for himself alone, but for forty generations of Englishmen thus foully slandered: he would answer in the words of the ancient liturgy brought from Rome by Augustine near a thousand years before: 'Spem in alium nunquam habui, praeter in te, Deus Israel.'[90]

The contrast with Burney's impersonal references to the polyphonic phenomenon could not be greater. Hawkins's timid suggestion that the motet was composed with an 'emulation to excel' had been fleshed out in the tale of the ducal challenge, but both are completely overshadowed by Collins's thundering rhetoric of religious persecution.[91] And, as Anderton observed, such changes in portrayals of the composer reveal as much about the differences in the angle of critical vision as they do about the music or the biography.

The relative lack of biographical information about Tallis renders him

---

[89] Collins, 'Thomas Tallis', 163.

[90] Collins, 'Thomas Tallis', 164.

[91] The concretization, as always, continues to change; Denis Stevens's 1982 'A Songe of Fortie Partes' presents a cooler, more political, although barely less speculative version of the composition of the motet.

particularly susceptible to such changes in critical vision. Maynard Solomon suggests that Shakespeare's similarly undocumented life leaves us free to 'fill in the outlines of his identity with projections of our own making',[92] and the question of Tallis's religious orientation is particularly vulnerable to the process of projection. John Bennett, in his 1988 article based upon documentary evidence contained in Joan Tallis's will, argues fairly convincingly that Tallis adhered to his Catholic faith throughout his life.[93] Prior to this, however, the question of Tallis's churchmanship had been decided almost exclusively by reference to his music. It is intimately linked to the relative aesthetic value assigned to the Latin and English works, which in turn, at least in the late nineteenth and early twentieth centuries, seems to have been strongly influenced by the religious beliefs of the authors.[94] W. S. Rockstro, one of the first to plead the merits of the polyphony over the Dorian Service, had converted to Catholicism in 1876;[95] Terry converted in 1896;[96] Flood was an Irish Catholic who had contemplated the priesthood before becoming organist at Belfast Pro-Cathedral;[97] and Collins was yet another convert.[98]

In the 300 years after Tallis's death, therefore, there were many changes in perceptions of the composer. Not only did the works considered to be most representative of Tallis's style or his finest achievements change, but they were approached at different times and in different contexts as canon, repertory, the subject of antiquarian interest and as a tender expression of religious faith. For Butler, and for the 'self-consciously learned' composers of the mid-eighteenth century, Tallis's motets were exemplars of good compositional practice; for the advocates of the Choral Revival in the nineteenth century, Tallis's music was the foundation upon which the liturgical music of the Anglican Church was built; for Catholic musicians in

---

[92] Maynard Solomon, 'Thoughts on Biography', *19th Century Music* 5 (1982): 276.

[93] John Bennett, 'A Tallis Patron?', *Royal Musical Association Research Chronicle* 21 (1988): 41–4.

[94] Peter Phillips's comments cited in the Introduction can also be seen as an example of religious projection.

[95] Rosemary Williamson, 'Rockstro [Rackstraw], W(illiam) S(mith) [Smyth]', *Grove Music Online*, accessed 22 May 2003.

[96] Timothy Day, 'Sir Richard Terry', 298.

[97] Alex Klein, 'Flood, W(illiam) H(enry) Grattan', *Grove Music Online*, accessed 23 May 2003.

[98] Eric Blom, 'Collins, H(enry) B(ird)', *Grove Music Online*, accessed 15 May 2003. The Anderton family had been Catholics since the time of the Reformation ('The Andertons and Religion', accessed 23 May 2003, <http://freepages.genealogy. rootsweb.com/~anderton/religion.html>), but I have been unable to clarify whether H. Orsmond Anderton was himself a Catholic. The correlation between the reassessment of Tallis's Latin music and the Catholic faith of these musicians will be examined further in Chapter 5.

the early twentieth century, his music expressed his deepest emotions about the religious turmoil through which he lived.

The image of 'such a man as Tallis' changed from the gentle, accommodating Tallis, 'setting the standard' for the music of the vernacular liturgy of the English church, to the defender of forty generations of slandered English Catholics, and the nature of the engagement with the composer changed too. The epitaph settings of the late eighteenth century constructed a musical monument to the composer, the biographies and images of the mid- to late nineteenth century gave him a face, and the more psychological analyses of the early twentieth century tried to give this face a smile (or perhaps in the case of Collins's Tallis, a frown). And as we shall see in the following chapters, these changes were reflected in the reception of individual works and in constructions of the history of English music.

CHAPTER 3

'This Mistake of a Barbarous Age':
Spem in alium

IN February 1878 the Rev. H. Fleetwood Shepherd wrote a letter to the editor of the *Musical Times*, which contained an account of the circumstances surrounding the composition and first performance of Tallis's 'Song of Forty Parts', *Spem in alium*. He had uncovered the account some twenty years earlier in the Cambridge University Library, in the Commonplace Book of a Thomas Waterbridge, who had recorded the story as told to him by Ellis Swayne on 27 November 1611, almost thirty years after Tallis's death:

> In Queen Elizabeth's time yere was a songe sen[t] into England in 30 parts (whence ye Italians obteyned ye name to be called ye Apices of ye world) wch beeinge songe mad[e] a heavenly Harmony. The Duke of — bearinge a great love to Musicke asked whether none of our Englishmen could sett as good a songe, and Tallice being very skilfull was felt to try whether he would undertake ye matter, wch he did and made one of 40 partes wch was songe in the longe gallery at Arundell house, wch so farre surpassed ye other that the Duke, hearinge yt songe, tooke his chayne of Gold from his necke & putt yt about Tallice his necke and gave yt him (wch songe was againe songe at ye Princes coronation).[1]

Very little else is known of the circumstances surrounding the origins of *Spem in alium*, although it has been the subject of much speculation.[2] The date of its

---

[1] Sheppard, 'Tallis and his Song of Forty Parts', 97. This letter is the subject of an extensive correspondence in the *Musical Times*, initiated by Elizabeth Roche, 'Tallis's 40-part motet', *Musical Times* 122 (1981): 230, and is discussed further in Denis Stevens, 'Songe of Fortie Partes', 172. Stevens suggests that Ellis Swayne must have been present at the 1610 performance.

[2] Hawkins suggests that it was written in an attempt to improve upon Ockeghem's thirty-six voice canon *Deo gratias* (*General History*, 456). Denis Stevens gives an essentially similar theory a political spin in 'A Songe of Fortie Partes, Made by Mr Tallys', *Early Music* 10 (1986): 171–81, although he believes that Striggio's *Ecce beatam* was Tallis's model. Stevens had previously suggested that the motet was composed in response to a royal payment to Tallis of forty pounds ('Tallis', *Die Musik in Geschichte und Gegenwart*, ed. Friedrich Blume (Basel: Bärenreiter, 1966)). H. B. Collins saw it as a protest on behalf of the 'forty generations' of English Catholics slandered by the Reformation ('Thomas Tallis', 164). Paul Doe, in his

composition is unknown, but is estimated at about 1570,[3] and Davitt Moroney has recently argued convincingly that Tallis's work was inspired by Alessandro Striggio's forty-part *Missa sopra Ecco sì beato giorno*.[4] Whatever its origins, Tallis's motet (in the English version, *Sing and Glorifie*) was indeed again sung at the coronation or creation as Prince of Wales of Henry in 1610, and in 1616 when his brother Charles (later Charles I) was made Prince of Wales after Henry's death in 1612.[5] An account of the 1616 performance shows that it was not performed during the actual ceremony, but at dinner afterwards:

> After the ceremonie [...] the King arose and went up to dinner; but the Prince with his Lords dined in the Hall, and was served with great state and magnificence [...] After some musique the Song of forty parts was song by the Gentlemen of the Chappell and others, sitting upon degrees over the Screene at the north end of the Hall.[6]

Ian Woodfield discusses these performances in some detail in his article '"Music of Forty Several Parts:" A Song for the Creation of Princes', and argues for the possibility of further performances at the creations as Prince of Wales of the future Charles II in 1638, and of George (later George III) in 1751.[7] His argument rests largely on the existence of scores copied at around these times, and will be discussed further below. No record exists of any other performance prior to the nineteenth century, when, despite the general lack of interest in Tallis's Latin

'Tallis's "Spem in alium" and the Elizabethan Respond-Motet', *Music & Letters* 51 (1970): 12, argues that the motet may have been composed for Elizabeth I's fortieth birthday in 1573. Elsewhere he suggests that, in addition to other possible motives, the work must have contained 'some element of personal fulfilment, satisfying that desire of so many composers in their old age to write a "masterwork" embodying the very finest of their art' (*Tallis*, 41).

3 Doe, *Tallis*, 41, and Stevens, 'Songe of Fortie Partes', 172.

4 Davitt, Moroney, 'Alessandro Striggio's Mass in Forty and Sixty Parts', *Journal of the American Musicological Society* 60 (2007): 1–70. Prior to the rediscovery of this mass, Striggio's forty-part motet *Ecce beatam lucem* was generally considered to have been the inspiration for Tallis's motet. The connection between the two works was first suggested by Iain Fenlon and Hugh Keyte in their article 'Memorialls of Great Skill: A Tale of Five Cities', *Early Music* 8 (1980): 329–34. It is discussed further by Ralph Leavis, 'Tallis's 40-part Motet', *Musical Times* 122 (1981): 230, Philip Brett, 'Facing the Music', *Early Music* 10 (1982): 347–50, and others.

5 Elizabeth Foster, *Proceedings in Parliament 1610*, vol. 1 (New Haven: Yale University Press, 1966), 98; John Nichols, *The Progresses, Processions, and Magnificent Festivities of King James the First*, vol. 3 (London, 1828), 213.

6 Nichols, *Progresses*, 213.

7 Ian Woodfield, '"Music of Forty Several Parts:" A Song for the Creation of Princes', *Performance Practice Review* 7 (1994): 61–4.

music, it was performed a number of times, and made a significant contribution to nineteenth-century perceptions of the composer.

The Song of Forty Parts had not been forgotten, however, despite the lack of performances, but had enjoyed a silent existence as the subject of curiosity and legend. Thomas Tudway, for example, writes in 1718: 'I have been often told of this Composition, but I could never believe ther [sic] was any such thing',[8] and copies of the score were made, collected and circulated. In his 1951 article 'The Manuscripts of Tallis's Forty-Part Motet', Bertram Schofield provides a detailed description of four of these copies, all dating from the eighteenth century or earlier.[9] He mentions several later scores, but concludes that, 'since they all descend indirectly from Egerton 3512 [the oldest surviving source] and throw no light on the manuscript, there is no need to enumerate them here.'[10] A. H. Mann described all the known manuscript copies of the Song of Forty Parts in the introduction to his 1888 edition of the motet, but the later scores appear to have aroused little interest since.[11] While they may not cast any further light on the 'correct' text of the work, a careful examination of all the surviving scores, together with records of performances, provides a detailed and informative picture of the 'afterlife' of the motet.

✥ *Early Manuscripts*

EGERTON 3512

THE earliest score still extant, now held in the British Library as Egerton MS 3512, dates from the early seventeenth century.[12] The scribe has not been identified, although Pamela Willetts has established that the same hand is found in Thomas Myriell's 'Tristitae Remedium' (British Library Add. MSS 29372–7) and other early seventeenth-century manuscripts. Willetts suggests that the scribe may

---

[8] Bertram Schofield, 'The Manuscripts of Tallis's Forty-Part Motet', *Musical Quarterly* 37 (1951): 177.

[9] Schofield, 'Tallis's Forty-Part Motet', 176–83.

[10] Schofield, 'Tallis's Forty-Part Motet', 182.

[11] Thomas Tallis, *Motet for 40 Voices*, ed. A. H. Mann (London: Weekes, 1888). Mann's discussion of the scores is a valuable resource and is the source of important information not available elsewhere. There are, however, occasional omissions and inaccuracies in his descriptions that have gone unchallenged, and several important scores with which he was unacquainted.

[12] The last record of what may have been the autograph is in the 1609 catalogue of the library of Lord Lumley (see Sears Jayne and Francis Johnson, *The Lumley Library – The Catalogue of 1609* (London: Trustees of the British Museum, 1956), 14, quoted in Woodfield, 'Music of Forty Several Parts', 56–7).

have been John Ward, but admits that the evidence is not conclusive.[13] The manuscript is arranged in score, with all eight soprano parts first, followed by the eight second sopranos, and so on, with a continuo part inserted after the twentieth voice part. The voices are numbered 1, 6, 11, 16, etc., indicating rather obliquely the division of the work into eight choirs of five voices. The words are not those of the Latin original, but of an unrelated English text in honour of Princes Henry and Charles.

> Sing and glorifie heavens high Maiesty
> Author of this blessed harmony
> Sound devyne praises
> With melodious graces
> This is the day, holy day, happy day
> For ever give it greeting
> Love and joy hart & voice meeting
> Lyve Henry/Long liv Charles Princly and mighty
> Harry lyve/Charles lyve long in thy Creation happy.[14]

The placement of the alternative texts, with the references to Harry written over those to Charles, but with neither consistently aligned with the rest of the text, indicates that both versions were included at the time of copying.

The complete original Latin text is written above the thorough bass part on the first folio. The final page bears the inscription:

> Mr Thomas Tallis, gentleman of King Henry the Eyght's Chaple, King Edward Queen Mary and of her Majesty that now is Queen Elizabeth, the maker of this Song of fourty partes.

The phrase 'her Majesty that now is' suggests that it was copied from an Elizabethan source. Schofield believed that the manuscript dates from before 1612, the date of Henry's death.[15] Although he does not explain his reasoning, it appears to be based upon the assumption that the text was in honour of the princes, and must therefore have been made while they were both still alive.[16] Willetts argues,

---

[13] Pamela J. Willetts, 'Musical Connections of Thomas Myriell', *Music & Letters* 49 (1968): 39–41. This attribution is considered further in Craig Monson, 'Thomas Myriell's Manuscript Collection: One View of Musical Taste in Jacobean London', *Journal of the American Musicological Society* 30 (1977): 438–9.

[14] Schofield, 'Tallis's Forty-Part Motet', 179–80. Also given in Woodfield, 'Music of Forty Several Parts', 59.

[15] Schofield, 'Tallis's Forty-Part Motet', 180, n. 16.

[16] Schofield appears not to have known of the records of the performances in 1611 and 1616.

even less convincingly, that 'the occasion for which this English adaptation' was made was Henry's creation in 1610, and that Charles is mentioned as well because of his 'prominent part in the festivities'.[17] Woodfield, on the other hand, suggests that the manuscript was produced as a type of record of the performances in 1610 and 1616, and that the reference to Charles places the date of copying after 1616.[18] Neither Schofield nor Willetts recognises the performance problem inherent in the alternate texts; their interpretations privilege the text, and are unconcerned with performances, while Woodfield assigns primacy to the performances, and sees the score as a record of past acts.[19]

By the beginning of the eighteenth century, however, these performances had been forgotten, and the score had come to be valued purely as an historical curiosity and collector's item. This position is captured in a much-quoted letter dated 1 May 1718 from Thomas Tudway to Humfrey Wanley, discussing the proposed donation of the score to Edward Harley, the second Earl of Oxford, by James Hawkins, organist of Ely Cathedral:[20]

> I think it will incomparably be proper to go along wth that great body of composition wch I have prepared for my Lord, a greater rarity there cannot be in its kind [...] & is indeed fittest to be laid up, among so many valuable manuscripts wch you have wth so much judgm^{t}, pains & Industry procur'd for my Lord. The designe of composeing it was not, we may be sure, to be perform'd; but to remain a Memoriall of ye great skill & ability of ye composer, who was able to find wayes for so many parts to move differently, in their own spheres.[21]

Sir John Hawkins cites this correspondence in his *General History*, but claims that the score was no longer amongst the Harleian manuscripts.[22] He appears to have mistaken the manuscript in question for the Latin autograph,[23] and some

---

[17] Willetts, 'Thomas Myriell', 39, n. 7.

[18] Woodfield, 'Music of Forty Several Parts', 60.

[19] This is quite different from the view of the score as a blueprint for future ideal performances implicit in the work-concept.

[20] This correspondence is quoted and discussed in some detail in Schofield, 'Tallis's Forty-Part Motet'.

[21] *GB-Lbl* Harl. 3782, fol. 95, quoted in Schofield, 'Tallis's Forty-Part Motet', 177.

[22] Hawkins, *General History*, 456–7.

[23] 'In the reign of the first or second Charles some person put to it certain English words, which are neither verse nor prose, nor even common sense; and it was probably sung on some public occasion; but the composition with Latin words coming to the hands of Mr. Hawkins [...] he presented it to Edward earl of Oxford' (Hawkins, *General History*, 456).

confusion about this continues right through to the preface of the edition produced in 1928 for the Carnegie Trust, which claims 'the original score, or set of
parts, with Latin words, was in the possession of James Hawkins of Ely'.[24] Schofield,
however, has identified an inscription on Egerton 3512 as being in Tudway's hand,
confirming that it was this copy rather than the autograph that was the subject of
the correspondence.[25]

While Hawkins was unaware of the location of Egerton 3512 at the time of
writing his *General History*, Charles Burney was better informed. He states in
his *History* that it had been 'attracted into the vortex of Dr. Pepusch; but is, at
present the property of Mr. Robert Bremner, Music-printer, in the Strand'.[26] As
Schofield observes, Bremner is known to have purchased the Fitzwilliam Virginal
Book at the sale of Pepusch's library in 1763, and it is therefore quite possible that
he acquired this score at the same time.[27] Burney appears to have purchased the
manuscript from Bremner, along with a modern copy: the *Catalogue* of the 1814
sale of Burney's music library after his death included two manuscript copies of
the score.[28] The 'original ancient score' (that is, Egerton 3512) was listed as item 405
and was purchased for five shillings by Robert Triphook, a bookseller in St James's
Street. It was advertised, again described as 'the original ancient score', in Triphook's catalogue of books for sale in 1815, with a healthy mark-up to one guinea,
but was absent from the 1817 catalogue.[29] There are no further known references
to its whereabouts until 1947, when it was presented to the British Library 'by a
lady resident in King's Lynn'.[30] All other copies still extant are derived from this
score.

R.M.4.g.1

The second copy listed in the catalogue of the sale of Charles Burney's library, at
item 406, is described as 'a fair modern copy of do. MS'. (See Figure 7 for a summary

---

[24] Thomas Tallis, *Spem in alium* (London: Oxford University Press, [1928]).

[25] Schofield, 'Tallis's Forty-Part Motet', 179.

[26] Burney, *General History*, 2:67, n. x.

[27] Schofield, 'Tallis's Forty-Part Motet', 179.

[28] *Catalogue of the Music Library of Charles Burney*, intro. A. Hyatt King (Amsterdam: Frits Knuf, 1973), 16. Burney's ownership of these scores was mentioned in
the Order of Service for the Tallis Commemoration service at St Alfege's Greenwich in 1885, but Schofield does not seem to have been aware of it.

[29] *A Catalogue of Books ... Now on Sale at Robert Triphook's, 37, St James's Street,
London* (London, 1815), 24, item 414.

[30] Schofield, 'Tallis's Forty-Part Motet', 179. The unexpected reappearance of the
score and its donation to the British Library prompted the writing of Schofield's
article.

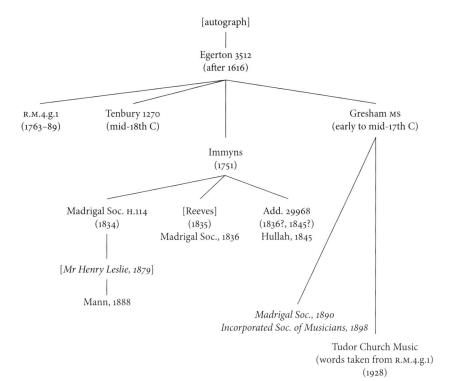

Figure 7. Relationship between copies of *Spem in alium*.
Dates of copying appear in parentheses; lost copies appear in square brackets;
details of performances that would have necessitated the preparation of parts
for performers appear in italics.

of the relationships between the scores.)[31] The words 'in Latin' have been added in the same hand that recorded the details of purchaser and price. Although it is unclear how this copy made its way into the Royal Music library, there seems little doubt that Burney's second copy is the manuscript now held in the British Library at R.M.4.g.1.[32]

R.M.4.g.1 appears to have been stored folded prior to binding; the Latin words are written at the top of the back page, and 'This belongs to Robt Bremner Music Printer London' is inscribed upside down at the bottom. When folded, both inscriptions would be the right way up, one on the back and the other on the front. At the top of the first folio is written 'as in the original', followed by an ascription to Tallis identical to that found in the Egerton manuscript, save for some modernised

[31] *Catalogue of the Music Library of Charles Burney*, 16, item 406.
[32] Hilda Andrews, *Catalogue of the King's Music Library: Pt 2, The Miscellaneous Manuscripts* (London: British Museum, 1929), 209.

spelling. The arrangement of the voices, with all eight parts of each voice type grouped together, is also the same as the Egerton manuscript, strongly suggesting that R.M.4.g.1 was copied from Egerton 3512, presumably while the latter was in the possession of Bremner.[33] Although the words of this copy, unlike Egerton 3512, are in Latin, the poor underlay is consistent with the substitution of a new text.[34]

Item 406 at Burney's sale was bought by the famous bass singer James Bartleman for one guinea (considerably more than the price paid for the so-called 'original'),[35] and a copy of 'Tallis's Song of Forty Parts' was purchased by an unknown buyer for £1/10/6 at the sale of his library on 21 February 1822.[36] The description in Bartleman's catalogue – 'in score, 17 pages, very large folio' – corresponds exactly with R.M.4.g.1. Press reviews of a performance in 1879 indicate that this copy was in the Buckingham Palace Library at that date.[37]

A newspaper cutting is pasted onto the flyleaf of this copy. Hilda Andrews claims that it contains information about the score's transcription,[38] but the cutting clearly refers to a different copy and will be discussed further below.

GRESHAM COLLEGE MS

Another copy of the motet survives from the early to mid-seventeenth century; it is now held at the Guildhall Library, London (MS G.Mus.420), but is part of the collection of the Library of Gresham College. It is not a score but a collection of parts, one part to a page, and is described in some detail by Schofield, who establishes that it was copied from Egerton 3512.[39] Again, the underlaid text is the

---

33 Andrews dates this copy from the late eighteenth-century copy, which is consistent with the suggestion that the copy was made after Bremner purchased the copy from Pepusch in about 1763, and before Bremner's death in 1789.

34 Schofield, 'Tallis's Forty-Part Motet', 179.

35 Neither copy was particularly well priced, compared to other items such as a 1613 edition of Ward's *First Set of English Madrigals*, which went for £2/5/–, or *Lady Nevel's Book* at £13.

36 *A Catalogue of the Very Valuable and Celebrated Library of Music Books, Late the Property of James Bartleman, Esq.* (London, 1822), 11, item 327.

37 See, for example, 'Choral Concerts', *London and Provincial Music Trades Review*, 15 Jun 1879, 2. This performance is discussed further below. A. H. Mann also refers to this as the Buckingham Palace copy in the preface to his 1888 edition (*Motet for 40 Voices*, i)).

38 Andrews, *King's Music Library*, 209.

39 Schofield, 'Tallis's Forty-Part Motet', 180–2. Philip Brett notes, in the preface to the revised Tudor Church Music edition, that a 'note-for-note collation of the two sources' supports this claim (Thomas Tallis, *Spem in alium nunquam habui: A Motet in Forty Parts*, rev. ed. Philip Brett (London: Oxford University Press, 1966)).

English 'Sing and Glorifie'; the Latin words are also reproduced in several places in the manuscript. Woodfield believes that this copy may have been produced for Charles II's creation as Prince of Wales in 1638. He refers to a claim by Anthony Wood in his *Athenae Oxoniensis* that Thomas Warwick, who was Gibbons's successor as organist at the Chapel Royal, had composed a song of forty parts, which had been performed for Charles I in about 1635;[40] Hawkins repeats this in his *General History*.[41] Woodfield argues that it is more likely that Warwick had conducted a performance of Tallis's motet rather than of a newly composed work of his own, particularly given the 'limited range' of his other compositions.[42] Thomas Oliphant reaches a similar conclusion in an annotation on a later score:

> Hawkins says that a Mr Thos. Warwick, organist of Westminster Abbey, *composed* a 40 part song, which was performed before Charles I. It is however, much more likely to have been this song of Tallis's with the English adaptation, as it is improbable that an obscure musician like Warwick should have attempted anything of the kind, within 50 years after Tallis.[43]

If the performance before Charles I in 'about 1635' was actually of Tallis's motet, rather than another 'song of forty parts' by Warwick, it may well have been on the occasion of the 1638 creation as Prince of Wales of the future Charles II, continuing the tradition established by his uncle and father. And this copy may have been in some way associated with such a performance, although Denis Stevens points out that, as the parts are copied one part to a page, on both sides of the paper, it was 'unperformable'.[44] This copy, like Egerton 3512, also includes the alternative references to both Charles and the long-dead Harry, suggesting that it was primarily a record of the past, rather than a resource for future performances.

The Gresham manuscript does not appear to have been widely known in the eighteenth and nineteenth centuries, nor to have been the source of any further copies. It could not really be described as lost, however: it bears the signature of E(dmund) T(homas) Warren, secretary of the Noblemen's and Gentlemen's Catch Club (1761–94), and it is also possible that Edward Taylor, Gresham Professor from 1837, knew of its existence: the Gresham Music Library was largely collected by Taylor, and one of his Gresham lectures in 1852 was on the subject of 'Tallis and

---

[40] Woodfield, 'Music of Forty Several Parts', 61–2.

[41] Hawkins, *General History*, 585.

[42] Woodfield, 'Music of Forty Several Parts', 62.

[43] This score, which was copied by John Immyns, is now missing, but the annotation was reproduced in Mann, *Motet for 40 Voices*, ii: Mann identifies this annotation as being in Oliphant's hand.

[44] Stevens, 'Songe of Fortie Partes', 175.

his Song of Forty Parts'.[45] The motet was listed, although inaccurately as 'for four Voices and a thorow Bass', in the catalogue of the Gresham College Library prepared in 1872.[46] This description is an example of the inadequacies of the catalogue, and in 1889 it was proposed that Dr A. H. Mann be asked to prepare a new catalogue.[47] Although there is no evidence that such a catalogue was ever compiled, this request may have led to Mann's discovery of the manuscript. It is not on the list of scores that prefaced Mann's 1888 edition of the Song of Forty Parts, but he must have found it shortly afterwards. A brief report of its performance by the Madrigal Society in June 1890 mentions that 'the "Forty-part Song" was edited for the occasion' by Mann, and refers to a copy in the Gresham library.[48] The Gresham manuscript was also the source of a score prepared by Mann for the Incorporated Society of Musicians in 1898;[49] these performances will be discussed further below.

IMMYNS (MAD. SOC. H.1.MS.100)

The second score that Woodfield associates with the creation of one of the Princes of Wales was made in the mid-eighteenth century by John Immyns, the founder of the Madrigal Society. Immyns was involved with the Academy of Ancient Music and worked as a copyist for Dr Pepusch; he probably copied this score from Egerton 3512 while it was in Pepusch's possession.[50] This score, still catalogued in the Madrigal Society collection in the British Library as H.1.MS.100, has been missing since 1966.[51] Fortunately Mann included a detailed description of this and other copies with which he was acquainted in the preface to his 1888 edition, and reproduced the following inscription:

> This Motett of forty parts was first composed to the Latin words following by Thomas Tallis, gentleman and Master of the Chappell to K. Henry ye 8th, K. Edward ye 6th, Q. Mary & Q. Elizabeth. Supposed to be fitted to the above

---

45 *Gresham Music Library: A Catalogue of Printed Books and Manuscripts Deposited in Guildhall Library* (London: Corp. of London, 1965), i; 'Syllabuses of Gresham Lectures', London, Guildhall Library.

46 *Catalogue of Books, Pictures, Prints, etc., Presented by Mrs Laetitia Hollier to, and also of Books and Music in, the Library of Gresham College London* (London, 1872), 47.

47 *Gresham Music Library*, i.

48 'Miscellaneous', *London and Provincial Music Trades Review*, 15 Jun 1890, 7.

49 'The Incorporated Society of Musicians', *Musical Opinion and Music Trades Review* 21 (1898): 323.

50 Schofield, 'Tallis's Forty-Part Motet', 178.

51 This score was loaned by the British Library to the Madrigal Society for an exhibition, and it was never returned (communication with Chris Banks of the British Library, 1 Dec 1997).

English words in ye Reign of James ye 1ˢᵗ by Orlando Gibbons, M.D., only at the writing over this score in ye year 1751 ye words [Prince Charles] were altered to [King George].[52]

The similarities to the inscription of Egerton 3512 are obvious. This copy again underlays the English words, and includes a figured bass line, but Immyns was the first copyist to reorder the voice parts into eight five-part choirs, reflecting the polychoral nature of the music more clearly than the original from which it was copied.

Woodfield has noted that the date of copying, 1751, was also the date of the creation as Prince of Wales of the future George III, and has suggested that this copy was prepared with a view to performance on this occasion. While the coincidence is suggestive, it is entirely consistent with Immyns's interest in early music – and indeed with the broader eighteenth-century interest in early polyphony noted in Chapter 1 – that he would have copied this work either for his own interest or for the Madrigal Society without necessarily being involved in a royal performance. The reference to 'King George' also seems inconsistent with a performance at the creation – 'Prince George' would have been more appropriate – and there is no reason to believe that the Hanoverian George would have known about or been interested in the practice of the Stuarts over a century earlier.[53]

The rearrangement of the voice parts and the updating of the words, however, indicate that Immyns, unlike the other early copyists, was oriented towards a potential performance, rather than producing an exact visual copy of the 'original'. This copy was, indirectly, the source of almost all the nineteenth-century performances.

TENBURY MS 1270

A third score of *Spem in alium* dating from the mid-eighteenth century is in the music collection of St Michael's College, Tenbury, now held in the Bodleian Library, Oxford.[54] The front page bears the following inscription, closely related to that found in the Egerton manuscript:

[52] Mann, *Motet for 40 Voices*, ii.

[53] Although his primary focus is the nineteenth century, David Cannadine argues that the current belief that the pageantry and ceremonial surrounding the British monarchy represents an unbroken tradition extending back for centuries is largely misplaced, and that prior to the twentieth century there was little interest or competence in the rituals of the monarchy ('The Context, Performance and Meaning of Ritual: The British Monarchy and the "Invention of Tradition", *c.* 1820–1977', in Hobsbawm and Ranger, *The Invention of Tradition*, 101–64).

[54] *GB-Ob* MS Tenbury 1270. The date is taken from E. H. Fellowes, *Catalogue of Manuscripts in the Library of St. Michael's College, Tenbury,* 2nd ed. (Paris: Éditions de l'Oiseau Lyre, 1933).

This song in 40 parts was first composed to the above Latin words by Mr Thomas Tallis Gentleman of King Henry ye 8[ths] Chappell. King Eduard ye 6th Queen Mary and of her Majesty that now is Queen Elizabeth. Mr Hawkins Organist of the Cathedral Church of Ely presented the late Lord Oxford with this Original and the same was deposited among his Lordship's MSS.[55]

This score differs from Egerton 3512 in a few minor details: the continuo part is inserted after the twenty-fourth voice part, as opposed to the twentieth, and the references to Prince Henry have been omitted, leaving the words 'Charles live long', even though Charles II had died in 1685. The voices, however, are arranged in voice parts, rather than in choirs, and are again numbered 1, 6, 11, 16, etc., as in the Egerton manuscript. The anachronistic inclusion of the phrase 'her Majesty that now is Queen Elizabeth' strongly suggests that it was copied from this source.

Mann had not seen this score himself, but his discussion of the scores includes a description of the manuscript by Frederick Arthur Gore Ouseley in which Ouseley states that it had been purchased by his father from an unknown source in about 1820.[56] A copy of *Spem in alium* taken 'from the original in Lord Oxford's collection' was sold to an unknown buyer on 8 June 1820 at the sale of the library of George Ebenezer Williams, organist of Westminster Abbey (1814–19).[57] The reference to Lord Oxford's collection is consistent with the inscription on the Tenbury manuscript, and this may well have been the same score. The provenance of Williams's score is unknown.

THE 'SILENT' SCORES

Five pre-nineteenth-century copies of the Song of Forty Parts survive, therefore,[58] but only the Immyns copy appears to be primarily concerned with the possibility of performance. The alternative texts of Egerton 3512 and the Gresham manuscript suggest that they were conceived as a record of past events. Both R.M.g.4.1 and Tenbury 1270 replicate the unusual distribution of parts found in Egerton 3512, and the decision by the copyist of R.M.4.g.1 to reinstate the Latin text at a time when almost all music written in a language other than English was performed

---

[55] Edward Harley died in 1741.

[56] Mann, *Motet for 40 Voices*, ii–iii.

[57] A. Hyatt King, *Some British Collectors of Music, c. 1600–1960* (Cambridge: Cambridge University Press, 1963), 27; *A Catalogue of an Extensive and Valuable Collection of Music Books … Part of which were the Property of the Late Mr G. E. Williams Organist of Westminster Abbey … Sold by Mr White, 2 June 1820 and Two Following Days* (London, 1820), 19, item 4: 'A curious MS Motett, of 40 parts by Tallis, fitted to English Words by O. Gibbons, a scarce copy from the original in Lord Oxford's Collection.'

[58] Assuming that the lost Immyns score still survives.

in English translation also points to a primarily historical orientation, as do the references to Elizabeth and Charles in Tenbury 1270. Only Immyns updated the text to refer to the reigning monarch, and reordered the voice parts to reflect the structure of the music, rather than the appearance of the original from which he was copying. The 'designe' of these early copies, if not of the work itself, therefore seems, as Tudway claimed, not to be performed, but to act as silent monuments to the 'ye great skill and ability of ye composer'.

An inscription on the Gresham manuscript remarks that the Song of Forty Parts was 'often seene, but seldome sung',[59] and Burney's description of the 'Polyphonic Phenomenon' also implies a visual engagement with a silent score:

> This wonderful effort of harmonical abilities is not divided into *choirs* of four parts [...] like the compositions *a molti chori*, of Benvoli, and others; but consists of eight trebles, placed under each other; eight mezzi soprani, or mean parts; eight counter-tenors; eight tenors; and eight basses.[60]

This is not a description of the musical structure of the work, nor of any performance, real or ideal, but simply of Egerton 3512. A similar conflation of the work and the score is found in Burney's statement that the Song of Forty Parts still 'subsists' and can be found 'in the possession of Robert Bremner'.[61]

A comment in a letter to Christoph Daniel Ebeling in 1771 makes Burney's essentially visual relationship with the score explicit: he writes that a 'long & laboured Fugue, *recte et retro* in 40 parts, may be a good entertainment for the *Eyes* of a Critic, but can never delight the *Ears* of a Man of Taste'.[62] Burney was not alone in this view: a similar observation was made in 1795 by William Mason in his *Essays on Church Music*, although he attributed the forty-part work to Bull: 'Dr Bull could produce to the astonished reader (not hearer, for the hearer would know nothing of the matter) a piece of harmony of full forty parts.'[63]

---

[59] *GB-Lgc* MS G.Mus.420.

[60] Burney, *General History*, 2:67.

[61] Burney *General History*, 2:67, n. x.

[62] Alvaro Ribeiro, ed., *The Letters of Dr Charles Burney*, vol. 1 (Oxford: Clarendon, 1991), 104; Burney's emphases. Unlike Tudway, Burney believed that a performance of *Spem in alium* was possible: he suggested in a footnote that this and other works by earlier English composers should be performed at the Annual Congress of Musicians, 'if ever any other compositions than those of Handel were to be performed' (Burney, *General History*, 2:68, n. z).

[63] Mason, 'Essays on Church Music', 100. This attribution probably stems from an anecdote in Anthony Wood's *Athenae Oxoniensis*, discussed in Stevens, 'Songe of Fortie Partes', 180–1, in which he recounts a tale of Bull adding an additional forty parts to an existing forty-part work. Mason made a similar comment about the aural unintelligibility of *I call and cry*, discussed in Chapter 1. These comments are,

The way in which a piece of music can be said to exist when it is not being performed has been the subject of much debate and philosophical speculation. Stanley Boorman provides a fairly commonsense response to this question when he argues that 'there is a sense in which the composition remains in existence [when it is not being performed] in the memories of the creator and earlier listeners.'[64] For most of the seventeenth and eighteenth centuries, however, both the creator of *Spem in alium* and the earlier listeners were long dead. Burney's misunderstanding of the polychoral nature of *Spem in alium* indicates that although his eyes may have been entertained, his ability to 'read' the score or to 'hear with his eyes' was limited.[65] This, combined with some of the odd features displayed by the score copies, suggests that the few people who had access to one of the rare scores had only an at best incomplete sense of its musical structure. Thus, prior to the nineteenth century, while the Song of Forty Parts may have 'subsisted', it was as a collector's item and curiosity, with 'little more than a historical existence.'[66]

❧ *The Nineteenth-Century Revival*

WHETHER the score copied by John Immyns in 1751 was prepared for a particular performance must remain a source of speculation, but almost a century after its foundation by Immyns, the Madrigal Society mounted the first documented performance of the Song of Forty Parts in over 200 years. There is, however, some confusion about the number of times and the dates on which the motet was performed. Although references can be found in the secondary literature to Madrigal Society performances in 1834, 1835 and 1836, the performance in 1836 is the only one that can unequivocally be proved to have taken place.

The 1834 performance can be easily dismissed: references to it seem to have been limited to the reviews of the performance by Henry Leslie's Choir in

---

of course, part of the broader debate between the 'ancients' and 'moderns'. Burney's views on the necessity of a score for the 'intellectual' understanding of music, and the discourse surrounding the tensions between visual and aural understanding of music is discussed in Irving, *Ancients and Moderns*, 174.

[64] Stanley Boorman, 'The Musical Text', in Cook and Everist, *Rethinking Music*, 405–6.

[65] For a discussion of some of the issues and assumptions surrounding what she terms 'silent listening', see Judd, *Reading Renaissance Music Theory*, particularly Chapter 1.

[66] This quote, and the review from which it is taken (*The Times*, 5 Jun 1845, 6) is discussed further below. Even if, as Woodfield argues, it was performed in 1751, the lack of contemporary records of such a performance indicate that it had little or no impact upon general perceptions of the motet.

Table 8 Reported nineteenth-century performances of Tallis's *Spem in alium*

Date	Choir/Occasion	Conductor	Venue
*Jan 1834[†]	Madrigal Society	William Hawes	
*15 Jan 1835	Madrigal Society	William Hawes	Freemason's Hall
21 Jan 1836	Madrigal Society	William Hawes	Freemason's Hall
4 Jun 1845	Hullah's Upper School	John Hullah	Exeter Hall
17 May 1879	Mr Henry Leslie's Choir	Henry Leslie	St James's Hall
*1888–9[‡]		A. H. Mann	
Jan 1889	Manchester Vocal Society	Henry Watson	
20 May 1890	Madrigal Society	Frederick Bridge	Holburn Restaurant
Jan 1898	Incorporated Society of Musicians	A. H. Mann	

* Performances that appear not to have taken place.

† 'Choral Concerts', *London and Provincial Music Trades Review*, 15 Jun 1879, 2. Versions of the same review were also found in *Figaro*, 21 May 1879; *Athenaeum*, 24 May 1879, 673–4; and *Dwight's Journal of Music* 39 (1879): 120.

‡ Bumpus, *Cathedral Music*, 40.

1879,[67] and were probably the result of incorrect information circulated at that concert. While I have found no evidence to support a performance in 1834, the evidence pointing to an 1835 performance is more substantial. A score currently held in the Madrigal Society collection in the British Library as Mad. Soc. MS H.114 contains the following unambiguous inscription:

> A Forty-Part Song/ composed by /Thomas Tallis/ circa 1575/ Originally written to the Latin "Spem in alium nunquam habui praeter in Te"/ and adapted to the English Words/ circa 1639/ Transcribed/ from/ a copy made by John Immyns AD 1751/ (the words Prince Charles being altered to King George/) by /Thomas Oliphant/ Hon[y] Sec[y] to The Madrigal Society/ AD 1834

> It was performed by the Madrigal Society and their friends, assisted by the Young Gentlemen of the Chapel Royal, St Paul's Cathedral, and Westminster Abbey, at their Anniversary Fest[l] on the 15th January 1835, held in the Freemason's Hall. It was noticed by most of the Newspapers.

This is followed by a list of the names of 115 singers (plus twenty-two unnamed boys) who were present.

A search for these newspaper notices, however, raises serious doubts about

---

[67] See, for example, 'Choral Concerts', *London and Provincial Music Trades Review*, 15 Jun 1879, 2.

whether this performance actually took place. The Madrigal Society Anniversary Festival in 1835 was reviewed in several newspapers,[68] including the *Morning Post* and the *Spectator*, but none of the reviews contains any reference to *Spem in alium* or the English version, *Sing and Glorifie*. The *Spectator* published a complete list of the works performed, from which the forty-part motet is conspicuously absent.[69] The music reviewer for the *Spectator* at this time was Edward Taylor,[70] an honorary member of the Society, whose name was included in the list of those present. Although his involvement with the Society raises questions about the impartiality of his reviews, it must also reduce the likelihood of error. The reviewer, presumably Taylor, observes that 'the selection was not, on the whole, so rich as last year; but it contained some pieces of unrivalled vocal grandeur, particularly Gibbons "O clap your hands."' Whilst *O clap your hands* is indeed a splendid piece, it is improbable that it would be considered 'unrivalled' by *Spem in alium*. The programme published in the *Spectator* is confirmed by a handbill from this festival that, by a great stroke of good luck, survives in the archival collection of the Royal College of Music (see Figure 8).[71]

An examination of the reviews of the Anniversary Festival for the following year confirms that the motet was not performed at the 1835 festival. The 1836 festival was reviewed in the *Standard*, the *Morning Post*, the *Musical Library* and the *Spectator*, these last two both listing the complete programme. *Sing and Glorifie* was performed at the end of the first half of the programme (after which dessert was served), and the *Musical Library* explicitly stated that it was 'an undertaking which, perhaps, had never before been attempted; certainly not within the memory of the oldest man living'.[72] The *Spectator* described the performance as 'an achievement without parallel in the history of modern vocal enterprise',[73] and a review in the *Morning Post* observes that it was remarkably well performed, 'when it is considered that the majority of the vocalists had never seen it before'![74]

What, therefore, are we to make of the record of performance found in Mad. Soc. H.114? There are several possibilities, all largely unsatisfactory. The

[68] Craufurd states that the Anniversary Dinners were reported in the press from 1834 ('Madrigal Society', 39).

[69] 'Music of the Week', *Spectator*, 17 Jan 1835, 60.

[70] Langley, 'Taylor, Edward'.

[71] I wish to express my gratitude to Mr Oliver Davies, who miraculously located this handbill.

[72] Supplement to the *Musical Library* 23 (1836): 43–4.

[73] 'The Madrigal Society', *Spectator*, 23 Jan 1836, 80.

[74] *Morning Post*, 22 Jan 1836, 3. An abbreviated version of this review was published in the *Standard*, 22 Jan 1836, 3.

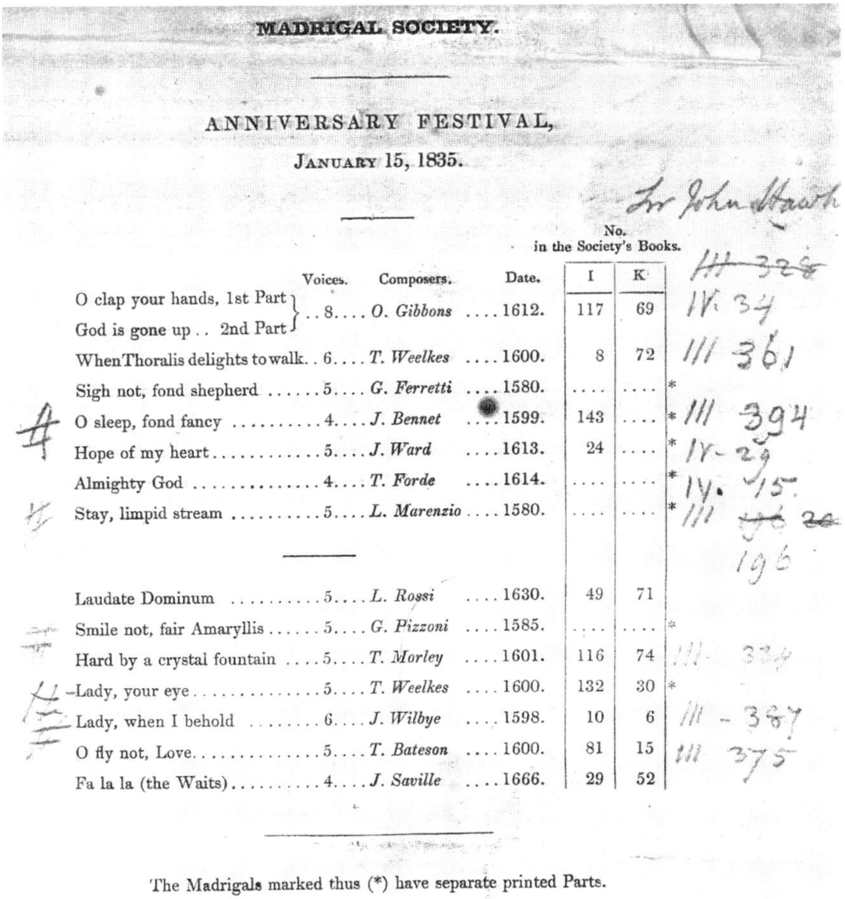

MADRIGAL SOCIETY.

ANNIVERSARY FESTIVAL,

January 15, 1835.

	Voices.	Composers.	Date.	No. in the Society's Books.			
				I	K		
O clap your hands, 1st Part / God is gone up .. 2nd Part	8	O. Gibbons	1612.	117	69	IV. 34	
When Thoralis delights to walk.	6	T. Weelkes	1600.	8	72	* III 361	
Sigh not, fond shepherd	5	G. Ferretti	1580.	....	....	*	
O sleep, fond fancy	4	J. Bennet	1599.	143	....	* III 394	
Hope of my heart	5	J. Ward	1613.	24	....	* IV. 29	
Almighty God	4	T. Forde	1614.	....	....	* IV. 15	
Stay, limpid stream	5	L. Marenzio	1580.	....	....	* III 24	
Laudate Dominum	5	L. Rossi	1630.	49	71		
Smile not, fair Amaryllis	5	G. Pizzoni	1585.	....	....	*	
Hard by a crystal fountain	5	T. Morley	1601.	116	74		
Lady, your eye	5	T. Weelkes	1600.	132	30	*	
Lady, when I behold	6	J. Wilbye	1598.	10	6	III - 367	
O fly not, Love	5	T. Bateson	1600.	81	15	III 375	
Fa la la (the Waits)	4	J. Saville	1666.	29	52		

The Madrigals marked thus (*) have separate printed Parts.

Figure 8. Handbill from Madrigal Society Anniversary Festival, 1835

simplest explanation would be that H.114 was actually used at the 1836 performance, but somehow the dates on the manuscript are incorrect. It is, however, possible to confirm from Madrigal Society records that the singers listed on the manuscript attended the 1835 rather than the 1836 Festival. For example, the *Spectator* review of the 1836 performance mentions 'Sir Andrew Barnard fresh from the Court of King William', but Sir Andrew is not found amongst the participants listed in H.114. The Madrigal Society financial accounts confirm that Sir Andrew was present at the Festival in 1836, but not in 1835.[75] Several other members, including Riversdale Grenfell, Charles S. Packer and George Duvall, are recorded as having paid to

---

75 Accounts of the Madrigal Society, 1832–9, *GB-Lbl* Mad. Soc. MS F.17. In 1835 Sir Andrew Barnard paid only £1 quarterage, but in 1836 he paid £1/15/–, which was the quarterly subscription plus 15 shillings for the Anniversary dinner.

attend the festival dinner in 1835 but not in 1836, and all are included in the listing in H.114.

A second possibility is that the motet was scheduled to be performed in 1835, but was for some reason postponed to the following year. It is, however, hard to imagine how such a detailed list of singers could have been compiled before the Festival took place, especially when eighty-eight of the 115 adult performers named were visitors, rather than members of the Madrigal Society.

The third possibility is that the score was annotated at a later date, the guest list being compiled from some record of those present at the 1835 Festival in the mistaken belief that the performance took place in 1835 rather than the following year. The records of the Madrigal Society currently held in the British Library do not, however, contain sufficient information to recover a complete list of the visitors present in 1835, so some other source would have been required. The suggestion that the list of performers was prepared retrospectively is also rendered less likely by the existence of another score, which, as described by Mann in his 1888 publication, sounds fundamentally similar to Mad. Soc. MS H.114, but records the correct details of the 1836 Anniversary Festival. Unfortunately I have been unable to locate this score, but Mann states that, like H.114, it was made by Oliphant from Immyns's copy, that it was dated 17 January 1836, bore the inscription 'This Motett was performed at the Anniversary Festival of the Madrigal Society 21st of Jan. 1836, by the undersigned members of the Society, and their friends' and included 'the signatures of all those present, performers & non-performers'.[76] Given the existence of a score that was a correct record of the 1836 performance, including signatures rather than just names of the participants, it seems unlikely that Oliphant would have erroneously compiled H.114 as a record of the same event.

None of these solutions is therefore very satisfactory, and for the moment the question of why Mad. Soc. MS H.114 records in such detail a performance that never took place must remain a mystery.

The impetus for the 1836 performance may well have been the acquisition of Immyns's score by the architect Joseph Gwilt, who was a member of the Society

---

[76] Mann, *Motet for 40 Voices*, iii. This score also included a piano or organ accompaniment derived by Oliphant from Immyn's figured bass line. Peter Holman has suggested that the thorough bass was part of Tallis's original conception ('"Evenly, Softly, and Sweetly Acchording to All": The Organ Accompaniment of English Consort Music', *John Jenkins and His Time: Studies in English Consort Music*, ed. Andrew Ashbee and Peter Holman (Oxford: Clarendon, 1996), 360), but despite the provision of this accompaniment in this score, and of the figured bass in the earlier scores, no mention is made of instrumental accompaniment in any of the reviews of nineteenth-century performances.

from 1812 until 1838.[77] Mann was unaware of how the copy came to be in the possession of the Madrigal Society, although he speculates that it may have been purchased from Immyns's widow, but mentions that it bore Gwilt's stamp.[78] The *Musical Library* review states that Gwilt had recently purchased the score, which he presented to the Madrigal Society on this occasion.

Gwilt was not, however, the first member of the Madrigal Society to have had access to a copy of the motet. George Ebenezer Williams, who appears to have owned the Tenbury copy before it was purchased by Ouseley, snr., joined the Society in 1814, and Bartleman, who at one stage owned R.M.g.4.1, was also a member.[79] While access to a copy of the score was, of course, a necessary condition for a performance, it was not therefore a sufficient one. The decision to perform the work at this time no doubt reflected both the prosperous state of the Madrigal Society in the late 1830s,[80] and the broader interest in early choral music that was starting to emerge at this time, and marked the beginning of a new phase in the motet's history. For the first time it was removed from its ceremonial role in the private chambers of the aristocracy and royalty and brought into the sphere of the musical enthusiast.

The Madrigal Society Anniversary Festivals fell into a grey area between the public and private realms. These occasions took place in a public hall and were commented upon in the press; but although originally known as 'Public Feasts', they were not open to the public.[81] The enjoyment of the performers, who normally greatly outnumbered the listeners, was paramount. The *Spectator* review of the 1836 festival claims that '200 people were present, of whom not less than 150 took part in the performance of the pieces', although the score prepared for the performance claims that there were 104 vocalists and twenty-four visitors,[82] and the *Musical Library* reported that the motet was performed by 'such of the company as were willing to take a part', divided into eight choirs of eleven singers.

---

[77] Thomas Oliphant, *A Brief Account of the Madrigal Society from its Institution in 1741, up to the Present Period* (London: Calkin & Budd, 1835), 18, and Accounts of the Madrigal Society, 1832–9, *GB-Lbl* Mad. Soc. MS F.17.

[78] Mann, *Motet for 40 Voices*, ii. Mann makes it clear that Immyns's score was still in the Madrigal Society library in 1888, although Rockstro claimed that it had 'hopelessly disappeared' ('Schools of Composition').

[79] Oliphant, *Brief Account*, 18; Oliphant describes Bartleman, who joined in 1793, as 'the first English bass singer of his time.'

[80] Craufurd, 'Madrigal Society', 42.

[81] Craufurd, 'Madrigal Society', 39.

[82] This figure comes from a description of the score in an advertisement in *Reeve's Catalogue of Music and Musical Literature* 9 (1882): 75, which is discussed further below.

The press reviews, particularly the review in the *Spectator*, which was presumably written by Taylor, catch the friendly, clubbish atmosphere.[83] The account in the *Spectator* begins with reminiscences of the 'old days', including a personal recollection of Horsfall, 'the hero of the meeting', and observed that 'there was the usual happy admixture of professionals and amateurs – clergy and laity – Whigs and Tories.' The reports in the *Morning Post* and *Musical Library* similarly focused on the chummy atmosphere, mentioning president John Leman Rogers's 'humorous exordium' on the history of the motet, and his joke with George Smart, then organist of the Chapel Royal, about Tallis's salary of 7½ d per day while holding the same position. These meetings, therefore, had little in common with the ideal modern concert performance, 'cut off completely from all extra-musical activities' and attended by a silent, non-participating audience.[84] The lack of rehearsal, together with the employment of eight sub-conductors,[85] who can have done nothing but 'marshal the beat', rather than a single conductor attempting to convey his own expressive interpretation of 'the musically meaningful content of a work', also suggest that this performance was not primarily dedicated to the deep aesthetic appreciation of a work of art.[86]

In general, however, the critical response to the performance, which, given doubts such as Tudway's and Burney's, must have been undertaken in the spirit of an experiment, was positive: the reviewers were obviously sympathetic to the Madrigal Society's goals and felt that they had been reached, or even exceeded. The *Musical Library* was positive about the performance – 'fewer mistakes occurred than could have been expected in the first trial of a composition so complicated in its formation' – but slightly disappointed with the motet:

Were the motet abridged about one-third, the remainder would rise in the estimation of all [...] But musicians are fastidious on this point, and,

---

[83] Thomas Day is rather scathing about the Madrigal Society's less than serious attitude towards the music they performed, at least in the period prior to 1820, noting that such societies were seen as a 'source of pleasant entertainment and companionship', and that 'good liquor mixed freely with good music' ('Old Music in England, 1790–1820', *Revue belge de musicologie* 26–7 (1972–3): 29).

[84] Goehr, *Imaginary Museum*, 236. Goehr has explored the problematic nature of the distinction of the 'musical', the 'extra-musical' and the 'non-musical' in 'Writing Music History', 187–90, and in *The Quest for Voice: On Music, Politics, and the Limits of Philosophy* (Berkeley: University of California Press, 1998), 6–18. Richard Taruskin also questions Goehr's use of the term (*Text and Act: Essays on Music and Performance* (New York: Oxford University Press, 1995), 17).

[85] *Spectator*, 23 Jan 1836, 80: the sub-conductors were listed as Messrs. Bellamy, Turle, Goss, Lucas, Elliott and Jolly and Sir G. Smart.

[86] Goehr, *Imaginary Museum*, 235.

generally speaking, rather consent to the death of a composition – than save it by the sacrifice of a limb.

The *Morning Post* review was more enthusiastic:

> This quadragintesimal harmony […] was performed – when it is considered that the majority of the vocalists had never seen it before – with astonishing skill, and the burst of the general choir, when all the parts were heard together, was perfectly electrical. It is to be hoped that another opportunity will be found of hearing 'Sing and Glorify' of Tallis. The company separated at 11 o'clock with unmixed feelings of delight.[87]

The next opportunity of hearing *Sing and Glorify* did not, however, present itself for another nine years, when it was performed by John Hullah's Upper Singing School. This occasion does not appear to have been a success.

John Pyke Hullah had begun massed singing classes at Exeter Hall in 1841, based upon the Wilhelm method taught in Paris, which, together with Joseph Mainzer's classes, generated a type of 'sightsinging mania'.[88] This mania was one of many factors contributing to the general revival of interest in choral music in the 1840s. It has been estimated that by July 1847 50,000 people were being taught by Hullah and his pupils;[89] the Upper Singing School concert was a showcase for his most advanced pupils.

A total of 1,500 singers were involved in a concert at Exeter Hall on Wednesday 4 June 1845. Tallis's 'Forty Part Song' was performed by a 'semi-chorus' of 500 singers. It was sung to *sol-fa* syllables as, according to *The Times*, the English words were 'too trashy for endurance',[90] and was reviewed in *The Times*, the *Morning Post* and the *Spectator*.

The provision of parts for a choir of this size must have presented a significant challenge. A collection of material purchased by J. Crampton for the British Museum from the Glee Club of London in 1876 for £5/5/– and now catalogued as Add. MS 29968 includes some of the copies used for this performance.[91]

---

[87] *Morning Post*, 22 Jan 1836, 3.

[88] For a brief description of the spread of the sightsinging movement, see Scholes, *Mirror of Music*, 3–19. A more extensive discussion is found in Bernarr Rainbow, *The Land without Music: Musical Education in England, 1800–1860, and its Continental Antecedents* (Novello: London, 1967).

[89] Frances Hullah, *The Life of John Hullah* (London: Longmans, Green & Co., 1886), 35. Scholes reports that Hullah had 50,000 pupils by July 1842 (*Mirror of Music*, 11).

[90] 'Exeter Hall', *The Times*, 5 Jun 1845, 6.

[91] *Puttick & Simpson Sales Catalogue*, 29 Feb 1876, lot 602. This manuscript had previously been in the possession of the bookseller R. E. Lonsdale. Crampton was a

It comprises a third copy of *Spem in alium* in the hand of Thomas Oliphant,[92] and seventy-six individual voice parts, in a variety of different hands and on different papers. The copy by Oliphant, unlike his other copies, is not in score: each of the eight five-part choirs is transcribed separately with the English words, slightly modified to read 'Live the King'. On the fly-leaf is pasted Burney's description of the work, 'printed for a few friends by J. Poplett, 43, Beech St, City', with the phrase 'although somewhat Gothic' omitted.[93] Mann believed that the sub-scores in Oliphant's hand were for the use of the sub-conductors of the individual choirs at the performance by the Madrigal Society. This seems plausible, as the reference to the King probably dates the copy prior to the accession of Queen Victoria in 1837.[94] He also argues that the individual parts, many of which bear names, were used by singers at the Madrigal Society performance, the names indicating that the singers wished to use the same copy at each rehearsal. This is most unlikely, as many of the names are those of women (Miss Wallis, Miss Jane Osborne, Mrs W. Jones, etc.), whereas the Madrigal Society performers were all male, and records of the Madrigal Society in the mid-1830s show that none of the men's names belonged to members at that time. Furthermore, the *Spectator* review of the 1836 performance notes Oliphant had copied the parts for that performance.[95] It is much more likely that these copies were used for Hullah's performance, as one of the copies (the tenor part of the eighth choir) bears the inscription 'Hullah's Upper School' in the upper right-hand corner, and the name of the Honorary Librarian, Charles Beevor, appears on another copy. These parts are listed in the 1850 *Catalogue ... of the Library of St Martin's Hall*, the hall built by John Hullah.[96]

The association of these individual parts with Oliphant's parts suggests that the copies for the 1845 performance were made from the materials Oliphant prepared for the Madrigal Society performance in 1836, which in turn had been based upon Immyns's copy.

---

dealer from whom the British Museum acquired a large quantity of music in the late 1870s: see Alec Hyatt King, *Printed Music in the British Museum* (London: Clive Bingley, 1979), 94.

92 The others are Mad. Soc. H.114 and the missing score created for the 1836 performance.

93 Howard Irving discusses both the overall negative connotations of the term 'Gothic', and Burney's more complex use of it in Irving, *Ancients and Moderns*, 165–74.

94 Mann, *Motet for 40 Voices*, i.

95 *Spectator*, 23 Jan 1836, 80. There is no trace of the many copies that must have been made for the singers at this performance.

96 *Catalogue of Music and Musical Literature Contained in the Library of St Martin's Hall* (London: Parker, 1850).

While the press reception of the Madrigal Society performance was generally warm, the response to Hullah's performance was icy. The *Times* review is the most positive, noting that it 'was a most creditable effort on the part of Mr. Hullah to train his pupils into the performance of a work that was at once so great a rarity and so admirable an exercise.' The reviewer concludes, however, that 'the work can never become popular, belonging in fact to those musical pedantries which existed in the early days of art, and […] therefore it may be many years before it is played again.'[97] The *Morning Post* review was considerably less kind:

> The great feature of the evening was expected to be Tallis's 'Forty Part Song', announced in the programme in imposing capitals. This composition chiefly owes its fame to tradition, while it remained unheard it might have retained its repute, but its merits will by no means stand the test of modern criticism. The *forty* parts so much talked about, are found, on examination, to consist of barely *four* – very ill written and ill digested – breaking off here and there to be resumed elsewhere, without the shadow of continuity. Forty parts may be easily written thus. The extreme obscurity of the harmony enhances the ill effect arising from the unskillful part writing, and the result was anything but satisfactory. All the singers in the world – and five hundred voices did their best for this last night – would never make the 'forty-part song' endurable to modern ears. Mr Hallah [*sic*], however, is to be praised for his perseverance in preparing so great a curiosity for public performance. It is not likely, we think, to be repeated.[98]

Once again, this is music that is best left unheard.

The reviewer for the *Spectator* – Taylor had relinquished the post in 1843 – was, if possible, even more critical, retrospectively damning the earlier performance as well:

> Tallis's 'Song of Forty Parts' was produced, probably as an exercise of the reading of the more select pupils. When performed at the Madrigal Society's Anniversary in 1836, it was found totally effectless; and this mistake of a barbarous age as to the principles of harmonious effect, it might be thought quite sufficient to have revived once as a curiosity. Its repetition on Wednesday seemed to put an end to its pretensions as a work of interest or entertainment; none present, we suspect, will ever want to hear it more.[99]

It is hard to shake the impression that the '*sol-fa'd*' performance by 500

97 'Exeter Hall', *The Times*, 5 Jun 1845, 6.
98 'Mr. Hullah's Classes', *Morning Post*, 5 Jun 1845, 3.
99 *Spectator*, 7 Jun 1845, 546.

recently trained singers left a lot to be desired. The Madrigal Society performance had quashed the doubts as to whether it could be performed, however, and
expectations of the 1845 performance appear to have been considerably higher
than they had been a decade earlier. The disappointed *Morning Post* reviewer, for
example, had expected the motet to be 'the great feature of the evening'. Hullah's
'great choral meetings' also seemed to have been closer to the modern concert,
dedicated to appreciation of 'each musical work for its own sake',[100] than the con-
vivial participatory anniversary dinners of the Madrigal Society. The *Times* review
may have been the kindest because it expected the least: *Spem in alium* was seen
as representative of 'the early days of art' and as an 'admirable exercise', but was
found to be aesthetically lacking. It was the motet's inability to 'stand the test of
modern criticism' that so disappointed the reviewers in the *Morning Post* and the
Spectator: as a curiosity it was interesting, as a 'work of interest or entertainment',
which was the spirit in which it was presented on this occasion, it was a complete
failure.

Whatever the reasons for the critical failure of the 1845 performance, it was
a long time before anybody heard the Song of Forty Parts again. The next performance, again in the English version, was by Mr Henry Leslie's Choir on 15 May
1879 at St James's Hall, thirty-four years later.[101] Sheppard's letter to the *Musical
Times* had been published the previous year, and it is possible that this account of
the impact upon the unnamed duke of 'hearing it sung' inspired Leslie to attempt
another performance, but this performance, and indeed Sheppard's decision to
publish an account that he had located twenty years earlier,[102] can also be seen as
an early sign of the renewed interest in Tallis's polyphony that took place around
this time.

Several reviews of this concert mention that it was conducted from a score in
the library of the Sacred Harmonic Society.[103] A copy of Tallis's 'Forty Part Song'
had been purchased for £8 at the sale of Thomas Oliphant's library on 25 April
1873 by William Henry Husk.[104] The inscription, which was reproduced in the
sales catalogue, identifies the manuscript as Mad. Soc. MS H.114. Husk, the author

---

[100] Goehr, *Imaginary Museum*, 237.

[101] Percy Scholes provides a brief history of this choir, taken largely from the pages of
the *Musical Times* (*Mirror of Music*, 28–30).

[102] Sheppard, 'Tallis and his Song of Forty Parts', 97.

[103] See, for example, 'Choral Concerts', *London and Provincial Music Trades Review*,
15 Jun 1879, 2. Mann had not seen this copy, but refers to the entry in the catalogue
of the library of the Sacred Harmonic Society.

[104] *Catalogue of the Important Musical Collections Formed by the Late Thomas
Oliphant, Esq. …*, Puttick and Simpson Sales Catalogue, vol. 155 (London, 1873),
43, item 589. This was by far the highest price paid for any item at the sale: the next

of the Tallis entry in Grove's *Dictionary*, was the librarian of the Sacred Harmonic Society from 1853 to 1887, and appears to have purchased the manuscript on behalf of the society: it is listed in the 1882 *Supplement to the Catalogue of the Sacred Harmonic Society Library*, which he compiled.[105] The Sacred Harmonic Society score was, therefore, Oliphant's score prepared for the putative Madrigal Society performance in 1835.

Although it was made up of amateurs, Mr Henry Leslie's Choir was extremely highly regarded – the *Daily Chronicle* described them as 'singularly perfect in those qualities that constitute good part-singing'[106] – and the standard of this performance seems to have been very high. The *London and Provincial Music Trades Review*, for example, observed that 'to properly conduct such a work, sung by the finest of our amateur choirs, was a stupendous task, and Mr. Leslie deserves the highest credit for its altogether successful accomplishment.'[107] The reviewer in the *Daily Chronicle* not only praised Mr Leslie for the successful execution of the music, but noted that it 'was evident that the utmost pains had been taken to secure an adequate interpretation of this curious work.' Unlike the 1836 performance, the music would have been extensively rehearsed: Henry Leslie believed that 'a difficult choral piece requires some eighty rehearsals, and an amount of labour greatly exceeding that necessary for the most elaborate orchestral symphony.'[108]

Despite this conscientious preparation, however, the Song of Forty Parts was not well received. The *Daily Telegraph* dismissed it as 'about as interesting and valuable as a set of Chinese concentric balls or a table made of a million bits of wood.'[109] This view is echoed in the *Musical Times* review, which, after downplaying the skill involved in writing in forty parts, concludes that it is

as interesting as any other ingenious, if not particularly useful, application of labour and patience. That it was successful in performance we cannot say. The complicated machine seemed to have become rusty, and creaked a good deal when set in motion.[110]

The reviews in the *Music Trades Review* and the *Daily Chronicle* were generally

most expensive items sold were Yonge's *Musica Transalpina* of 1588, which went for £4/5/–, and Wilbye's *Second Set of Madrigals* (1609) at £5.
[105] It is unclear when this copy was returned to the Madrigal Society collection.
[106] 'Mr. Henry Leslie's Choir, *Daily Chronicle*, 16 May 1879, 5.
[107] 'Choral Concerts', *London and Provincial Music Trades Review*, 15 Jun 1879, 2.
[108] Scholes, *Mirror of Music*, 29.
[109] 'Mr. Henry Leslie's Choir', *Daily Telegraph*, 17 May 1879, 5.
[110] 'Mr. Henry Leslie's Choir', *Musical Times* 20 (1879): 311.

more positive, but the former was forced to admit that 'the effect of this marvel-lous work is, in performance, perhaps more astonishing than pleasing to modern ears',[111] while the latter observed that 'applause at the conclusion was by no means so hearty as that invariably awarded to the performance by this choir of such pieces as Mendelssohn's eight-part psalm, "Judge me, O God."'

The Song of Forty Parts appears to have disappointed the reviewers and failed 'the test of modern criticism', but once again the bar had been raised. While the Madrigal Society performance was a musical experiment among friends, and the Hullah performance to *sol-fa* syllables demonstrated the newly acquired skills of hundreds of students, Leslie's performance was the first by a highly respected and thoroughly rehearsed choir as part of their regular concert programme. Reviews of the concert record that the hall was crowded 'in every part' by 'an enormous audi-ence' who had turned out to hear the work.[112] At this time, however, works such as the Mendelssohn psalm setting and Robert Lucas Pearsall's ten-part *Sir Patrick Spens* were still more to the taste of the audience.[113]

Despite the poor critical response, Leslie's decision to include the motet in one of his concert programmes indicates in itself a new willingness to approach this music in aesthetic, rather than historic, terms, and interest in the 'polyphonic phe-nomenon' continued to grow. Shortly after Leslie's performance William Reeves, a bookseller and music publisher based in Fleet Street,[114] advertised a proposal to publish a subscription edition of *Spem in alium*. The edition was to be based upon the score prepared by Oliphant for the 1836 Madrigal Society performance. Although this manuscript is now lost, Reeves provided a detailed description of it in the call for subscriptions.[115] This advertisement is the source of the newspaper

[111] 'Choral Concerts', *London and Provincial Music Trades Review*, 15 Jun 1879, 2.

[112] 'Choral Concerts', *London and Provincial Music Trades Review*, 15 Jun 1879, 2, and 'Mr. Henry Leslie's Choir', *Daily Chronicle*, 16 May 1879, 5.

[113] A brief review of this concert in 'Notes on News', *Musical Opinion and Music Trades Review* 2 (1879): 8, recommends *Sir Patrick Spens* as 'an effective piece in a programme, and one which choirs in search of novelty might make note of.'

[114] For more information on William Reeves, see James B. Coover, 'William Reeves, Booksellers/Publishers, 1825–', *Music Publishing and Collecting: Essays in Honor of Donald W. Krummel*, ed. David Hunter (Champaign, IL: University of Illinois, Urbana-Champaign, 1994), 39–67.

[115] *Reeves' Catalogue of Music and Musical Literature*, vol. 9 (London: Williams Reeves, 1882), 75. Similar or identical advertisements were found in several other catalogues printed at about this time. The advertisement includes a complete transcription of Oliphant's historical introduction, dated 17 January 1836, and of a note on p. 28 of the manuscript that announces: 'This Motett was performed at the Anniversary Festival of the Madrigal Society 21st Jan. 1836, by the undersigned members of the Madrigal Society and their friends'. The advertisement records

clipping on the flyleaf of r.m.4.g.1, and describes the transcription of this score by Oliphant, rather than the score to which it is attached.[116] Mann also describes the score, which he says is in the possession of William Reeves, noting that it 'is a beautifully written work, and certainly ought to be in the possession of its undoubtedly original owners, the Madrigal Society.'[117]

The proposed edition was to have been engraved from this score and printed on 'fine, thick paper' at a cost of 21 shillings or less to subscribers, and £2 to non-subscribers, with the possibility of a price rise one month after the subscription list was closed. There is no sign, however, that this publication ever took place, and James B. Coover argues that there is no evidence that Reeves had the capacity to engrave music at this time.[118]

Although Reeves's attempt at publication was unsuccessful, in 1888 A. H. Mann published an edition of the Song of Forty Parts, placing it, according to the *Musical Times*, 'within the reach of all who are interested in the preservation of these monuments of musical history.'[119] Again, this publication is descended, via Oliphant, from Immyns's 1751 copy: Mann explains that he based his edition upon a score he prepared from vocal parts lent to him by Henry Leslie.[120] The English words, with the modification 'Long live George', apparently taken from Immyns's 1751 copy, are included in the scholarly introduction, but the Latin text is underlaid in the edition.

Mann's 1888 edition is modest in size, cost and presentation. Its quarto size, possible due to its arrangement with only four choirs per page, is considerably smaller than modern editions, and the price of five shillings is significantly less than that proposed by Reeves. The preface includes a brief biography of Tallis and a scholarly discussion of all the available scores, and concludes with a list of forty-seven subscribers who each purchased five copies, and nine who purchased single copies. The list of subscribers includes Ouseley, Bumpus, J. A. Fuller Maitland,

that this was followed by the signatures of the 106 singers and twenty-four visitors present, and that a plan of the arrangement of the choirs, and the 'names of the Vocalisti' was found on p. 29.

[116] Although I have not been able to locate the exact issue of *Reeves' Catalogue* from which this cutting was taken, the text is identical with that found in Issue 9. The placement on the page is slightly different, but there can be no doubt that one of these catalogues is the source.

[117] Mann, *Motet for 40 Voices*, iii.

[118] Coover, 'William Reeves', 50.

[119] 'Motett for Forty Voices', *Musical Times* 29 (1888): 487.

[120] Mann, *Motet for 40 Voices*, iii. By 1890 these voice parts were said to be in the possession of Rev. Dr Mee of Oxford (*London and Provincial Music Trades Review*, 15 Jun 1890, 7).

William Monk and W. Barclay Squire. Also listed are a Mrs Beevor, presumably a relation of Charles Beevor, Hullah's librarian, and J. E. Street, Secretary of the Madrigal Society; J. P. Street, had been the Madrigal Society Librarian at the time of the 1836 performance.[121]

Bumpus claims that Mann conducted a performance shortly after the 1888 publication, although he gives no further details.[122] I have found no evidence of this, but it was performed by the Manchester Vocal Society under Dr Henry Watson in January 1889. This performance was not widely reviewed, but a brief paragraph in the *Musical Times* praised Watson for his 'boldness' in presenting this 'specimen of ingenious part-writing – much more talked about than known', which had 'so lately become accessible through the exertions of Dr. Mann of Cambridge.' The reviewer claimed that the forty-part motet presented 'no difficulty of execution', except for the strain arising from 'entrusting each part to a single voice', and concluded that 'the performance was very interesting and drew together a large number of students of counterpoint.'[123]

Another performance was mounted by the Madrigal Society at their 150th Anniversary Festival on 20 May 1890 at the Holborn Restaurant under the direction of Frederic Bridge, attended by 'the duke of Edinburgh and many distinguished musicians and a large number of ladies'.[124] The review in the *Musical Times* claims that prior to Leslie's 1879 performance it had only been performed twice 'in the present century';[125] no mention is made of the Manchester performance. Once again, the critical response was tepid:

> As an example of ingenuity it is most interesting, as a piece of music it is by no means so effective as might be expected. Some pains had evidently been taken to prepare the work, but the result, to say the least, was disappointing.

[121] See Craufurd, 'The Madrigal Society', 40, 46, where he notes: 'THE FAMILY OF STREET, which is still represented in the Society, and since the time of J. P. Street, has done the Society many services.'

[122] Bumpus, *Cathedral Music*, 40. Edward Dent claimed, some years after that event, that Mann gave a 'very mediocre performance' at Cambridge in 'about 1898', but as he also claims that 'Mann never got a score of the Tallis printed', these recollections must be approached with caution (Andrews, *Westminster Retrospect*, 11). Mann did, however, conduct a performance at the ISM in 1898, which will be discussed further below. I am grateful to Ian Burk for bringing this reference to my attention.

[123] 'Music in Manchester', *Musical Times* 30 (1889): 92.

[124] 'The Madrigal Society', *Musical Times* 31 (1890): 348.

[125] 'The Madrigal Society', 348. This supports the argument that the motet had not been performed in 1835, although, as the current discussion shows, reviews written such a long time after the event were hardly reliable.

The difficulty of bringing together a choir sufficiently competent and numerous to perform it is, perhaps, the reason why it is so seldom heard, and the amount of trouble involved in preparation is by no means commensurate with the result produced. It may therefore be well regarded as a monument of patience and skill, the more noteworthy when it is considered that it was supposed to be written three centuries back.

A brief mention of this performance in the *Music Trades Review* notes that 'the "Forty-part Song" was edited for the occasion by Dr. Mann'.[126] If, as previously suggested, Mann had discovered the Gresham copy sometime between 1888 and 1890 (this review also contains the first reference I have found to the copy in the Gresham Library), it seems likely that Mann's parts for this performance were based on this newly discovered manuscript.[127] If this speculation is correct, this would have been the first modern performance not based in some way upon Oliphant's copies of Immyns's score.

In line with Madrigal Society tradition, the soprano parts were performed by boys from Westminster Abbey. Edward Pine recalls: 'we frequently met at the rooms of the old Madrigal Society in Lyle Street, where for our singing we were rewarded with a glass of port, a buttered biscuit, and two shillings.'[128] The reward for the performance of *Spem in alium* was, however, more generous: 'each boy was delighted to receive, besides refreshments, a beautifully bound copy signed by the President, Lord Beauchamp, and the secretary, Edward Street.'[129] It is unclear whether this refers to Mann's published edition, or to the version prepared for the performance.

In January 1898 A. H. Mann conducted a choir of about 400 singers in a performance at the Congress of the Incorporated Society of Musicians in London in January 1898. The *Musical Times* observes that 'it is not a work that one yearns to hear twice, but it is a remarkable example of the glorification of early contrapuntal ingenuity.'[130] A review of this performance in the *Musical Opinion* notes that:

The work, despite the fact that only two rehearsals had been held, was given in a highly commendable manner; and at the close the audience so much appreciated it that a repetition was asked for, but time did not permit.

---

[126] 'Miscellaneous', *London and Provincial Music Trades Review*, 15 Jan 1890, 7.

[127] The Preface to the 1928 Carnegie Trust edition also mentions that Mann borrowed the Gresham manuscript 'when preparing an edition of the Motet for a performance by the Madrigal Society'.

[128] Pine, *Westminster Abbey Singers*, 202.

[129] Pine, *Westminster Abbey Singers*, 212.

[130] 'The Incorporated Society of Musicians', *Musical Times* 39 (1898): 101.

Dr. Mann's services, however, were recognised by the ladies of the choir, who afterwards presented him with a handsome dressing bag.[131]

That one would not 'yearn to hear twice' a performance by a choir of this size after only two rehearsals seems quite reasonable.

The score that Mann constructed for this performance was based upon the recently 'rediscovered' Gresham College manuscript, which he described in a review of the performance as 'the oldest MS. copy at present known'. Mann speculated that 'this version was arranged for some occasion when the two princes went into London, possibly after the Gunpowder Plot, or when Prince Henry was created the thirteenth prince of Wales.'[132] The 1928 edition for the Tudor Church Music series was based on this copy, although Tenbury 1270 and British Library Add. MS 29968 were also collated and R.M.4.g.1, the oldest known source with Latin words, was used as the source of the text underlay.[133]

❧ A Work of Interest or Entertainment?

IT can be seen from this survey of nineteenth-century reviews of *Spem in alium* that, despite increasingly frequent performances, the process of its acceptance as 'a work of interest or entertainment' was a slow one. Michael Talbot has identified three essential attributes of the musical work: discreteness, reproducibility and attributability.[134] Although *Spem in alium* unambiguously meets Talbot's primary requirements, there is still a serious question as to whether it was, during the nineteenth century, regarded as a *musical* work. Goehr has observed that under the work-concept, musicians began to see musical masterpieces as

transcending temporal and spatial barriers. [...] Works were not to be thought about as expressive or representative of concrete historical moments,

---

[131] 'The Incorporated Society of Musicians', *Musical Opinion and Music Trades Review* 21 (1898): 323.

[132] 'The Incorporated Society of Musicians', *Musical Opinion and Music Trades Review* 21 (1898): 323.

[133] Preface to Carnegie Trust Edition. The editor notes, however, that 'The underlaying of the words follows a later practice than that of Tallis's day, and is in places so perverse that it appears like an attempt on the part of an unknown editor to fit the Latin words to the English adaptation.' Of course, once Egerton 3512 came to light in 1947, this speculation was confirmed.

[134] Michael Talbot, 'Introduction', in Talbot, *Musical Work*, 3. Talbot's position differs somewhat from Goehr's: these distinctions will be examined further in the following chapter.

but as valuable in their own right as transcending all considerations other than those of an aesthetic/spiritual nature.[135]

References to timeless spiritual transcendence were conspicuously absent from reviews of performances of *Spem in alium*. In fact, the reverse was true: review after review approached the motet predominantly as an example of the 'musical pedantries which existed in the early days of art', a 'mistake of a barbarous age' or, at best, 'the glorification of early contrapuntal ingenuity.'[136] If a musical work is timeless and transcendent, the Song of Forty Parts conspicuously failed to qualify.

Around the turn of the twentieth century, however, this attitude began to change. Ernest Walker, for example, writing in 1907, explicitly challenges the prevailing view of the motet as an example of ingenuity, rather than beauty:

> In sheer technical facility the famous forty-part motet 'Spem in alium non habui' – written for eight choirs of five parts each – is equal to anything that the great music of any century or country can show; but the really most astonishing thing about it is that it is a splendid work of art also. [...] following the bad example of early historians, most writers have confined themselves far too exclusively to its purely ingenious qualities, which, very remarkable as they are, have always been well within the reach of the highly skilled mathematical musician, whether a genius like Tallis or a mere trifler. Of course, the more the purely technical difficulty presses, the greater is the chance that the artistic element will drop aside; and it is really extraordinary that in spite of the superlative risk of his endeavour Tallis should have produced in this motet a work so finely organized in form, so large and striking in thematic material and, on the whole, so varied in harmony and expression.[137]

In 1928 a new edition was published by the Carnegie Trust, which was a reprint of the edition prepared for the Tallis volume of the Tudor Church Music series. This edition prompted H. B. Collins's passionate argument, discussed in Chapter 2, that in *Spem in alium* Tallis did not merely 'attempt a feat hitherto unheard of [...] to exhibit his superb technical skill', but constructed a heartfelt and personal protest against 'forty generations' of persecution of English Catholics.[138]

---

[135] Goehr, *Imaginary Museum*, 246.

[136] 'Exeter Hall', *The Times*, 5 Jun 1845; *Spectator*, 7 Jun 1845; *Musical Times* 39 (1898): 101.

[137] Walker, *Music in England*, 45–6.

[138] Collins, 'Thomas Tallis', 164.

Despite the academic re-evaluation of the merits of Tallis's polyphony, performances in the early years of the twentieth century were rare,[139] but this new publication prompted a performance of *Spem in alium* on 15 May 1929 by the Newcastle-
upon-Tyne Bach Choir.[140] The programme, conducted by W. Gillies Whittaker,
included Byrd's four-part mass and the Song of Forty Parts, which was given three
times: 'an excellent way of doing something to make up for the neglect of the work,
and also a help to its understanding by the audience. No doubt performers and
hearers alike did it the fullest justice at the third time of asking.'[141] In his account of
the performance, entitled 'An Adventure', Whittaker describes his motivations:

> The appearance of the Tallis volume of the Carnegie Series last summer cre-
> ated an absolutely irresistible desire to tackle the forty-part Motet – *Spem in
> alium nunquam habui*. As a boy I had often looked longingly at Dr. Mann's
> 1888 edition […] and wondered whether I should ever have the opportunity
> to penetrate its mysteries, and the new score, fascinating with its countless
> minute notes and delicate lines, was as seductive as the map of Treasure
> Island.[142]

The cost of purchasing eighty copies of the publication was, however, prohibi-
tive, and an enthusiastic member of the choir hand-copied the two copies of each
part that were required. After describing the structure of the work and the 'disposition of the choir', Whittaker addresses the great question: 'Is it merely a technical
feat? Is there any real musical interest?'

> I can truly answer that few works have moved me so powerfully in rehearsal
> and performance. The serious beauty of themes, the range of emotions, the
> variety of the music, tender, massive, exhilarating by turns, the rich colour-
> ing owing to the large proportion of male voices, the numerous changes of
> shade and power obtained by the treatment of various groupings, and the
> consummate ease with which the composer leads his multitudes through
> their pilgrimage, make the Motet of living interest from start to finish. […]
> Whether viewed as an architectural scheme, a contrapuntal feat, an experi-
> ment in colour, an expression of emotion, or as an essay in musical thought,
> *Spem in alium* is undoubtedly a work of genius.[143]

---

139 Anderton, in 1914, lists all the 'recorded' performances, the last of which was the
     ISM performance in 1898 ('Thomas Tallys', 283).
140 W. Gillies Whittaker, 'An Adventure', *Collected Essays* (London: Oxford University
     Press, 1940), 86–9; first published in the *Dominant* 2 (May–June 1929): 40–2.
141 'Tallis's Forty-Part Motet', *Musical Times* 70 (1929): 551.
142 Whittaker, 'An Adventure', 86.
143 Whittaker, 'An Adventure', 89.

E.C., writing for the *Musical Opinion*, expressed a similar view:

> Perhaps the best possible compliment one can pay the motet is to say that, despite its extraordinary multiplication of parts, it did not compare unfavourably with the Byrd Mass. [...] The marvel of the motet, however, is not its technical ingenuity, but its musical success. Not only does the counterpoint come off, but the musical effect aimed at does so in a wonderful degree. The choir, in singing with feeling, sincerity and beauty, only reflected qualities inherent in the work.[144]

Spem in alium had finally, and unambiguously, been granted the status of musical work.

The unique size and complexity of the Song of Forty Parts ensure that it must always be a special case, and there are several aspects of its reception that defy expectations. It was revived by the Madrigal Society in 1836 at a time when even polyphonic anthems such as *I call and cry* were disappearing from the repertoire, and continued to be performed, if somewhat irregularly, throughout the nineteenth century in the face of consistently poor press reviews. The contrast between the criticism levelled at Tallis, the composer of *Spem in alium*, and the adulation, examined in the next chapter, of Tallis, the composer of the Responses, could hardly be stronger. Yet it is possible that there is a direct link between the Madrigal Society performance in 1836 and the renewed interest in Tallis's liturgical music in the 1840s. The Westminster Abbey organist, James Turle, was a close friend of the Society's president, John Leman Rogers, and was one of the sub-conductors at the 1836 performance. He is reported to have initiated the Tallis Days at Rogers's suggestion.[145] Oliphant's edition of the *Full Cathedral Service*, published under the auspices of the Society, was used at the Tallis Days, and another of the early editors of the Responses, John Bishop, was also involved with the Madrigal Society performance, and is listed on Mad.Soc. MS H.114. The successful performance of *Sing and Glorifie* in 1836 may well have led to the decision to dedicate a special 'day' to Tallis and his music just a few years later, and sparked the subsequent revival of interest in Tallis and his music. Yet, while this performance of the Song of Forty Parts may have provided the spark, it was Tallis's English service music, and in particular the Preces, Responses and Litany, that fuelled the interest in Tallis for at least the next fifty years.

---

[144] E.C., 'Music in Newcastle-on-Tyne', *Musical Opinion and Music Trades Review* 53 (1929): 914. The reference to the Byrd Mass points to the remarkable rise in popularity of Byrd's music in the first decades of the twentieth century.

[145] 'Tallis', *Musical Journal* 2 (1840): 250.

CHAPTER 4

'A Solid Rock of Harmony':
The Preces and Responses

R ICHARD Turbet wrote in 1985 that, with few exceptions, no piece of British music 'attracts more excitement than Tallis's gigantic *Spem in alium*'.[1] In the nineteenth century, however, it was not the Song of Forty Parts, nor any of his now highly regarded Latin motets, but Tallis's modest settings of the Preces, Responses and Litany that were identified as 'the principal means of conferring immortality upon Queen Elizabeth's organist'.[2] These fragments of harmonised plainchant were more frequently published and performed, more intensely debated and more highly regarded than any other portion of Tallis's output, or indeed almost any other piece of sixteenth-century music.

The responsorial portions of the Anglican liturgy, described by the Rev. John Jebb as 'the deepest, most affecting, and most comprehensive prayers that have ever been framed in the Church of Christ, under the guidance of the Spirit of God',[3] were the subject of a great deal of interest in the nineteenth century. Their prominence was reflected in the first edition of Grove's *Dictionary*, which contains articles on 'Response' (written by John Stainer), 'Litany' and 'Versicle' (both by Rockstro). Stainer observes that 'The musical treatment of such Versicles and Responses offers a wide and interesting field of study', and defines a 'Response' in its 'widest sense, as any musical sentence sung by the choir at the close of something read or chanted by the minister'. In its 'more limited sense' he applies the term to four groups, each with its own conventions of accent and melody:

> (1) those which immediately precede the Psalms, called also the Preces; (2) those following the Apostle's Creed and the Lord's Prayer; (3) those following the Lord's Prayer in the Litany; (4) and the Responses in the first portion of the Litany.[4]

The responses after the Creed, Stainer's second group, are frequently referred to

---

[1] Turbet, 'Thomas Tallis', 50.

[2] 'Meeting of the Charity Children', *The Times*, 4 Jun 1858, 12.

[3] John Jebb, *The Choral Responses and Litanies of the United Church of England and Ireland,* vol. 1 (London: George Bell, 1847), 1. A second volume was published by R. Cocks & Co. in 1857.

[4] Stainer, 'Response', 116. Tallis did not set the responses following the Lord's Prayer in the Litany; his setting of the Litany therefore falls into the last group.

simply as the Responses; groups one and two together are therefore known as the Preces and Responses.

The litany, preces and responses were also discussed at length in several extended articles dealing with the history of English church music, including J. Powell Metcalfe's 'The Music of the Church of England, as Contemplated by the Reformers', G. A. Macfarren's 'The Music of the English Church', and, somewhat later, J. M. Duncan's 'The Preces, Responses, and Litany of the English Church: A By-Way of Liturgical History',[5] all of which will be discussed further below.

Tallis's settings of the Preces, Responses and Litany occupied a unique position in these discussions. Rockstro, for example, devotes a substantial portion of his 130-word 'Versicle' article to Tallis's setting, claiming that although these responses were set by Continental composers such as Vittoria, 'none of them will bear any comparison with the matchless English Responses, in all probability set originally to the old Latin words, by our own Tallis, whose solemn harmonies have never been approached, in this particular form of music.'[6] In his *Substance of Several Courses of Lectures on Music*, William Crotch cites the Litany as 'a perfect speci-men of pure sublimity',[7] and, as mentioned previously, S. S. Wesley exempted Tal-lis's 'fine Responses' from his general criticisms of Tallis's music.[8]

The Responses and Litany were not only admired in theory, but were also much appreciated in performance. A letter to the *Harmonicon* in 1831, for example, urges the organisers of the Festival of the Sons of the Clergy to include Tallis's Responses in the forthcoming Festival, and incidentally provides an intriguing insight into early nineteenth-century performance practice:

> Every one must recollect, who has ever attended divine service on the three great festivals of our church at St Paul's Cathedral, the magnificent effect produced in Tallis's responses as played by the highly talented organist of that establishment on the splendid instrument at which he presides; and if so, it must be apparent that, with the addition of a strong and efficient chorus, and still more, with wind instruments, the effect must be such, that

---

[5] Metcalfe, 'Music of the Church of England', 157–60; Macfarren's 'The Music of the English Church' was published in the *Musical Times* in twelve instalments in 1867–8; the Responses are discussed at 13 (1867): 69–71; J. M. Duncan, 'The Preces, Responses, and Litany of the English Church: A By-Way of Liturgical History', *Musical Times* 61 (1920): 692–4.

[6] There is no evidence that the Preces or Responses were originally set to Latin texts: Rockstro's claim appears to be an example of his desire to embrace Tallis's Roman Catholicism, discussed in Chapter 2 above.

[7] William Crotch, *Substance of Several Courses of Lectures on Music (1831)*, intro. Bernarr Rainbow (Clarabricken: Boethius Press, 1986), 82.

[8] Wesley, *Few Words*, 45–6.

the introduction of these responses at the approaching festival must ever be remembered in the annals of church music.[9]

Vincent Novello considered the 'charming and expressive Responses by Tallis to be one of the very finest specimens of the *real Cathedral style*, both as to devotional melody and grand simplicity of harmony, that was ever produced.' He continues, 'I never miss an opportunity of hearing them performed as often as possible, and always with much delight and admiration.'[10]

A rare complaint about Tallis's Responses is found in a letter to the editor of *The Times* in 1879 by 'A Churchman', who argued against any musical setting of the responses and litany, claiming that although 'music is a sweet thing' it is no more appropriate to use it to excess than it is to add sugar to soup, fish and meat.[11] He concludes, in an argument strongly reminiscent of Philip Stubbs's 1583 *Anatomie of Abuses*, that a better example should be set for those 'whose juvenile tastes are so easily led away by novelties and sweets in any form, however much they may regret the consequences afterwards.'[12]

Martin Skeffington and W. H. Monk immediately sprang to the defence of the practice of singing these portions of the liturgy. Skeffington wrote that 'Tallis's glorious music to the Responses and Litany [...] has never yet been equalled or surpassed', while Monk argued that 'no Church, continental or insular, Roman or Greek, ancient or modern, can produce music, used in a similar way, of so grand and spiritual a type as this.'[13]

Throughout the nineteenth century Tallis's setting of the Preces and Responses was a standard feature at large choral festivals and services, such as the Charity

---

[9] 'Festival of the Sons of the Clergy', *Harmonicon* 9 (1831): 119.

[10] *GB-Lbl* Add. 33239, fol. 8v.

[11] 'A Churchman', 'Music in the Church Service', *The Times*, 1 Jan 1879. His views were supported by 'A Sufferer', who complained that choral services were a 'mockery in the House of God' ('Music in the Church Service', *The Times*, 4 Jan 1879).

[12] Philip Stubbs, *Anatomie of Abuses* (1583): 'I Say of Musick as Plato and Aristotle, Galen, and many others have said of it; that it is very il for yung heds, for a certeine kind of nice, smoothe sweetnes in alluring the auditorie to niceness, effeminancie, pusillanimitie, and lothsomnes of life, so as it may not improperly be compared to a sweet electuarie of honie, or rather to honie it-self; for as honie and such like sweet things, received into the stomack, dooth delight at the first, but afterward they make the stomack so quasie, nice and weake, that it is not able to admit meat of hard digesture: So sweet Musick at the first delighteth the eares, but afterward corrupteth and depraveth the minde ...' Quoted in Richard Leppert, *Music and Image: Domesticity, Ideology, and Socio-Cultural Formation in Eighteenth-Century England* (Cambridge: Cambridge University Press, 1988), 17–18.

[13] Martin S. Skeffington, 'Church Music', *The Times*, 2 Jan 1879; W. H. Monk, 'Music in the Church Service', *The Times*, 4 Jan 1879, 11.

Children's services and the Three Choirs Festivals. An 1865 report of the annual Sons of the Clergy Festival noted:

> That the 'suffrages' were by Tallis may be taken for granted. A century hence it might be foretold that any reporter of the 311th anniversary of the Festival of the Sons of the Clergy would have to write the same sentence, or words to the same effect. [...] on the 'Preces and Responses' of Thomas Tallis time has written 'no wrinkle'.[14]

A *Musical Times* review of the 1863 Festival of the Charity Children at St Paul's Cathedral was even more enthusiastic:

> The 'Preces' and 'Responses' were those of our Elizabethan Tallis – whose music to this part of the Church Service seems to be a solid rock of harmony, against which the waves of time are likely to beat, for century after century, without producing any appreciable effect. There it has been; there it is; and there it is likely to remain – massive, solid, and indestructible, because built upon the eternal principles of truth.[15]

The immense popularity of the Responses at this time can also be seen in the large number of nineteenth-century editions of the Litany and Responses. The British Library *Catalogue of Printed Music* lists eleven publications of the Litany and/or Responses during the 1840s and a further twenty-four between 1850 and 1914.[16] This number is particularly remarkable when compared with the modest list of publications of anthems by Tallis discussed in the first chapter, and the complete absence of editions of the settings of other 'Tudor' composers such as Byrd or Gibbons.[17] These editions varied widely in cost, format and presentation, ranging

---

[14] 'Festival of the Songs of the Clergy', *The Times*, 18 May 1865, 14.

[15] 'The Charity Children at St. Paul's', *Musical Times* 11 (1863), 83. A review of the 1865 Sons of the Clergy Festival makes a similar claim, stating that the performance of the Responses could be 'taken for granted', and that they would probably still be performed at the festival a hundred years later ('Festival of the Sons of the Clergy', *The Times*, 18 May 1865, 14).

[16] *The Catalogue of Printed Music in the British Library to 1980*, ed. Laureen Baillie (London: K. G. Saur, 1982), 55:315–16. This is unlikely to be a complete list: for example, the Guildhall Library holds a copy of *The Choral Service of Ely Cathedral as Arranged for Use by Thomas Tallis ...*, edited by the organist at Ely, Robert Janes, that is not in the British Library. The following discussion is based upon the editions held by the British Library.

[17] The Responses by Byrd, Tomkins, Smith, etc., which became the staples of the twentieth-century cathedral repertoire after the publication of *Six Settings of the Preces and Responses by Tudor Composers*, ed. I. Atkins and E. H. Fellowes (London: SPCK; Oxford University Press, 1933), were not published at all in the

from Jebb's monumental two-volume *Choral Responses of the United Church of England and Ireland*, with its exhaustive historical and analytical introduction, to a single folded sheet selling for threepence.[18]

The extraordinary number of editions of the Litany and Responses indicates not only the popularity of these settings, but also a distinct lack of agreement about the correct form of this music, for these editions differed not only in matters of presentation, but also in the actual notes on the page. Debate raged well into the twentieth century about whether Tallis had composed the Litany and Responses in four or five parts: numerous settings of both are to be found in the nineteenth-century editions, and three-part and unison arrangements were also published. Pages of prefaces were devoted to passionate and minutely detailed analyses of the sources, and to heated debates about the relationship between the harmonised settings and the plainsong, and widely differing conclusions were reached.[19]

Thus, despite the powerful image of the Responses as solid, monumental and immutable, an examination of the nineteenth-century editions uncovers a multiplicity of versions, and the 'solid rock of harmony' crumbles into something fragmentary, fluid and elusive.

☙ Early Sources

IN order to understand the editorial confusion that reigned in the nineteenth century, we must first examine the early sources upon which these nineteenth-century editions were based. No authentic source of the Preces and Responses survives from Tallis's lifetime: the earliest extant sources date from the early seventeenth century, roughly half a century after his death. Tallis left two sets of Preces and two sets of Responses, both of which are included in volume 13 of the Early English Church Music series; the EECM numbering will be adopted

---

1800s except in Boyce and in Jebb's *Choral Responses*. The British Library holds no separate nineteenth-century editions of Byrd's Short Service, and the earliest complete publication of Gibbons's popular 'Service in F' dates from the 1880s. As late as 1920 Byrd's setting of the Responses appears to have been largely unknown: Duncan claimed that Byrd's Responses 'seem to the writer to be superior to those of Tallis [...] and would well be worth the attention of any enterprising choir on the look-out for something off the beaten track' (Duncan, 'Preces, Responses and Litany', 692).

[18] John Bishop, ed. *Choral Responses at Morning and Evening Prayer ...* (London: R. Cocks & Co., [1859]).

[19] The issues and arguments surrounding the sources of the Responses and Litany are similar: in the following discussion I will focus primarily upon the Preces and Responses, but most of the conclusions reached apply equally to the Litany.

Table 9   Pre-civil war sources of Tallis's Preces and Responses

Source	Date*	Preces	Responses
RCM 1045–51	early 17th C	I	I
Peterhouse 'Former'	1635	I	I
Peterhouse 'Latter'	1635	II	II
Pembroke Mus. 6.1–6	1640	I	I
Christ Church Mus. 1220–4	after 1640	I	II
Barnard	1641	I	II

*Approximate dates taken from Daniel and le Huray, *Sources of English Church Music*.

here.[20] The earliest sources of these settings consist of a set of manuscript partbooks copied by John Barnard (RCM MSS 1045–51), his 1641 publication *Selected Church Musick*, and incomplete sets of manuscript parts at Pembroke and Peterhouse Colleges, Cambridge, and Christ Church, Oxford.[21] Both settings of the Preces and Responses are found in these sources in various combinations (see Table 9), but Barnard published Preces I and Responses II, and it is these that are generally referred to as 'The Tallis Responses'. The second Preces and first Responses were not published at all during the nineteenth century except in Jebb's collection, and have no further relevance to this discussion.

Modern scholarly editions, such as the Early English Church Music series edition, are based on these early five-part versions, which are fundamentally in agreement, and there is no reason to believe that they are not reliable representations of Tallis's original settings. In the discussion that follows, however, I will refer to this version as Barnard's as a reminder that there is no version of the Responses that can be unequivocally attributed to Tallis.

After the Restoration several completely new versions of the Responses were produced, considerably muddying the waters. Edward Lowe included a set of preces and responses in his 1661 *Short Direction*, under the title 'Extraordinary Responalls upon Festivalls in Foure Parts', and the nineteenth- and twentieth-century habit of referring to Tallis's Responses as the 'Festival' or 'Festal' Responses

---

[20] *Thomas Tallis: English Sacred Music: II. Service Music*, ed. Leonard Ellinwood, rev. Paul Doe, Early English Church Music 13, rev. ed. (London: Stainer & Bell, 1974): hereafter EECM 13. Duncan ('Preces, Responses, and Litany', 626) argues that, although the two sets of Preces are clearly independent, the second set of Responses is merely a variation of the first set: 'in the course of time, as the taste for melody grew at the expense of polyphony, the original was gradually modified, set II and "Church Musick" representing two stages in this process.' However, the two versions are included as separate entities in EECM 13.

[21] *GB-Cpc* Mus. 6.1–6; *GB-Cp* 33, 34, 38, 39; and *GB-Och* Mus. 1220–4.

appears to stem from this title. The Responses after the Creed are essentially a four-part arrangement of Barnard (see Example 13). The Preces, however, were drawn from several sources. The first response, 'And our mouth', is similar to Barnard; the second, 'O Lord, make haste', is a simplified four-part version of the same response from Byrd's Second Preces; 'As it was' is loosely based on Byrd, both in harmony and melody; and 'Praise ye the Lord' is a simplified reworking of Tallis as given in Barnard (see Example 14).[22] As Craig Monson has observed, however, Byrd appears to have modelled his Preces upon Tallis's, and this final response could also be interpreted as being based upon Byrd.[23] There is no reference to Tallis in the publication, and the Preces clearly owe more to Byrd than they do to Tallis, yet Lowe's version of both the Preces and Responses were consistently and unquestioningly attributed to Tallis by nineteenth-century writers.[24]

Lowe's *Short Direction* also included a four-part arrangement of the Litany, although again the earliest sources, including Barnard's *Church Musick*, Durham A5 and the 'Latter' Peterhouse set, are all in five parts. The soprano, tenor and bass parts given by Lowe are basically the same as Barnard's version,[25] while the alto part is a simplified combination of Barnard's two alto parts.

Ian Spink notes that four parts became the norm for cathedral music after the Restoration,[26] and Dean Aldrich also left two closely related four-part versions of the Preces and Responses in Christ Church MSS Mus. 9 and 48. In Mus. 48 the treble part from Mus. 9 has been transposed down an octave to become a second alto part. This manuscript bears the note: 'No need of a second Counter tenor, if there be boys to sing his part 8 notes higher.' In this version the Responses are virtually identical to Lowe, but the Preces have even less in common with Barnard than Lowe's version (see Example 14). They are, nonetheless, clearly attributed to Tallis.

---

[22] To accommodate the changed text for the 1662 Prayer Book, Lowe replaced this final response in his *Review* of 1664 with a simple plagal cadence.

[23] Craig Monson, 'The Preces, Psalms and Litanies of Byrd and Tallis: Another "Virtuous Contention in Love"', *Music Review* 40 (1979): 257–71.

[24] For example, Rimbault, *Order of the Daily Service*, ix. In his article 'J. Guggenheim as Music Publisher: Tallis and Byrd Restored', *Brio* 41 (2004): 49, Richard Turbet describes Lowe's edition as simply a combination of Byrd's Second Preces and Tallis's Responses.

[25] Barnard's version does, however, contain several errors, which will be discussed further below.

[26] Spink, *Restoration Cathedral Music*, 75.

Example 13. Comparison of Lowe's and Barnard's
versions of the Responses after the Creed

Example 14. Comparison of pre-nineteenth-century versions of the Preces

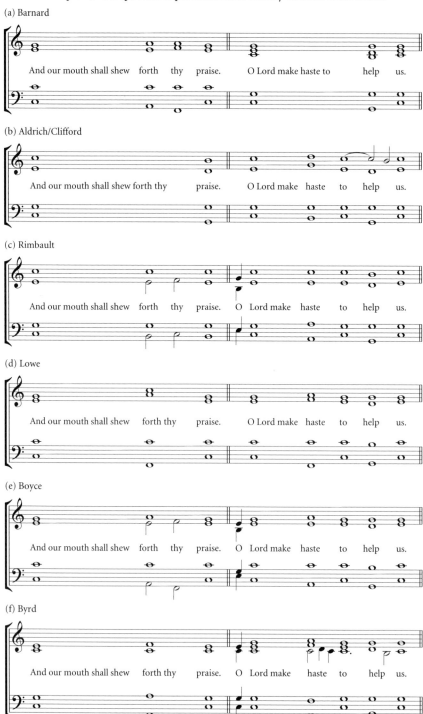

Example 14 continued.

Example 14 continued.

(a) Barnard

Praise ye the Lord, praise ye the Lord.

(b) Aldrich/Clifford

The Lord's name be prais - - - - - ed.

(c) Rimbault

The Lord's name be prais - - - - - ed.

(d) Lowe

Praise ye the Lord, praise ye the Lord.

(e) Boyce

The Lord's name be prais - ed.

(f) Byrd

Praise ye the Lord, praise ye the Lord.

Edward Rimbault reproduced an essentially similar version in the preface to his *Order of the Daily Service*,[27] which he claims he took from a manuscript 'in the hand-writing of James Clifford'. James Clifford, a native of Oxford, was a minor canon at St Paul's from 1661, best known for his 1663 collection of the words of anthems used in St Paul's and other cathedrals.[28] Rimbault attributes high authority to this source, arguing that as Clifford was a pupil of Byrd, 'his means of procuring *correct copies* of this great master's works were more favorable than those of many of his contemporaries',[29] yet this manuscript does not appear to have been known to anybody except Rimbault, nor to have survived. Rimbault's integrity (as well as his reliability as a scholar) is not above question,[30] and given the inclusion of the following items in a spoof catalogue for the sale of one Doctor Rainbeau, apparently modelled on Rimbault, the authority of such a manuscript must be treated with caution:

101 Forgeries by a well-known Antiquary—MS.
111 Forgeries of Musical Works, Anecdotes, Letters, &c., a large bundle.[31]

Even if the Clifford manuscript is genuine, it is still just another copy of a version that was circulating in Oxford in the late seventeenth century. Its authority was, however, widely accepted in the nineteenth century, and it is frequently cited in discussions of the relative merits of the various versions of the Responses and Litany, including Rockstro's 'Litany' entry in Grove's *Dictionary*.[32]

The next, and by far the most influential, publication of Tallis's Litany, Preces and Responses appeared in William Boyce's *Cathedral Music* of 1760.[33] Boyce's version of the Litany was basically the same as Barnard's, but the Preces and Responses were a curious amalgam of Barnard and Lowe that differed from all previous ver-

---

[27] Rimbault, *Order of the Daily Service*, xvii. This version can also be found in *GB-Lbl* R.M.24.c.11.(26.) and is very similar to that given as the 'New College Commemoration Responses' in Jebb's *Choral Responses*. Rimbault also published a four-part version of the Litany, ostensibly taken from the same source, as an appendix to his *Full Cathedral Service*.

[28] James Clifford, *The Divine Services and Anthems usually sung in His Majesties Chappell, and in all Cathedrals and Collegiate Choires in England and Ireland* (London, 1663 and 1664).

[29] Rimbault, *Order of the Daily Service*, xviii.

[30] Percy Scholes, for example, could find no record of the LL.D. that Rimbault is frequently claimed to have held (*Mirror of Music*, 771). See also Richard Turbet, 'Quack Doctor', *Musical Times* 137 (1996): 4.

[31] *Catalogue of the Music Library of Edward Francis Rimbault ... with the Library of Dr. Rainbeau*, intro. A. Hyatt King (Amsterdam: Frits Knuf, 1975).

[32] Rockstro, 'Litany', 152.

[33] Boyce, *Cathedral Music*, 1–2, 16–19.

Table 10 Summary of early versions of Tallis's Preces and Responses

Source	Date	Preces				Responses			
		version	plainsong	note	parts	version	plainsong	note	parts
Barnard	1641	Barnard	Tr/T*	G	5†	Barnard	T (mod)	F	5
Lowe	1661/4	Lowe	–	–	4	Barnard	T	F	4
Aldrich/ Clifford	late 17th	Aldrich	T	G	4	Barnard	T‡	G	4
Boyce	1760	Lowe	–	–	4	Barnard	T (mod)	G	5

* The plainsong, as given by Merbecke, is in the tenor on C in the first response, is in both the treble and tenor in the second and third responses, and is absent from the final response.

† However, the first response, 'And our mouths', is in only four parts.

‡ 'And with Thy spirit' starts with an E in the Tenor in Lowe, *GB-Och* Mus. 9, and *GB-Lbl* RM.24.c.11. (26.), but in Clifford the first note is a G, maintaining the plainsong.

sions. The Preces are in four parts, and are similar, although not identical, to Lowe, while the Responses are in five parts, and are essentially the same as Barnard. They were, however, transposed up a tone, as they were in Aldrich's version (see Table 10). Of the Preces, therefore, only the first response is common to both Boyce and Barnard (see Example 14), with the second and third having no common material, and the fourth only a loose similarity. Boyce's version of the Preces contains very little material that can actually be attributed to Tallis yet, as we will see, by far the majority of nineteenth-century editions were based upon it in some way. As Tallis's Responses were known primarily through Boyce's edition, it is not surprising that Lowe's 'Responalls upon Festivalls', upon which Boyce's version of the Preces seems to have been modelled, were so readily identified with Tallis.

In addition to the differences in the number of parts and variations in harmonies, the pre-nineteenth-century sources also differed in the degree of strictness with which they adhered to John Merbecke's English adaptation of the plainsong, particularly in the Responses. While the plainsong is generally in the tenor in Barnard's version of the Responses, there are several points where it is not strictly maintained (see Example 15).[34] Boyce reproduces Barnard's tenor exactly, while in Lowe and Clifford's versions the tenor line replicates the plainsong.

By the beginning of the nineteenth century, therefore, there were four different versions of the Preces and Responses: Barnard, Lowe, Aldrich/Clifford and Boyce. All versions of the Responses are closely harmonically and melodically related, although with variations in the number of parts and pitch. The versions of the

[34] Rimbault makes a similar, although more limited comparison in his *Order of the Daily Service*, x–xi.

Example 15. Variations in the treatment of the plainsong in versions of the Responses

Preces, however, are substantially different, and it is only their common attribution to Tallis that connects them.

❧ The Nineteenth-Century Editions

A s we saw in Chapter 1, Thomas Oliphant produced a new edition of Tallis's Service, including the Responses, for the Tallis Days in 1841. Until this time Boyce's *Cathedral Music* had remained the principle source of Tallis's service music, and Oliphant's edition, like the vast majority of the nineteenth-century editions, was based upon Boyce (see Table 11).[35] Oliphant's edition was one of the first of the deluge of editions of the Responses, often published with the Short Service,[36] that flooded the market in the 1840s, and formed part of a more general resurgence of interest in early liturgical sources. In 1843, for example, William Dyce published his influential edition of the *Order of Daily Service*, an arrangement of Merbecke's *Book of Common Prayer Noted*.[37] The 'sumptuous' presentation, 'with its vermilion rubrics, graceful border, and exquisitely carved text' seems to have inspired subsequent editors,[38] and was shortly followed by editions of Merbecke by William Pickering (1844), Rimbault (1845) and Robert Janes (1847); Rimbault also republished Lowe's *Review* in 1845.[39]

Two new editions of Boyce's *Cathedral Music* were also published in 1849: one edited by Thomas Warren, and the other by Vincent Novello.[40] Novello's preface

---

[35] Oliphant halved the note values in his edition. In general, the rhythmic notation has been ignored in the following discussion as the responses and the plainsong upon which they are based are essentially in free rhythm, although a great deal would no doubt be revealed about nineteenth-century editorial and performance practice by a close examination of this feature.

[36] Stainer points out that the Preces and Responses are not technically part of the service, and this distinction is maintained in Barnard's publication, which starts with Services, followed by Preces and Psalms, Responses and the Litany.

[37] William Dyce, *The Order of Daily Service, the Litany and Order of the Administration of the Holy Communion with plain tune, according to the use of the United Church of England and Ireland* (London, 1843). For more on this edition, see Rainbow, *Choral Revival*, 79–83.

[38] Frederick Oakeley, quoted in Rainbow, *Choral Revival*, 81. Rainbow also gives a sample page from Dyce's edition.

[39] E. F. Rimbault, *The Order of Chanting the Cathedral Service; with Notation of the Preces, Versicles, Responses, &c., &c., as Published by Edward Lowe, A.D. 1664* (London: Chappell, 1845).

[40] Joseph Warren, ed., *Cathedral Music ... Selected by Dr. William Boyce, Newly Edited and Carefully Collated and Revised ...*, 3 vols. (London: R. Cocks & Co., 1849); Vincent Novello, ed., *Cathedral Music ... Selected and Revised by W. Boyce ... Revised and the Organ Accompaniment Added by V. Novello*, 3 vols. (London:

Table 11 Nineteenth-century editions of Tallis's Preces and Responses

Boyce

Unmodified

Oliphant	1841	The Full Cathedral Service
Bishop	1843	The Order of the Daily Service
Rimbault	1845	*The Full Cathedral Service
Rimbault	[1846]	*The Order of the Daily Service
–	1854	The Order for Morning Prayer and the Litany
South Shropshire Choral Union	1888	*The Versicles and Responses at Morning and Evening Prayer
Martin	1903	Tallis's Festal Responses and Litany (NB Voice parts are transposed to give 2SATB)

Arranged for four parts

Rimbault	1850	The Order of Morning and Evening Prayer … (rearranged)
Hopkins	1868	Tallis's Festival Responses …
Barnby	1893	Tallis's Preces and Responses
Stainer	1900	Tallis's Preces and Responses
Pettman	1900	Tallis's Responses

Arranged for reduced number of voices with keyboard accompaniment

Pearsall	1843	The Hymns of the Church
Westbrook	1865	Tallis's Preces and Responses, arranged for three treble voices

Barnard

Bishop	1859	Choral Responses at Morning and Evening Prayer
SPCK	1869	*Preces, Responses, & Litany
SPCK	1901	*The Festal Preces and Responses

Aldrich/Clifford

Havergal	1847	The Preces & Litany set … for four voices … from MSS. of Dean Aldrich

Significantly different versions which may have been based on Boyce

Elvey	1846	Tallis's Litany and Responses

*Tenor part has been modified to correspond with the plainsong

attributed the 'present progress in Church Music' to the 'men like Boyce', and their perseverance in the 'seemingly hopeless battle against bad taste, ignorance, and indifference'. Warren's edition was produced 'under the immediate patronage of His Royal Highness the Prince Albert' in response to 'the increase in the

Novello, 1849). For more on Novello's antiquarian activities, see Olleson and Palmer, 'Publishing Music'.

Choral Service of the Church', and was advertised as 'new and corrected'. The preface declares that 'authentic documents' had been consulted in its preparation, the most important of which was Barnard's *Church Musick*. The main difference between this version and Boyce's, however, was that the tenor part in the Responses had been 'corrected' to conform to the plainsong. Warren acknowledges the assistance of several people, including Jebb and Husk, but particular mention is made of 'the Editor's sincere friend, Mr. John Bishop of Cheltenham'.[41]

In 1843, just two years after Oliphant's edition, Bishop had published his own edition of Tallis, *The Order of Daily Service*, dedicated to the Bishop of Gloucester and Bristol, and again based upon Boyce. Like many of these early editions, it is a beautifully presented volume, printed in red and black, with red-bordered, gilt-edged pages and an extended preface. The prefaces to these editions provide a valuable insight into the editorial, historical and ecclesiological orientations of their producers, and were the forum for a heated debate about the sources of the Preces, Responses and Litany. Bishop's preface typically locates his publication within the liturgical and musical concerns of the day:

> the increased attention which has of late been given to all matters connected with the ritual of the Anglican Church, has had its beneficial influence on the musical portion of the service. This has manifested itself, in many places, not only by the introduction of harmonized responses [...] but also by a return to those sublime strains of our venerable church writers, having been too long superseded by the flimsy compositions of modern times. Hence, despite the objections of those whose judgment is regulated solely by that which best pleases their fancy, the simple sublimity of the sixteenth and early part of the seventeenth century is rapidly gaining the consideration to which it is so justly entitled.[42]

In this preface Bishop announces his important discovery that 'certain portions [...] have been uncorrectly [*sic*] ascribed to Tallis' in Boyce,[43] and he identifies the origin of the response 'O Lord, make haste to help us' and the 'Gloria Patri', not with Tallis, but in Byrd's Second Preces. He also addresses the question as to whether the Litany and Responses had been originally written in five parts, as in Barnard, or four, as in Lowe. He concludes that to attribute the extended open fifth on 'O holy blessed and Glorious Trinity' (see Example 16) in Lowe's version of the Litany to Tallis

---

[41] Warren, *Cathedral Music*, i.

[42] Bishop, *Order of the Daily Service*, ix.

[43] Bishop, *Order of the Daily Service*, x.

Example 16. Lowe's version of 'O Holy, blessed and glorious Trinity'

is a libel upon his name. […] Much more of the Litany is given in the same naked harmony; for which reason, and from the fact that Barnard's books were published so long before Lowe's work appeared, the Editor cannot but consider the former the highest authority – no earlier printed work containing Tallis's service being known.[44]

Two other publications produced at around this time seem to have been based directly upon Bishop's edition: the service book of the College of St Peter, Radley (1847), and a Novello edition of *The Order for Morning Prayer and Litany* (1854).[45] These two editions are extremely similar; neither acknowledges an editor, and both include Bishop's continuation of the Litany.[46] The Novello edition is very plainly presented, and in keeping with Novello's aim of producing cheap music was, at one shilling, the cheapest of the priced copies examined from that period.[47]

The next substantial editions of Tallis's Preces and Responses were published in 1845/6 by Edward Rimbault. He published two related volumes, both with the same preface: *The Order of the Daily Service* and *The Full Cathedral*

[44] Bishop, *Order of the Daily Service*, xix.

[45] *The Order for Morning Prayer, and the Litany, as Used in the College of St Peter, Radley, Together with that by Thomas Tallis for the Feasts of the Church* (London, College of St Peter, 1847); *The Order for Morning Prayer and the Litany, Noted by Thomas Tallis* (London: J. Alfred Novello, 1854). Rainbow gives a brief account of the musical services at Radley (est. 1847) in his *Anglican Choral Revival*, 233–4.

[46] Tallis did not set the second part of the litany, known as the second suffrages, and many modern editions contain a harmonised version of the chant, allowing the entire litany to be performed.

[47] The price continued to drop, however, and the editions published by Stainer and Barnby published at the turn of the twentieth century, discussed below, were priced as low as 1½ d.

Service.[48] They are ornately presented, again printed in red and black, with decorative borders throughout and a comprehensive twenty-page 'Historical Introduction'. This introduction, as discussed in Chapter 2, provides a survey of Tallis's biography, works and sources. It also introduces Rimbault's influential argument that the Litany and Responses were originally composed in four parts, an argument that spawned a debate about the correct form of this music that continued well into the twentieth century.[49]

Rimbault argues that no '*authentic*' copy of Tallis's service survives, and that Barnard's version is corrupt:

> That this copy has undergone, in the Responses and Litany, considerable alterations, must be evident, from the knowledge that Tallis, as well as every other church musician of the sixteenth century, *harmonized the Responses with the melody or plain-song in the tenor*; whereas, in Barnard and Boyce (in accordance with more modern usage), the melodies of the first Preces and Litany have been transposed to the treble or upper part.[50]

Unfortunately, Rimbault does not reveal the source of his 'knowledge' of the practices of sixteenth-century composers, which is the crux of his argument.[51] He also quotes a statement by Hawkins that Tallis added three parts to the plainchant in the Responses,[52] and cites a letter from Dean Aldrich to Dr Fell, claiming that 'Tallis's magnificent Litany was *originally* written in *four* parts, with the plain-chant in the tenor: Barnard was the *first* who *despoilt* it.'[53] He claims that all the '*ancient* MS copies of the same that the Editor has seen', together with Lowe, are in four parts.

According to Rimbault, Barnard corrupted the Litany by moving the plainsong between the tenor and the treble, and by adding a fifth part. He points out that the treble and the *decani* tenor parts move in consecutive octaves for two notes at the

---

[48] Rimbault, *Order of the Daily Service* and *The Full Cathedral Service as Used on the Festivals and Saint's Days of the Church of England* (London: D'Almaine, 1845). The Preface to both editions is dated 6 October 1846.

[49] As late as 1920 Duncan was still heavily influenced by Rimbault's arguments.

[50] Rimbault, *Order of the Daily Service*, ix.

[51] Byrd, for example, in his Second Preces departs considerably more from the plainsong than any of the versions of Tallis.

[52] Hawkins, *General History*, 457: 'but Tallis has improved them [the Responses] by the addition of three parts'.

[53] Rimbault cites his own edition of Merbecke as the source of this quote, although the location of the letter is not identified there either. This quote was repeated by Bumpus (*Cathedral Music*, 44), Duncan ('Preces, Responses, and Litany', 626) and others, but I have been unable to locate the original letter.

Example 17. Error in Barnard's version of the Litany,
'O God the Son, Redeemer of the world'

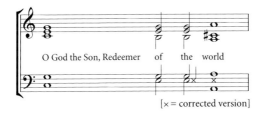

[× = corrected version]

end of the several of the responses in Barnard (see Example 17), although this is
obviously a typographical error and does not occur in the *cantoris* tenor partbook.
He argues that this error is a residue of the transposition of the plainsong from
the tenor to the treble, and concludes, rather unconvincingly, that 'The knowledge
of this fact alone proves that the plain-song was *originally in the tenor*.' He also
seems to feel that this transposition 'account[s] for the "naked harmony"' in Lowe's
version of the Litany:[54] his logic at this point is unclear, but is obviously intended
as a rebuttal of Bishop's argument.

Furthermore, Rimbault argues, Barnard not only moved the plainsong from the
tenor and added the extra part, but in the process corrupted the plainsong itself; he
quotes the places where Barnard's tenor deviates from the plainsong as evidence
(see Example 15).

Rimbault then reproduces the Preces, Psalms and Responses as given by
Clifford (fortunately, given the manuscript's subsequent disappearance), claiming
that 'They are much more likely to be as Tallis left them, than the cumbersome
harmonies given by Barnard.'[55] He includes Clifford's version of the Litany as an
appendix to *The Full Cathedral Service*; he believes this to be the 'most ancient
copy preserved', arguing that 'Tallis's adaptation of the Litany (not the cumbersome one in five parts in general use) was *never published*.'[56]

Yet Rimbault, despite the obvious strength of his own feelings on the subject,
also based his edition upon Boyce's five-part version. His only concessions to his
own arguments are minor 'corrections' to the tenor line to bring it into line with
the plainsong.[57] He admits that

it would certainly have been desirable to have restored the ancient Preces at
the commencement, the original four-part harmony of the Responses after

---

54 Rimbault, *Order of the Daily Service*, ix–x.
55 Rimbault, *Order of the Daily Service*, xi.
56 Rimbault, *Order of the Daily Service*, xvii.
57 The harmonies are such that the tenor part can be adjusted without needing to
make modifications to the other parts.

the Apostle's Creed, and the original Litany, with the plain-song in the tenor. The beauty, simplicity, and uniformity of this arrangement must be apparent to everyone; but it would have been hazardous to have attempted such an arrangement, when we consider the *long-established use* of the present form. The Editor has therefore contented himself with pointing out some of the discrepancies of the latter in this Preface, and has reprinted the 'Litany in four parts', as an Appendix to the 'Full Service.'[58]

Therefore, despite his concerns about the lack of reliability of Barnard and Boyce, and his conviction that Tallis had originally composed the Responses and Litany in four parts rather than five, Rimbault felt compelled by the weight of 'long-established use' to reproduce Boyce's version yet again. The minor changes to the tenor part seem to be the sole basis of an advertisement claiming that this version was 'the only correct one offered to the public.'[59]

Although Rimbault stopped short of publishing the four-part version of the Responses that he considered the most likely to be authentic, the Rev. Henry E. Havergal, chaplain at Christ Church, Oxford, put Rimbault's arguments into practice in his 1847 *The Preces and Litany set by Thomas Tallis for Four Voices ... from the MSS of Dean Aldrich.*[60] This edition is based upon Christ Church MS Mus. 48, which Havergal argues 'has every evidence of authenticity',[61] with the second alto transposed up an octave, so that the Preces and Responses are in agreement with the version attributed to Clifford by Rimbault.[62] It is therefore the first to be based upon an identified source other than Boyce. Havergal seems to have been strongly influenced by Rimbault, whom he cites throughout the preface. He claims that 'Dr. Rimbault has proved from the nature of Barnard's errors, his [Tallis's] version to have been originally for *four* voices', and suggests that Aldrich, Clifford and Lowe, who were all associated with Oxford, were probably 'acquainted with some one genuine copy of Tallis then and there existing.'[63] The Oxford-based Havergal appears to have been exhibiting a certain amount of local chauvinism in this edition, which also contains twenty-one single psalm chants, a

[58] Rimbault, *Order of the Daily Service*, xvii.

[59] Contained in advertisements found in both editions. This generates an interesting resonance with the advertisements for Boyce, in which accuracy was also a major selling point.

[60] Henry E. Havergal, *The Preces and Litany set by Thomas Tallis for Four Voices, Now First Printed with Some Chants of the xvi and xvii Centuries, from the MSS of Dean Aldrich* (Oxford, 1847).

[61] Havergal, *Preces and Litany*, 1.

[62] The transposition renders this version identical with that found in *GB-Och* Mus. 9, but Havergal does not appear to have been familiar with this manuscript.

[63] Havergal, *Preces and Litany*, 1.

simplified form of chanting the Litany and Responses in 'general use in the choirs of Oxford', and the *Veni Creator*, discussed in Chapter 1 above.[64] The publication concludes with a modest subscription list of fifty-five, including Sir Frederick A. G. Ouseley, Vincent Novello and Frederick Helmore, and multiple sets for Canterbury Cathedral (10), St Paul's Church, Oxford (12), and Christ Church, Oxford (20).

In the same year, Jebb published the first volume of his *Choral Responses*, dedicated to Rev. David Williams, Warden of New College, Oxford. The two-volume publication, of over 350 pages, is a fascinating undertaking worthy of a more detailed examination than is possible here. It is particularly notable for its replication in full of many sources of the same music, an example of editorial thoroughness that looks forward to the concerns of the late twentieth century. Tallis is given pride of place in the collection. The first volume is divided into three sections: Tallis's Service; Services by Other Composers; and an Appendix of 'obsolete' versions (i.e. settings of superseded versions of the Prayer Book). The first section includes four versions of Tallis's Preces and Responses, including Boyce's version and Aldrich's 'alto' Responses, and several versions of the Litany.

Jebb begins his substantial Preface by claiming that the publication 'is intended to serve the twofold purpose of a record, and of a book for actual use in the Choir',[65] although it is hard to imagine that many choirs would have found much use for such a weighty volume. With so many variants of the same music, it is much more like a modern collected edition than an edition to be used in everyday performances by the choir.[66] The issue of size becomes even more important when it is borne in mind that, unlike many contemporary editions, it did not include the full Service, but only the Preces, Responses and Litany.

Jebb outlines his motivation for this unusually comprehensive undertaking in the preface:

> The Editor would wish it to be distinctly understood, that he has no theories of his own or of others to propose, as to the manner of conducting these essential parts of the Choral Service. Nor is it any part of his plan to promote, by adaptation or suggestion, congregational or parochial chanting;

---

[64] It may be significant that the *Veni Creator* was first attributed to Tallis by Crotch, then Heather Professor at Oxford, in a publication that was also strongly oriented towards the local practice at Oxford, and dedicated to the University Church, Oxford.

[65] Jebb, *Choral Responses*, 1.

[66] The subscription list to vol. 2 includes many of the cathedral and collegiate choirs, but very few multiple copies were purchased, suggesting that although it may have been the source of other copies, its 'actual use in the choir' was limited.

his simple design being to ascertain and record, what has been the actual practice of the *English* Church.[67]

Jebb's introduction includes an exhaustive discussion of the merits of the sources with which he is familiar. He dismisses Aldrich's four-part arrangement of the Preces as 'the most meagre of all that have been adapted since the last Review', and concludes that Barnard's five-part version was the 'most faithful exhibition now extant of Tallis's harmonies':

> The ordering of the fifth part surely came from the same hand which con-ceived the rest of the harmony. There is an unity of conception throughout. If we allow this part to have been inserted by another, then we are placed in the same difficulty with those who ascribe the Homeric poems to more than one individual: we must suppose two geniuses of equal powers. It is observable, that the various four part harmonies [...] do not agree among themselves, as to the arrangements of the internal parts. Had the original been in four parts only, why should these discrepancies have existed? In fact, in these versions we perceive marks of adaptation, by inferior hands, who were not at unity among themselves, even in the correction of the real or supposed inaccuracies of *Barnard*.[68]

Jebb is clearly rebutting the arguments of Rimbault and Havergal: he explicitly rejects Havergal's suggestion of a superior Oxford source, claiming that 'it seems but reasonable to suppose, that an edition prepared in *London* [i.e. Barnard], where the original was composed, by a member of a Metropolitan choir, was more likely to be correct than an *Oxford* MS written by an unknown hand, and stamped with no public authority.'[69] Yet he also acknowledges the assistance of Havergal and Bishop in the preparation of his *Choral Responses*.

Despite this endorsement of Barnard's authority, however, Jebb opens his collec-tion with Boyce's version, 'called, for distinction's sake, "*Tallis's Festival Responses*"', and omits Barnard's version altogether.[70] He argues that Boyce's version, which he claimed 'exceeds even Barnard's in richness, solemnity, and profound devotional character',[71] was the best adaptation available for the 1662 Prayer Book, and that

---

[67] Jebb, *Choral Responses*, 1.

[68] Jebb, *Choral Responses*, 9.

[69] Jebb, *Choral Responses*, 6.

[70] Jebb, *Choral Responses*, 9. Jebb justifies this omission with reference to a forthcom-ing separate publication that appears not to have taken place (*Choral Responses*, 6). Barnard's Preces and Psalms are included in the second volume.

[71] Jebb, *Choral Responses*, 8.

'its insertion here may facilitate collation to the student, and may also make the present work more complete and convenient for the Choir.'[72]

The second volume of Jebb's *Choral Responses*, published in 1857, included the Peterhouse version of Tallis's Responses and Litany, presumably unknown to Jebb at the time of publication of the first volume, and settings of the litany and responses by other composers such as Tomkins, William Smith, Aylward and Amner. It also included 'unisonal' and harmonised settings in 'Common Use' at the Cathedrals, and reprints of early 'obsolete documents' such as Lowe's *Short Direction* and Merbecke's *Book of Common Prayer Noted*, thus achieving Jebb's goal, stated in the first volume, of recording the practice of the English Church.

During the 1840s, while Jebb, Rimbault and Bishop were debating the respective merits of the various sources, several other editions were published with a rather less scrupulous editorial approach.

The edition with the most limited connection with any identifiable source was George Elvey's *Tallis's Litany and Responses Arranged for the Daily use of Cathedral and Collegiate Churches* (1842).[73] There is no introduction, and the music bears only the most tenuous relationship with any of the sources discussed above. The Preces, which have been transposed up a tone, are very loosely related to the version published by Boyce (see Example 18), but bear no resemblance to any of the other versions:

'And our mouths'	no connection
'O Lord, make haste'	reharmonisation of treble
'As it was'	no connection
'world without end'	same bass and treble, different harmonisation
'The Lord's name'	the same

The Responses after the Creed, however, are in a minor mode, and are completely different, both harmonically and melodically, from all other sources. The plainsong does not appear in any part. The Litany is more closely related to that found in Boyce, although it is still substantially different. Why Elvey, described on the title page as 'Private Organist to Her Majesty and organist of St George's Chapel, Windsor', felt entitled to refer to these Responses as Tallis's is a mystery. The collection concludes with some additional responses for the Restoration of the

---

[72] Jebb, *Choral Responses*, 5.

[73] G. I. Elvey, *Tallis's Litany and Responses Arranged for the Daily Use of Cathedral and Collegiate Churches* (London: R. Mills, [1842]). Even more idiosyncratic is an edition published in about 1847 by R.H.L. (identified in the CPM as Robert Hunter Lyon), *The Order for Chanting the Morning and Evening, Wednesday and Friday, and Eucharistic Services, Arranged Chiefly from Tallis*. The connection with Tallis is so tenuous that it will not be examined here.

Example 18. Comparison of Boyce's and Elvey's versions of the Preces

(a) Elvey (originally in D)

And our mouth shall shew forth thy praise. O Lord make haste to help us.

(b) Boyce

And our mouth shall shew forth thy praise. O Lord make haste to help us.

(a) Elvey

As it was ... shall be, world with - out end. A - men. The Lord's name be prais - ed.

(b) Boyce

As it was ... now ... shall be, world with - out end. A - men. The Lord's name be prais - ed.

Royal Family, and the Queen's Accession, and it is likely that this royal affiliation would have lent this collection a certain authority.

In 1843 Francis Paget, Bishop of Oxford, and Samuel Pearsall, from Lichfield Cathedral, published *The Hymns of the Church Pointed as they are to be Sung or Chanted ... as Set to the Music by Thomas Tallis*.[74] The preface contains instructions on performing Anglican chant, and a novel pointing system, but no reference to

74 Samuel Pearsall, *The Hymns of the Church, Pointed as they are to be Sung or Chanted: with the Versicles, Creed of S. Athanasius, Litany, Commandments, etc. as Set to Music by Thomas Tallis*, comp. F.E.P. [Francis Edward Paget] 2nd ed.

the source of the Preces and Responses, which are essentially a keyboard arrangement of Boyce's version. Although the harmonies are fundamentally unchanged, they are arranged to fall comfortably under the hand, without concern for continuity of part writing. No attempt appears to have been made to ensure the integrity of the plainsong, and in places crotchet divisions of the minim beat are only notated in the upper line, suggesting that it was expected that the congregation would sing this part, rather than the plainsong.

The practice of the congregation singing the treble line rather than the plainsong appears to have been widespread, and was the subject of much complaint. A review in the *Musical Times* of the 1852 Charity Children's Festival is typical:

> The responses [*sic*], as sung by the children, are altogether a mistake. They sing the ornamental melody added for choirs by Tallis; instead of this the whole choral body, children and adults, should sing the *Plain Song itself* [...] We are continually losing the Plain Song in this way, and *listening* instead to a melody supplemental to it.[75]

The Rev. John Bacchus Dykes referred to this 'most objectionable' practice in an address to the Church Congress in 1865,[76] and a letter to the Anglican newspaper *The Guardian*, from the Precentor of Grahamstown Cathedral in South Africa, claims that it could still be heard 'even in England' as late as 1900.[77]

G. A. Macfarren described a related phenomenon in his 1867 survey of 'The Music of the English Church':

> I have heard of more than one living cathedral organist, who, knowing nothing of the Plain Song, wholly uninformed that this constituted the Church Part of the performance of service, having a disrelish for the antique harmony of Tallis diluted by Barnard,[78] [...] has taken for a *canto-fermo* the top line of Barnard's alteration of Tallis's counterpoint, written entirely new harmony under this, and thus altogether expunged the venerable *Cantus Ecclesiasticus*, which, however deformed, however obscured, however ignored,

(London: James Burns; Rugeley: John Thomas Walters, 1843). Paget produced an earlier edition without Pearsall's help, which I have been unable to locate.

[75] 'Cantor', 'The Annual Meeting of Charity Children, at Saint Paul's Cathedral', *Musical Times* 5 (1852): 44.

[76] *Church Congress Reports*, Norwich 1865, 302–3.

[77] The Precentor of Grahamstown Cathedral, 'Choral Practice of Congregations', *Guardian* 55 (1900): 747.

[78] Macfarren's arguments about the origins of the Responses are examined further in Chapter 5.

had till then still dragged on a degraded existence in the secret recesses of the tenor part [...][79]

A published example of this practice can be found in W. J. Westbrook's *Tallis's Preces and Responses, Arranged for Three Treble Voices*,[80] which takes the treble line from Boyce, adds two alto parts, not taken from Boyce, and completes the harmonies in the accompaniment.

An attempt to provide a solution to this problem of treating Boyce's treble line as the 'melody', prepared in response to a unison performance at the 1847 Charity Children's Festival, was provided by the Manchester organist Benjamin S. John Baptist Joule in his *Directorium Chori Anglicanum*.[81] In the extensive preface, Joule argues that 'during the great Rebellion the People gradually forgot their song [...] and even church-musicians seemed at length to be ignorant of the true principle upon which the ancient services were constructed.' He wishes to remedy this situation, and in order to let 'this important, this essential feature, the Birthright of the People, be religiously and accurately preserved', he provides a harmonisation with the plainsong in the treble.[82] Joule's edition is a lavish production: the title page is printed in blue, red and black, the pages are gilt-edged and the front cover is embossed in gold. It is comprehensive in scope, covering all the services of the Church of England, including the Churching of Women. It is, strictly, an arrangement rather than an edition of the Tallis Responses – there is no mention of Tallis in the title, and he admits that he has modified some of the endings to facilitate the pitching of the priest's intonations – but Joule acknowledges that his harmonies are 'principally' taken 'from ancient sources, from versions which are attributed to *Tallis*'.[83]

A different solution to the ongoing problem of congregational performance of the treble line can be found in about 1850 in Rimbault's *The Order of Morning and Evening Prayer ... the Plainsong of the Church being in the Tenor, According to the Ancient Usage*, 'compiled from authentic documents in the library of the editor'. Again, there is no mention of Tallis in the title, but the Preces and Responses are a rearrangement of Boyce (see Example 19) with the tenor and treble parts exchanged in the Preces, and an amalgamation into one of the two alto parts in the

---

[79] Macfarren, 'Music of the English Church', 70.

[80] W. J. Westbrook, *Tallis's Preces and Responses, Arranged for Three Treble Voices, with Accompaniment for the Organ, Harmonium or Pianoforte* (London: Alfred Whittingham, 1865).

[81] Benjamin S. John Baptist Joule, *Directorium Chori Anglicanum* (London: Novello, 1849), xvii.

[82] Joule, *Directorium Chori*, x.

[83] Joule, *Directorium Chori*, xii.

Example 19. Comparison of the Preces from Rimbault's
Order of Morning and Evening Prayer and Clifford

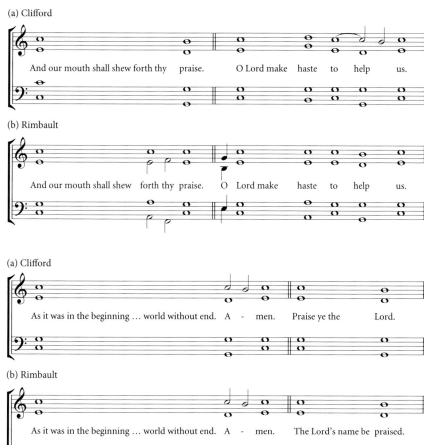

(a) Clifford

And our mouth shall shew forth thy   praise.   O Lord make   haste   to   help   us.

(b) Rimbault

And our mouth shall shew   forth thy praise.   O   Lord make   haste   to   help   us.

(a) Clifford

As it was in the beginning ... world without end.   A - men.   Praise ye the   Lord.

(b) Rimbault

As it was in the beginning ... world without end.   A - men.   The Lord's name be praised.

Responses.[84] The plainsong was printed in a larger size, with the instruction: 'It will be understood that the Notes in *large characters* are to be sung by the *people*; the Notes in *small characters* above and below are for the choir',[85] and the introduction contained an emotional plea that 'the ancient Melodies of the Church, coeval with Christianity itself, ought to be religiously preserved: and that, too, in such a way, that *all* can join in the "with one accord!"'.[86] Despite his firmly held

[84] The Litany is the four-part version, taken from Clifford and published in the Appendix to the *Full Cathedral Service*.

[85] Edward Francis Rimbault, *The Order of Morning and Evening Prayer with the Musical Notation in Harmony of Four Parts, the Plainsong of the Church being in the Tenor, According to the Ancient Usage* (London: Novello, [1850]), iv.

[86] Rimbault, *Morning and Evening Prayer*, iii.

and passionately argued beliefs, however, Rimbault was still unable to shake off the influence of Boyce's version.

A similar effort to distinguish the plainsong visually was made in 1859 by John Bishop in his *Choral Responses at Morning and Evening Prayer*, his second edition of Tallis's Preces and Responses.[87] It comprised a simple folded sheet, with headings in Old English type, printed in red and black on three staves, with the plainchant on a separate stave. Bishop had argued in the Preface to his 1843 *Order of Daily Service* that Barnard's version was the most authoritative, and had identified the portions of Boyce's version not based on Tallis. Bishop's *Choral Responses* is the first of the very few nineteenth-century editions to be based primarily upon Barnard; it gives both Barnard's version of the Tenor part and an alternative 'corrected' version, with the note: 'The small notes in the Tenor are preferred by some, as tending to preserve the plainchant on which the Responses are evidently constructed.' It cost only threepence, making it one of the cheapest editions of its day.

The number of 'scholarly' editions of the Litany and Responses dropped off around the middle of the century, but in about 1869 the Society for Promoting Christian Knowledge (SPCK) published another substantial edition of the Preces, Responses and Litany based upon Barnard, arranged so that the plainsong is consistently in the tenor.[88] The plainsong in Barnard's version of the Litany moves relatively freely between the tenor and the treble, and a degree of rearrangement is therefore required to produce a version with the plainsong in the tenor. It was prefaced by a long and detailed introduction, largely devoted to describing the many changes to Barnard's version necessary to meet this goal, which notes that 'the term *basis* is used advisedly, as this is by no means a mere reproduction'.

The argument for basing the edition upon Barnard seems to be taken largely from Jebb's *Choral Responses*, 'to which invaluable work the Editor [...] desires to acknowledge his deep obligation'.[89] Aldrich's letter to Fell is also quoted, but this time in support of the five-part version. The editor argues that, 'as we have, in the Dean's own handwriting, at least two copies of the Litany *in the five part* [...] version', the four parts mentioned must be in addition to, rather than inclusive of, the plainsong.

Unlike Jebb, however, the unnamed editor is overtly trying to promote congregational singing of the plainsong. The plainsong, 'corrected' so that it corresponds with Merbecke, is printed in diamond-headed type, and it is recommended that

---

[87] John Bishop, *Choral Responses at Morning and Evening Prayer* (London: Cocks, 1859).

[88] Thomas Tallis, *Preces, Responses and Litany* (London: SPCK, [1869]). Another fundamentally similar edition was published by the SPCK in 1901.

[89] Tallis, *Preces, Responses and Litany*, 1.

Example 20. 'Glory be' and 'The Lord's Name' from the SPCK edition of 1867

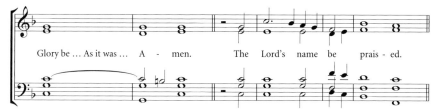

it 'should be played upon a *solo* or *reed* stop, so as to indicate the familiar melody (known to every frequenter of Cathedrals) that should be sung by the congregation at large.'[90] The 'Glory be' has been reinstated, despite being assigned to the priest in the 1662 prayer book, and 'The Lord's name be praised' is a more direct adaptation of Barnard than Boyce (see Example 20).

Despite these arguments in favour of Barnard's five-part version, four-part arrangements of Boyce became increasingly common towards the end of the century. One of the first such arrangement was Edward J. Hopkins's edition of *Tallis's Festival Responses* (*c.* 1868).[91] Hopkins, the organist at the Temple Church, appears to have been heavily influenced by Rimbault, and he cites Rimbault's reference to Aldrich's letter to Dr Fell as evidence that the Litany was composed in four parts.[92] But he also adopts Jebb's belief that Boyce's adaptations of the Preces 'far exceed in richness, solemnity and devotional character the versions of Barnard and Tallis'.[93] His edition of the Preces and Responses amalgamates the two alto parts from Boyce's Responses into one, while the Litany is based upon Aldrich's four-part version.

Hopkins states that Tallis's Preces, Responses and Litany had long been esteemed for their 'rich harmony, striking modulation, and sweet flowing melody', but again laments the fact that this often led to the neglect of the 'still higher merit of carrying with or within them the pure and simple plainchant', with the result that the 'accompanimental vocal harmonies were reduced from the lofty and sacred purpose to which they had been dedicated to the lower level of being simply beautiful music.'[94] He concludes that

[90] Tallis, *Preces, Responses and Litany*, 2.

[91] Edward J. Hopkins, *Tallis's Festival Responses Consisting of the Versicles, Preces, &c., and Litany, the Plainsong being Restored Throughout, and the Whole Reduced to the Original Number of Four Parts* (London: Weeks, [1868]).

[92] Hopkins, *Tallis's Festival Responses*, 3.

[93] Hopkins, *Tallis's Festival Responses*, 3. It is not clear exactly what Hopkins means by the 'version of Tallis'.

[94] Hopkins, *Tallis's Festival Responses*, 3.

it is obvious that it formed no part of Tallis's design to supersede or silence the congregational song during the celebration of Divine Service on the Church Festivals, but, on the contrary, to clothe it, as the audible medium to which prayer and praise were offered up, in the most devotional and edifying harmony his great knowledge of the musical art was capable of producing.[95]

Several four-part editions based on Boyce were published around the turn of the century. Edgar Pettman, the organist of St James's Church, Piccadilly, published an essentially similar edition in 1900,[96] based upon Boyce, but with slightly modified rhythms and carefully marked dynamics, and Novello published editions by Barnby and Stainer in 1893 and 1900 respectively that were fundamentally similar to Hopkins's. Both were four-part arrangements of Boyce, with 'corrected' plainsong. Stainer's was set a tone lower than usual ('in the key of F'), but with the exception of pitch, they are very similar in presentation, layout and content (both also contained the so-called 'Ely' confession). Duncan claimed that in 1920 Barnby's four-part arrangement of Boyce was the version 'in common use',[97] but the domination of the four-part version was not complete. George Martin published a five-part version of Boyce, arranged for two Trebles, Alto, Tenor and Bass in 1903, for example,[98] and Bumpus claimed that the five-part version was, in 1908, 'almost universally adopted'.[99]

From at least the time of Bishop's 1843 *Order of Daily Service*, therefore, it was widely known that Boyce's version of the Preces and Responses were at best a flawed representation of Tallis's intentions. Despite the confusion generated by Rimbault's claims for the four-part versions, the authority of Barnard's version was widely accepted. Yet well into the twentieth century, most editions of Tallis's Responses continued to be based upon the version published by Boyce in 1760.[100]

---

[95] Hopkins, *Tallis's Festival Responses*, 5.

[96] Edgar Pettman, *Tallis's Responses: A Simplified Arrangement as Sung at St James's Church Piccadilly* (London: Houghton, 1900).

[97] Duncan, 'Preces, Responses, and Litany', 692.

[98] George Martin, *Tallis's Festal Responses and Litany as Sung at St Paul's Cathedral …* (London: Novello, 1903).

[99] Bumpus, *Cathedral Music*, 43.

[100] Watkins Shaw's *Two Setting of the Preces and Responses at Morning and Evening Prayer by Thomas Tallis …* (London: Novello, 1957), discussed further below, can be seen as one of the final stages of this tradition.

♪ *Text or Act?*

IT would be easy to dismiss these nineteenth-century editions of Tallis's Responses as being of little consequence. Nicholas Temperley, in his survey of nineteenth-century British cathedral music, quite reasonably dispatches the Responses with the observation that 'a version believed to be Tallis's was often sung'.[101] It would also be easy to dismiss the nineteenth-century editors of the Responses as incompetent, arrogant or ill informed. Philip Brett, for example, takes a similar route in his discussion of the early Breitkopf & Härtel collected editions:

> They [nineteenth-century editors] aimed at a text that would reflect the composer's intentions, of course, but their ways of going about it were circumscribed by the lack of agreed standards and methods, by the desire for completion, and also, in some cases, by a certain arrogance.[102]

That is, Brett assumes ('of course') that the goal of editors of early music in the nineteenth century was essentially the same as our own – the creation of a 'text that would reflect the composer's intentions' – and that for various reasons they failed to meet these goals. I believe, however, that this survey of the nineteenth-century editions of Tallis's Responses suggests that reflecting the composer's intentions was not, in fact, their primary editorial goal, and that the nineteenth-century attitude towards early choral music was fundamentally different from our own. Again, Lydia Goehr's work-concept provides a useful way of examining this change in practice. By the end of the twentieth century, even music as distant from the 'Beethoven paradigm' as Tallis's Responses had been well and truly brought under the conceptual umbrella of the work-concept. Yet Goehr admits that, despite her watershed date of 1800, 'conceptual change, like the change in practices, has no sharply defined beginning or end'. She sees the nineteenth century as a transitional period, when the regulative force of the work-concept was beginning to be felt even in non-paradigmatic arenas such as early choral music, but was still less than complete.[103] Many of the more enigmatic aspects of the nineteenth-century

---

[101] Temperley, 'Cathedral Music', 175.

[102] Philip Brett, 'Text, Context and the Early Music Editor', *Authenticity and Early Music: A Symposium*, ed. Nicholas Kenyon (Oxford: Oxford University Press, 1988), 87.

[103] Goehr, *Imaginary Museum*, 110, 206. Jim Samson's 'The Practice of Early-Nineteenth-Century Pianism', in Talbot, *Musical Work*, 110–27, also examines an area in which musical practice was relatively independent of the work-concept in the nineteenth century. Samson argues that in many senses the musical work did not 'emerge triumphant' until around the middle of the nineteenth century ('Musical Work', 24).

reception of the Responses can, I believe, be attributed to the fact that there were some aspects of the reception of the Responses in which an idealised conception of a musical work loomed unexpectedly large, while there are others, in particular with respect to the continued importance of their liturgical function, in which the Responses failed to comply with the aesthetic ideals of the musical work.

Michael Talbot has argued that the 'point' of the indiscriminate use of the term 'work' is that it can be applied, regardless of 'size, specification or purpose'. A wide range of music could therefore qualify as works of Beethoven, for example, provided that '(a) they are musical products of some sort and (b) Beethoven wrote them.'[104] By this broad definition Tallis's Responses are undisputedly 'works', and they enjoy just this kind of status in the Early English Church Music edition of Tallis's English service music. They are included because they are music and they are by Tallis: there is nothing in the presentation or commentary to distinguish them from the other 'works' – anthems, canticles, psalms – in the edition.

Yet in many ways Tallis's Preces and Responses are extremely poor candidates for workhood; the extent to which the Responses meet Talbot's key attributes of musical works – discreteness, reproducibility and attributability – is in each case debatable.

At even the most fundamental level of discreteness, or work-as-object, the Responses are problematic. Are (Is?) Tallis's Preces and Responses one 'object' or two, or is each individual response a complete entity in itself? The Preces and Responses were historically regarded as separate items – Barnard, for example, groups the Preces with the Psalms, quite separately from the Responses – but by the nineteenth century the Preces and Responses were regarded as a single unit,[105] and the combination of Tallis's settings of what are now known as the first Preces and second Responses was universally accepted as comprising 'Tallis's Responses', even though Tallis certainly never intended them to be paired in this way. Talbot discusses the problem of levels of separability, but the examples cited – Bach's Preludes and Fugues and the songs on The Beatles' *Sergeant Pepper's* album – are rather less problematic than the Responses.[106]

Goehr takes a rather different approach to the question of what constitutes a work. She argues that the possession of particular attributes is not an essential

---

[104] Talbot, 'Composer-Centredness', 171–2. Talbot cites the tendency to group all products of a particularly composer indiscriminately (Beethoven bagatelles 'lumped together' with *Fidelio*) as evidence for his restatement of Goehr's work-concept as a move towards composer-centredness.

[105] This is still the case: see, for example, *Settings of the Preces and Responses by Byrd, Morley, Smith, Tomkins*, ed. and arr. Watkins Shaw, Church Music Society Reprints 48 (Croydon: RSCM, 1985).

[106] Talbot, 'Introduction', 3.

requirement for 'workhood' – that 'no form of musical production is excluded a priori from being packaged in terms of works' – but rather that work-like characteristics may be 'assigned' where they are lacking.[107] Yet for Goehr, one of the essential features of musical works is the absence of any 'extra-musical' function. The role of the imaginary museum is two-fold: it acts as a marker of an object's status 'as a work of fine art', and serves to 'frame' the object, to 'strip it of its local, historical, and worldly origins' so that 'only its aesthetic properties would metaphorically remain.'[108] Yet in the nineteenth century Tallis's Responses were not stripped of their historical origins and liturgical function, but were rather celebrated because of them.

Goehr's insistence on the relationship between work-character and the absence of the extra-musical function has, however, been the subject of criticism. Reinhard Strohm, for example, considers 'the idea that function or relevance for social practices should, generally, have been a hindrance to music's possession of work-character' to be the 'greatest flaw' in Goehr's exposition of the work-concept.[109] Harry White also takes issue with her 'tale' of music's emancipation from the extra-musical:

> No-one can usefully deny that Bach's cantatas were more immediately indentured to social function than the keyboard compositions of Beethoven, but this does not mean that *Wachet auf, ruft uns die Stimme* is less emancipated *in musical terms* than the 'Waldstein' sonata. To suggest otherwise, as Goehr does, is to mistake the social function of music for its meaning.[110]

While the Responses are undoubtedly less musically 'emancipated' than Bach's cantatas, much of the nineteenth-century rhetoric surrounding the Responses suggests strongly that they were nonetheless perceived in work-like terms. In particular the image of the 'solid rock of harmony' implies an idealised conception of the Responses that transcends the fragmented nature of the music itself and the profusion of competing versions – in other words, a work. Goehr argues that the projection of such an ideal object, 'a construction that exist[s] over and above its performances and score', is a direct consequence of, and indeed the purpose of, the regulative work-concept.[111]

Furthermore, the Responses were seen not only as a rock, but one uniquely able

---

[107] Goehr, *Imaginary Museum*, 244.

[108] Goehr, *Imaginary Museum*, 173.

[109] Reinhard Strohm, 'Looking Back at Ourselves: The Problem with the Musical Work-Concept', in Talbot, *Musical Work*, 139.

[110] White, 'If It's Baroque', 100.

[111] Goehr, *Imaginary Museum*, 105–6, 173–4.

to withstand the 'waves of time', upon which 'time has written "no wrinkle"', 'an heirloom, beyond the powers of time to antiquate'. While *Spem in alium* was dismissed as the 'mistake of a barbarous age', Tallis's harmonisation of the Responses were believed to have been 'built upon the eternal principles of truth'.[112] Again, the parallel with Goehr's claim that idealised works were seen as 'transcending temporal and spatial barriers' as a result of their 'ability to probe and reveal the higher world of universal, eternal truth' is striking.[113] The Responses were therefore perceived in work-like terms as an ideal object transcending particularities of version, score or performance, and revealing the timeless and unchanging principles of truth, yet they achieved this status not, like the *St Matthew Passion*, when they were transported from the church to the concert hall,[114] but within the context of the Anglican liturgy.

This co-existence of work-character and liturgical function may have been possible, at least in part, because the distance between the church and the concert hall is not always as great as is assumed. Even today it is not hard to find examples of blurred boundaries between the two, such as the annual broadcast of the Service of Nine Lessons and Carols from King's College, Cambridge, or concert tours and recordings by collegiate and cathedral choirs and, in the nineteenth century, the stranglehold of the concert hall over musical practice was less complete. Jeremy Gregory has argued that the church continued to play an integral role in English culture throughout the eighteenth century and into the nineteenth and, citing C. S. Lewis, that the chasm between a Christian and secular culture lies 'somewhere between us and Waverley novels'.[115] Jeremy Dibble claims that until late in the nineteenth century, the main focus of the music degrees at Oxford and Cambridge was the training of church musicians.[116] Certainly for most of the nineteenth century the Church of England, and particularly the services at St Paul's Cathedral, Westminster Abbey and the Chapel Royal, continued to play a significant part in

---

[112] Metcalfe, 'Music of the Church of England', 159.

[113] Goehr, *Imaginary Museum*, 246, 153.

[114] See Goehr, *Imaginary Museum*, 248.

[115] Jeremy Gregory, 'Christianity and Culture: Religion, the Arts and the Sciences in England, 1660–1880', *Culture and Society in Britain, 1660–1800*, ed. Jeremy Black (Manchester: Manchester University Press, 1997), 116–17. For a discussion of the social and political power of the Church of England, also see John Wolffe, *God and Greater Britain: Religion and National Life in Britain and Ireland, 1843–1945* (London; New York: Routledge, 1994), 128–30.

[116] Jeremy Dibble, 'Grove's Musical Dictionary: A National Document', *Musical Constructions of Nationalism*, ed. Harry White and Michael Murphy (Cork: Cork University Press, 2001), 35.

the musical life of London, and the intersection between the roles of musical antiquarian, scholar and church musician was substantial.

The overlap between the liturgical and the aesthetic was particularly marked
in events such as the Charity Children's Festivals, which were the source of many
of the quotes about the timeless quality of the Responses. The Charity Children's
Service, while consisting of a service of worship in St Paul's Cathedral, had many
of the features of a concert. The choir was composed of up to 6,000 children from
the London schools, and the paying 'audience' numbered in the thousands. The
service was regularly reviewed in the press: Berlioz attended the Anniversary in
1851 and produced a rapturous account of the event, couched entirely in terms
of visual and aural spectacle, with little evidence of other than a purely aesthetic
assessment. He concludes that this celebration of 'the sublimity of *monumental
music*' would be impossible in Paris, for a number of reasons, including a lack of
faith in 'Art'.[117]

A similar picture of liturgy-as-concert emerges from an extract from the 'Recollections' of William Gardiner included in Bumpus's *Cathedral Music*, showing how
'a Sunday in London might be spent by a lover of Church music' in the 1830s.[118]
The account begins with a trip to Westminster Abbey to hear the Whit-Sunday
performance of the 'responses of Tallis' – 'grand specimens of the simple evolu-
tions of harmony' – followed by the masses of Haydn and Mozart at the Bavarian
Chapel in Warwick Street, a quick visit to the Chapel Royal, where he often met up
with Sir George Smart, Sir John Rogers and other luminaries from the Madrigal
Society, and a 'leisurely drive' to St Paul's for the evening service, where, 'fortunately, the anthem was one of all others I wished to hear'. Such accounts show
that the social, historical, liturgical and aesthetic were far from mutually exclusive
aspects of musical experience.

The ongoing liturgical function of the Responses is, however, not the only
feature that muddies their work-status. The relationship between text and performance is central to discussions of the ontology of the musical work, and again,
the Responses can be seen to lie at a considerable conceptual distance from the
Beethoven paradigm in this respect.

The importance of the score is inherent in Talbot's second requirement of reproducibility; he admits that he personally subscribes, 'more or less', to the view that
within the Western European Classical Tradition the work *is* its score.[119] White
interprets Goehr's 'Beethoven paradigm' as referring to the 'absolute sovereignty

---

[117] Hector Berlioz, 'The Charity Children's Anniversary at St. Paul's Cathedral', trans.
    Sabilla Novello, *Musical Times* 7 (1855): 67–70.

[118] Bumpus, *Cathedral Music*, 392–3.

[119] Talbot, 'Introduction', 6.

of the musical text as the status quo to which the concept of performance was sub-servient',[120] while Willem Erauw goes so far as to suggest that 'during a classical concert, musicians are interpreting musical texts instead of playing music.'[121]

Inherent in these formulations is the idea that a performance is a realisation of a pre-existing score. The early history of the harmonised responses of the Angli-can liturgy, however, can be best understood in terms of a performance tradition captured in, rather than defined by, the texts. Duncan, in his *Musical Times* article, which relies heavily on the prefaces to Jebb's *Choral Responses*, notes that choirs tended to improvise their own harmonies to the responses, which were then writ-ten down 'for uniformity's sake' (many of these are recorded in the 'Common Use' versions published in Jebb's second volume). He reports that 'in his [Jebb's] time the Gloucester choir still sang the responses from oral tradition.' The overlap between Tallis's Responses and this oral tradition can be seen in 'the curious use of Wells Cathedral', which performed 'a combination of Tallis and the Westminster use', the result of the organist, C. W. Lavington, writing down his recollection of 'how it was done' at Westminster Abbey.[122] Tallis's Responses can be seen as simply a special case within this broader tradition.

The confusing array of versions of Tallis's Responses that confronted the nine-teenth-century editors therefore represented not so much a series of definitive scores, but rather a rich and varied performance tradition. Thus Lowe's 'Extraordi-nary Responsalls upon Festivalls' and the other late seventeenth-century four-part versions of Tallis's Responses represent a direct response to the changes in practice that took place at the Restoration, particularly the general transition from five- to four-part choirs and the changes to the 1662 Prayer Book. Even in the nineteenth century, editors were often motivated by fidelity to liturgical practice rather than fidelity to a text. Those who believed that the congregation had an inalienable right to sing the liturgy placed a high premium upon a consistent and 'correct' treatment of the plainsong within the Responses.[123] Others, such as Jebb, who saw the per-formance of the liturgy on behalf of the congregation as the role of the choir, were content to accept the freer treatment of the chant found in the earlier sources.[124]

---

[120] White, 'If It's Baroque', 97.

[121] Erauw, 'Canon Formation', 115.

[122] Duncan, 'Preces, Responses, and Litany', 552.

[123] This practice, however, was in itself concerned with fidelity to the plainsong as encapsulated in Merbecke's text.

[124] Rainbow argues that for Jebb the choral service was 'synonymous' with the cathe-dral service, and that he was opposed to congregational participation in the serv-ice, except for 'soft singing by those of the people who really understood how to chant' (*Anglican Choral Revival*, 31).

And for all these editors, Boyce's version represented the dominant nineteenth-century practice.

The early history of the Responses is then one of process, rather than product, of act rather than text. The nineteenth-century editors were motivated by respect for the liturgical traditions and practice of the church as well as for the early sources and the composer's intentions and these conflicting motivations can be traced in their editions. Some, such as Oliphant's Madrigal Society edition seem to have been the result of predominantly antiquarian interest that was becoming increasingly important in the 1840s. Others, like Jebb's *Choral Responses*, were more sociological, recording as comprehensibly as possible the actual practice of the church.[125] These early editors also appear to have been willing to give more weight to their own aesthetic judgements than is now considered appropriate (perhaps the 'arrogance' to which Brett refers). They valued Boyce's version because, to use Jebb's words, 'it exceeds even *Barnard's* in richness, solemnity, & profound devotional character.'[126]

Somewhat paradoxically, it was Rimbault, despite his dubious ethics and his now discredited conclusions, who was most concerned with creating a text that he believed would 'reflect the composer's intentions'. Although he never completely abandoned Boyce's traditional version, Rimbault was at least in principle less concerned with maintaining the traditions of the church than most of the other nineteenth-century editors. Although his arguments were misguided, his attempt to reinstate the four-part version of the Responses and Litany was driven by a desire to undo the corruption that he attributed to Barnard, and to retrieve the original version in line with the evidence of his 'original documents' and with what he believed to be Tallis's intention.

As we have seen, the process whereby Barnard's version of Tallis's Responses gradually replaced Boyce's was a long and slow one, and despite the efforts of Bishop and the SPCK was far from complete by the turn of the twentieth century. As late as 1957 Watkins Shaw produced an edition that, while encouraging the adoption of Barnard, still recognised the claims of the older traditions. Byrd's setting of 'O Lord, make haste to help us', upon which Lowe and Boyce are based, is included as an alternative, to 'allow for its continued use where desired'. It is, however, given in Byrd's original version and clearly attributed to him. The final response of the Preces is reproduced 'as set by Tallis for the Prayer Books of Edward VI': an arrangement of the same music to the text of 1662 Prayer Book is provided

---

[125] For a useful discussion on editorial orientations, see Peter Shillingsburg, *Scholarly Editing in the Computer Age: Lectures in Theory and Practice* (Duntroon, ACT: Royal Military College, 1984).

[126] Jebb, *Choral Responses*, 8.

as an alternative.[127] The first settings of the Preces and Responses are grouped together followed by the second to encourage a performance that more closely reflects the earliest sources, but again traditional practice is acknowledged in the prefatory notes, which suggest that the combination of the first Preces and second Responses 'should be maintained where the claims of familiarity are paramount'. While this edition is obviously intended for liturgical use, it is markedly more concerned with recapturing Tallis's intentions (and recognising the contribution of Byrd) than the earlier editions. Even in the choir stalls, fidelity to the composer and the early sources was overtaking fidelity to tradition.[128]

Although Tallis's compositional intentions were not the first concern of most nineteenth-century editors, however, the role of Tallis in the reception of the Litany and Responses was far from insignificant. While every other feature of the Responses (the number of voices, the role of the plainsong, the harmonies) was open to debate, the fact that they were Tallis's was almost never questioned,[129] and any perceived deficiencies were attributed to the incompetence or malice of later scribes and editors rather than to Tallis himself. The reality of the Responses may have been a confused mess of competing versions, but the image of the 'solid rock of harmony' transcended this reality, and Tallis's role as author of this 'heirloom' similarly transcended the complexities of actual practice.

As the 'Father of Church Music', who 'set the standard' of English liturgical music, Tallis's role as composer was, however, both greater and smaller than that of a traditional composer. He was, as discussed in Chapter 1, granted authorship, in the Amens, of the plagal cadence, but at the same time he was seen less as an independent creator than as a conduit of divine will and of the age-old traditions of worship. In his liturgical music Tallis is not valued for his compositional originality, but for completing a process begun in antiquity.[130] The plainsong had its roots in Roman oratory, the 'noble confessor' John Merbecke adapted it to the English liturgy, and Tallis 'brought to work to perfection' by adding

---

[127] Shaw, *Preces and Responses*, 2.

[128] This process is complete by the EECM edition of 1972. The one concession to liturgical practice in this edition is the inclusion, as an alternative, of the text from the 1662 Prayer Book under the final response of the Preces. In general, however, even in liturgical performances within the Anglican service, fidelity to the composer's original text is given high priority, and the original words of these and other early settings of the Responses are now usually sung.

[129] Two exceptions are Charles Child Spencer, 'Historical doubts as to the Genuineness of Tallis', *Parish Choir* 1(1847): 121–2, and J[ohn] C[rowdy], 'On the Choral Treatment of the Litany', *Musical Standard* 5 (1866): 144–5.

[130] This is in direct contrast to the new emphasis on originality in the 'Beethoven Paradigm' (Goehr, *Imaginary Museum*, 220–3).

harmony.[131] The ambiguity of Tallis's role is reflected in the title pages of many of the editions of the Responses: Bishop and Rimbault describe the Responses as 'arranged' by Tallis;[132] Havergal and Pearsall both use the term 'set'; and the 1854 Novello edition refers to them as 'noted' by Tallis. Although the Litany and Responses were not seen as the products of a single creative act, but rather as the result of an extended process of musical evolution and collaboration, Tallis's contribution to the process was still seen as unique and essential. Metcalfe concludes that 'there never was an English musician in any age so fitted to settle the musical service of the Church of his country as Thomas Tallis', and takes 'fresh confidence that God was specially over-ruling our Reformation, each time we think of the men raised up to bring the work to perfection'.[133]

The importance of attributability is particularly notable when Tallis's 'Festal' Responses are compared with the 'Ferial' Responses. Although they are indisputably the same type of 'thing' as Tallis's Responses (being simply a different harmonisation of the plainsong), they conspicuously do not meet Talbot's attributability requirement. It is not merely that the composer is unknown: they are perceived as a form of crystallised practice, essentially unattributable, in the same way that Talbot argues folk song is unattributable.[134] The vital importance of attributability can be seen in Duncan's observation: 'As might be expected from the circumstances of their origin, the Ferial Responses exhibit few signs of inspiration, and could without much difficulty be improved upon.'[135] When these Ferial Responses are compared with the simplified four-part versions of Tallis's Responses, particularly the Aldrich/Clifford version, it is hard to see sufficient qualitative difference to justify this judgement. The role of Tallis in the reception of the Responses is vital.

Both Goehr and Talbot acknowledge the status associated with the work-concept. Goehr has argued that as a result of the 'conceptual imperialism' of the work-concept, it is often believed that the more closely music 'embodies the conditions determined by the romantic work-aesthetic, the more civilized it is'; Talbot refers to the 'dignity and meaningfulness of high art'.[136] There can be no doubt that Tallis's Responses were viewed as civilised, meaningful and dignified in the nineteenth century, yet their work-status was at best equivocal. They were never 'stripped' of

[131] See Macfarren, 'Music of the English Church', 69, and Metcalfe, 'Music of the Church of England', 158–9. The nationalist subtext of this argument, particularly as expounded by Metcalfe, is examined in greater detail in Chapter 5 below.

[132] Rimbault, *Order of the Daily Service*, and Bishop, *Order of the Daily Service*.

[133] Metcalfe, 'Music of the Church of England', 158–9.

[134] Talbot, 'Introduction', 4.

[135] Duncan, 'Preces, Responses, and Litany', 552.

[136] Goehr, *Imaginary Museum*, 248–9; Talbot, 'Composer-Centredness', 172.

their liturgical function (even in the twentieth century, their small size and fragmentary nature have prevented them from making the transition to the concert
hall or the recording studio),[137] but were valued because of their unique place in
the history of Anglican music. They were the 'solid rock of harmony' upon which
the Anglican liturgy was built, and they enjoyed a popularity that largely transcended differences of class and churchmanship and, it must be said, the purely
musical interest of these few simple chords. Despite their monolithic status in the
popular imagination, the lack of a single, universally recognised text allowed them
to be taken up, in their various manifestations, by a broad cross-section of English
musical society from the village choir to St Paul's Cathedral, by choral traditional-
ists such as John Jebb and by advocates of congregational participation in the liturgy, and to be adopted by diverse groups who could each project their own meanings onto these few disputed notes. In the final chapter, I will examine some of the
historical narratives associated with Tallis's setting of the Litany and Responses,
and with his music in general, in an attempt to uncover these meanings, and to
come a little closer to understanding Tallis's significance in nineteenth-century
English musical life.

[137] Both settings of the Preces and Responses are found on vol. 6 of the Chapelle du
Roi recording of Tallis's complete works. This provides a nice example of the kind
of unquestioning drive for completeness discussed by Talbot. On the recordings,
a pseudo-liturgical ordering of items has been observed, but reviews published on
the Signum Records website still indicate a level of discomfort with the enterprise.
David Allinson, for example, notes that the '"completist" urge behind the recording inevitably means that a few items are not "concert-friendly", being working
liturgical music', while Allison Bullock commends the choir for 'managing not to
sound bored (for this must indeed be dull music to record)' (*Thomas Tallis: The
Complete Works, Volume 6 – Music for a Reformed Church*, accessed 6 Jan 2007,
<http://www.signumrecords.com/catalogue/sigcd022/reviews.htm>).

CHAPTER 5

'The Englishman's Harmony': Tallis and national identity

L EO Treitler begins his article 'Gender and Other Dualities of Music History' with the claim that

> Music is, among other things, a discourse of myth through which 'Western civilization' contemplates and presents itself. This is said, not in order to question the truth value of music-historical narratives, but to emphasize their aspect as stories of traditional form that the culture tells in its desire to affirm its identity and values.[1]

The idea of the concretization – that in the perceptions of a particular collective an individual work or the works of a given composer will assume a distinct shape that can be identified and that will change with time and circumstance – has underpinned this discussion so far. In this concluding chapter, however, I will take an essentially different approach: I will shift my focus away from perceptions of Tallis and his music to the 'discourses of myth' that surrounded them and the stories that were told about them. I will concentrate on the intersection of Tallis's Responses with myths of English national and religious identity, paying particular attention to the claim that the harmony with which Tallis 'clothed' the plainsong was, in some sense, inherently English. I will also examine the implications of the belief that the reign of Elizabeth was a golden age, particularly for church music, which was followed, more or less inevitably, by a period of corruption and decline. I will then look briefly at the ways these myths of religious and national identity were recast by the predominantly Roman Catholic musicians mentioned in Chapter 2, and at how the new stories that began to be told about the church music of the sixteenth century allowed a reassessment of the value of pre-Reformation English music.

---

[1] Leo Treitler, 'Gender and Other Dualities of Music History', *Musicology and Difference: Gender and Sexuality in Music Scholarship*, ed. Ruth A. Solie (Berkeley: University of California Press, 1993), 23–45.

❧ 'Natural' Harmony and the 'Rude Nations' of the North

THE claim that the English possessed a 'natural' taste for harmony is made most explicitly in an 1865 article by the Rev. J. Powell Metcalfe, 'The Music of the Church of England, as Contemplated by the Reformers'. Metcalfe was a relatively minor figure in English musical circles, identified at the head of the article as the 'Editor of the "School Round Book," "Metrical Anthems," and Joint Editor [with Rimbault] of the "Rounds, Catches, and Canons of England."' Although published in the primarily secular forum of the *Musical Times*, the article is strongly religious in tone. Metcalfe's argument is complex but revealing, and I will quote from it at some length.

Metcalfe begins by establishing the religious and nationalist foundations of his argument, addressing the question: 'What was the Reformation?'

> Nothing more, yet nothing less [...] than a movement to Anglicize the Church Catholic – to adapt ancient usage and universal doctrine so as to form the 'particular or national Church' [...] of sober, thoughtful, independent-minded Englishmen.

The role of music in this Reformation, he explains, was to make the liturgy particularly amenable to English taste, to help it 'to touch the deeper feelings of the Englishman's heart, and aid it in vibrating to the appeals of God's awful truth'.[2] Hence the music to which the English liturgy was set must be quintessentially English; it must contain within it that which is most sympathetic to what he perceives to be a distinct English national character.

After establishing that the role of music 'as Contemplated by the Reformers' was to render the liturgy essentially and unmistakably English, Metcalfe discusses the liturgical music of the English Church, which he divides into six styles: the monotone, preces, chant, services, anthems and the metrical psalms.[3] He starts with the monotone, comparing it to the technique used by classical orators. He then moves on to the Preces and Responses, locating the origins of the chant in the recitative used in ancient Roman drama, taking care to distinguish it from modern Italian opera, 'the source of all that is florid and brilliant and flighty'. While he considered the very antiquity of these origins to be sufficient to ensure 'veneration by our Reformers', he argues that the harmonisation of the chant, 'while preserving the original character [...] yet render[ed] it more agreeable to the English ear – more

---

[2] Metcalfe, 'Music of the Church of England', 157.

[3] An identical taxonomy was used by Ouseley in his 'The History and Development of Church Music', *Church Congress Reports*, Manchester 1863, 161–70, discussed further below.

moving to the English heart'. He distinguishes the 'natural' harmony with which the chant was 'enriched', however, from the *arithmetical* harmony' that preceded the Reformation. This 'harmony of imitation', or *'counter*-point', he argues, consisted of 'intricate contrapuntal puzzles', turning 'the lovely winning Polyhymnia into a parcel of dry bones.' What he calls 'simple' harmony, or 'the Englishman's harmony', came from

> the unlearned – the common people, whose natural tastes had taught them harmonies to the burdens of their dearly loved ballads, even before the learned clerk had begun to potter over his fleshless musical arithmetic and cramp sweet sounds in the stocks of fugue.

The ancient Roman recitative and the 'natural' English harmony were therefore brought together at the Reformation by 'those wise old Fathers of our Church': the Preces and Responses were 'clothed with the Englishman's harmony',[4] allowing the 'holy old words, instead of being bleared with fuging' to 'creep into the Englishman's heart on the breath of his native harmony'. He assures us that while Merbecke performed a great service in adapting the plainsong to the English liturgy, 'it needed the far greater work of a Thomas Tallis to fit it for the highest form of the English Churchman's worship.' He concludes, with a typical example of the purple prose devoted to Tallis's Responses in the nineteenth century:

> May we not take fresh confidence that God was specially over-ruling our Reformation, each time we think of the men raised up to bring the work to perfection. Probably, there never was an English musician in any age so fitted to settle the musical service of the church of his country as Thomas Tallis, the personal friend of Archbishop Parker [...] To Tallis we owe that great perfecting of Merbecke's work that has given to our Church an heirloom that seems beyond the power of time to antiquate, that stands out the more majestically for each attempt to supplant it that successive generations of musicians have made.[5]

His argument, then, can be summarised thus: the Church of England has taken the best of the Catholic tradition, with its roots in Greco-Roman antiquity,

---

4 See also Hopkins, *Tallis's Festival Responses*, 5: Tallis's purpose in the Responses was to 'clothe' the congregational song 'in the most devotional and edifying harmony his great knowledge of the musical art was capable of producing.' For a general discussion of the use of the term 'clothed in harmony', see Grant Olwage, 'Hym(n)ing: Music and Masculinity in the Early Victorian Church', *Nineteenth-Century British Music Studies*, ed. Peter Horton and Bennett Zon, vol. 3 (Aldershot: Ashgate, 2003), 36.

5 Metcalfe, 'Music of the Church of England', 158–9.

and made it peculiarly English. This has largely been achieved, in musical terms, by harmonising the plainchant of the Responses in simple, 'natural' harmonies, which are particularly well suited to an instinctive English affinity for harmony. This should not be confused with the, by implication, 'unnatural' counterpoint that characterised the period before the Reformation.[6] Just as England was widely believed to have been selected by God for the 'especial guardianship of Christianity',[7] Metcalfe believed that Tallis had been divinely chosen to bring this great work to fruition, which he did in his harmonisation of the Preces and Responses, seen by Metcalfe as a unique, divinely inspired embodiment of the history of the Church of England.

Although echoes of this association of the English with simple homophony can be found in the fame of the *Contenance Angloise* in the fourteenth and fifteenth centuries, this belief in an inherent English musicality sits rather uncomfortably with the more widespread appellation of England as the Land without Music.[8] It does, however, function as a music-historical version of a more widespread English historical narrative: that of an innate simplicity and purity corrupted by foreign Catholicism and restored at the Reformation. An examination of the traditional narratives of English ethnic and religious history helps illuminate the political and religious resonances of Metcalfe's argument.

The most influential of the myths about England's religious and ethnic origins were first articulated by Geoffrey of Monmouth in his twelfth-century *Historia Regum Britanniae* or *History of the British Kings* (hereafter *British History*). In summary, Geoffrey claimed that Britain was named after Brutus the Trojan, grandson of Aeneas, who came to the island in about 1170 BC.[9] There followed a long line of British kings, the greatest of whom was Arthur, who conquered the invading Saxons, the Picts, the Scots, Ireland, Iceland, Sweden, the Orkneys, Norway, Denmark and finally Gaul. He was on his way to conquer Rome when he was called back by news of a rebellion at home and fatally injured. His

---

[6] See Irving, *Ancients and Moderns*, 163–74, on the associations of the term 'Gothic' and harmony with learned counterpoint, in comparison with this 'natural' harmony.

[7] George Croly, *England the Fortress of Christianity* (London, 1839), cited in Wolffe, *God and Greater Britain*, 17.

[8] For two quite different analyses of the widespread anxiety about the lack of innate English musicality in the mid- to late nineteenth century, see Rainbow, *Land without Music*, and Stradling and Hughes, *English Musical Renaissance*. William Gatens also briefly addresses the same question (*Victorian Cathedral Music in Theory and Practice* (Cambridge: Cambridge University Press, 1986), 18–19).

[9] In this chapter, therefore, the term 'British' generally refers to the ostensible descendants of Brutus before the arrival of the Anglo-Saxons, rather than inhabitants of modern-day Great Britain.

descendants, the Britons, continued the war with the Saxons, but were eventually overcome and retired to Wales and Cornwall. Merlin, however, prophesied that the Red Dragon of the Britons would one day rise up and conquer the White Dragon of the Saxons. The accession of the Welsh Henry VII to the throne in the late fifteenth century was seen by many as the fulfilment of this prophecy.[10]

Over the following centuries a series of specifically religious myths was overlaid onto this framework, particularly relating to the establishment of the English church. Until at least the eighteenth century, there was a firm belief in the apostolic foundation of the Church of England: the origins of the English church were variously attributed to Joseph of Arimathea, who was believed to have built the first English church in Glastonbury, St Paul, St James, Simon Zelotes and others. When the Britons were driven into Wales by the 'ravages of the pagan Saxons', they continued to practice their indigenous form of Christianity, resisting, ultimately unsuccessfully, the attempts of Augustine to bring them under the authority of the Church of Rome.[11] The Protestant perspective on the Augustinian mission is captured by Foxe in his 1563 *Actes and Monuments*:

> religion remained in Britain, uncorrupt, and the word of Christ truly preached, till about the coming of Augustine and of his companions from Rome, many of the same Britain-preachers were slain by the Saxons. After that began the christian [*sic*] faith to spring among the Saxons after a certain Romish sort.[12]

The English Reformation, under the Tudor monarch Henry VIII, was seen, then, not as a spurning of the one true church, but a purging of foreign contamination

---

[10] T. D. Kendrick, *British Antiquity* (London: Methuen, 1950), 7–9. For a discussion of the continued power of these beliefs and their role in later political and religious developments, also see Glanmor Williams, 'Some Protestant Views of Early British Church History', *History* 38 (1953): 219–33, and Sydney Anglo, 'The *British History* in Early Tudor Propaganda', *Bulletin of the John Rylands Library* 44 (1961): 17–48.

[11] Colin Kidd, *British Identities before Nationalism* (Cambridge: Cambridge University Press, 1999), 99–101. For a discussion of myths about the origins of British Christianity, and a reproduction of John Hamilton Mortimer's late eighteenth-century *St Paul Preaching to the Britons*, also see Sam Smiles, *The Image of Antiquity: Ancient Britain and the Romantic Imagination* (New Haven, CT: Yale University Press, 1994), 97–9, 103–8.

[12] Foxe, *Actes and Monuments*, 1:516, as quoted in Williams, 'Some Protestant Views', 225. A similar point is also made in Peter Roberts, 'Tudor Wales, National Identity and the British Inheritance', *British Consciousness and Identity: The Making of Britain, 1533–1701*, ed. Brendan Bradshaw and Peter Roberts (Cambridge: Cambridge University Press, 1998), 20, although this refers back to Williams.

of an ancient and indigenous religious heritage, and a fulfilment of the Galfridean prophecy.[13]

These views were espoused by important Reformation figures, such as Archbishop Parker, the 'personal friend' of Tallis, who was convinced that the origins of the English episcopacy lay with Joseph of Arimathea rather than Rome.[14] They continued to hold sway for a considerable time: Colin Kidd claims that well into the seventeenth century 'the descent claimed by the Church of England from the apostolic church of the ancient Britons remained crucial to the defence of Anglican legitimacy'.[15] Glanmor Williams argues that the belief in an early British church, independent of Rome, survived into the nineteenth century, although 'pruned of its more palpably mythical accretions'. As tensions between the Church of England and the Church of Rome mounted in the nineteenth century, the idea of an early and indigenous English church took on renewed significance.[16] While these myths may no longer have been accepted as fact, they continued to resonate strongly throughout the nineteenth century. The Arthurian legend, for example, was particularly popular in Victorian England,[17] and was the subject of William Dyce's frescoes in the new Parliament House, while E. T. Parris won £100 for his unsuccessful submission of *Joseph of Arimaethea Converting the Britons* for the same purpose.[18] Resonances of such myths can also, I believe, be traced in some nineteenth-century discussion of Tallis and of early Anglican music.

The source of Metcalf's claim that the English had a natural affinity for harmony is the following much-cited passage from Gerald of Wales's, or Geraldus Cambrensis's, *Descriptio Cambriae*:

> The Britons [i.e. the Welsh] do not sing in unison, like the inhabitants of other countries; but in many different parts. So that when a company of singers among the common people meets to sing, as is usual in this country, as many different parts are heard as there are performers, who all at length

[13] Williams, 'Some Protestant Views', 221–2.

[14] Williams, 'Some Protestant Views', 226.

[15] Colin Kidd in 'Protestantism, Constitutionalism and British Identity under the Later Stuarts', in Bradshaw and Roberts, *British Consciousness*, 327–8. Kidd recognises the tensions that existed between England's 'predominantly Saxonist' political identity, and the reliance of the Church of England upon myths of ancient British Christianity (*British Identities*, 99).

[16] Williams, 'Some Protestant Views', 229–30. Anglo-Catholics were also keen to distance themselves from *Roman* Catholicism (see Gatens, *Victorian Cathedral Music*, 5, 62).

[17] See Barczewski, *Myth and National Identity*.

[18] Smiles, *Image of Antiquity*, 105–6.

unite in consonance, with organic sweetness. In the northern parts of Great Britain, beyond the Humber, on the borders of Yorkshire, the inhabitants use the same kind of symphonious harmony; except that they only sing in two parts, the one murmuring in the base, and the other warbling in the acute or treble. Nor do these two nations practice this kind of singing so much by art as habit, which has rendered it so natural to them, that neither in Wales, where they sing in many parts, nor in the North of England, where they sing in two parts, is a simple melody ever well sung. […] But as not all the English sing in this manner, but those only of the North, I believe they had this art at first, like their language, from the Danes and Norwegians, who used frequently to invade and so occupy, for a long time together, those parts of the island.[19]

This account dates from the turn of the thirteenth century, postdating by about sixty years the *British History*, with which Gerald of Wales was acquainted.[20] Although contemptuous of some of the *British History*'s more extravagant flights of fancy, Gerald accepted its basic premises about the ethnic origins of the British people, and included the description of the fictional gilded roofs of Caerleon in his itinerary as though he had seen them for himself.[21]

In Gerald's description, the ancient Britons are identified as the possessors of an instinctive and natural musicality, transformed by Metcalfe into the 'Englishman's harmony'. However, this passage offers a dual explanation of the ethnic origins of this natural harmony, which appears to have been simultaneously indigenous to the British inhabitants of Wales, and to have been introduced into the North of the country by the Danish invaders. This is typical of the tension that has existed throughout English history, identified by Colin Kidd as 'a major ambiguity in English conceptions of nationhood',[22] between the need to embrace the characteristics of the various waves of invaders, particularly the Anglo-Saxons, and the wish to preserve the unique identity of the ancient British. It is also part of a broader understanding of England as ethnically linked to the northern nations of Europe, which is central to the Anglo-Saxon identity.

---

[19] Translation taken from Burney, *General History*, 1:483.

[20] Paul J. Nixon, 'Giraldus Cambrensis on Music: How Reliable are his Historiographers?', *Proceedings of the First British-Swedish Conference on Musicology: Medieval Studies, 11–15 May 1988*, ed. Ann Buckley (Stockholm: Royal Swedish Academy of Music, 1992), 274, and Kendrick, *British Antiquity*, 4.

[21] Kendrick, *British Antiquity*, 12.

[22] Kidd makes this point repeatedly, claiming that the tension was even more pronounced in attempts to reconcile ecclesiastical with temporal history (Kidd, *British Identities*, 83; see also p. 104 for the peculiarly religious aspects of this dilemma).

There has been considerable debate about the reliability and interpretation of the musical details of the passage from Gerald of Wales cited above,[23] but it was widely known in the eighteenth and nineteenth centuries and many nineteenth-century writers appeared happy to accept that it described a natural tendency to sing in spontaneous, improvised harmony that was still observable in the North of England and in Wales.

In an address to the Church Congress in Nottingham in 1871, for example, the Rev. Dykes stated emphatically:

> Harmony is of Northern origin. And it is strange how in many parts of the North (take, for instance, parts of Yorkshire) the choirs cannot tolerate continuous unison singing. They reject the Gregorian chants, because they do not come to them in harmonised form.[24]

G. A. Macfarren attributes his experience of spontaneous harmonisation in Scottish hymn-singing, which he compared unfavourably to the sound of an orchestra tuning up, to this Northern affinity for harmonisation:

> I am aware, too, that the early inhabitants of this land of Britain, in common with those of the Northern countries whence they emigrated hither, had the gift of what may be called natural harmony; I mean that, whereas the Greco-Gregorian Plain-Song of the Church was chanted in unison, the priesthood who imported this classic pagan form of musical art into our latitudes found the peoples to whom they taught Christianity accustomed to sing their national songs in three-part harmony [...] Yes, the art of musical combination originated in the North, not among Greek philosophers, not among ecclesiastical scholars, but among the rude nations of these wild regions whose instinct for beauty was their only teacher.[25]

The passage from the *Descriptio Cambriae* cited above forms the culmination of Ouseley's chapter on 'Early English Church Music' in the English edition of Emil Naumann's *The History of Music*,[26] and Ouseley cited Gerald of Wales as his authority for exempting Northerners from his general comments on unison hymn singing at the Leeds Church Congress in 1872:

---

[23] See, for example, Nixon, 'Giraldus Cambrensis', 264–89, esp. 276 ff.

[24] Rev. Dr. Dykes, *Church Congress Reports,* Nottingham 1871, 376.

[25] Macfarren, 'Music of the English Church', 26. He cites Charles Kingsley's novel *Hereward* as having 'rendered popularly familiar this notable fact in music history'.

[26] Emil Naumann *The History of Music*, trans. F. Praeger, ed. F. A. Gore Ouseley, vol. 2 (London: Cassell, [1882]), 397–402.

A hymn is essentially congregational. In most parts of England it should be sung by the people in unison, although accompanied by the organ in harmony. This does not apply, however, to the very musical part of England in which we are now assembled, where the people appear to sing harmony by Instinct, and to have done so from the time of Giraldus Cambrensis.[27]

Ouseley had explained his views on the Northern origins of harmony at much greater length in a lecture on the development of Church Music given to the Church Congress at Manchester in 1863.[28] He states that the aim of his lecture is to examine the origins of church music, with a view to providing a 'rational account of musical progress and development [...] to guide us in our judgement as to the present state of the art, and its future in connection with the Church of England'. It is divided in two halves: the first outlines the general history of church music, and attempts to set right what Ouseley considers 'the wildest and most untenable theories [that] have been put forward on this subject';[29] the second deals specifically with the 'English school of cathedral music'.

The development of harmony appears to form the foundation of his argument and he begins his lecture by 'proving' that the Arabs, the Egyptians, and the Jews could not have known harmony.[30] The Arabs, he claims, are very resistant to change, and in 'those nations of the present day who have changed their manners and customs the least, we shall find in almost every case, that not only are they devoid of all acquaintance with harmony, but that harmonized music is absolutely painful to their ears.' He argues, as did Metcalfe, that the use of microtones in the scales of these countries rendered harmony impossible, and that the influence of the Egyptians on the Jews would make it unlikely that they would have

---

[27] Ouseley, *Church Congress Reports*, Leeds 1872, 333.

[28] Ouseley, 'Church Music', 161–70.

[29] Ouseley, 'Church Music', 161. He does not explicitly identify what these theories are, but implies that they refer to the origins of plainsong in the music of the Jewish temple. He addresses this question more extensively and explicitly in his 'Considerations on the History of Ecclesiastical Music of Western Europe', *Proceedings of the Musical Association* 2 (1875–6): 30–2, where he argues that plainchant *must* have descended from the Greeks, rather than the Hebrews (referred to in the Church Congress lecture as the 'Oriental Jews') as they are unarguably Eastern. Treitler examines the racial and historical implications of the claim for Greek origin of plainsong in 'The Politics of Reception', 283, 292–4. The Jewish origins of plainsong were widely accepted: see Bennett Zon, *The English Plainchant Revival*, Oxford Studies in British Church Music (Oxford: Oxford University Press, 1999), 217, 329.

[30] He appears to have based these ideas at least partly on the writings of Fétis, but he had also travelled very briefly to Tangiers in 1851 (F. W. Joyce, *The Life of Rev. Sire F. A. G. Ouseley, Bart.* (London: Methuen, 1896), 70).

used harmony either.[31] He therefore divides ancient music into two classes: the simple or Greek, from which he believes plainsong was derived, and the ornamental (Egyptian and Syrian), which he dismissed as 'so overcharged with ornaments and minute variations of pitch and pace, that distinct melody is well nigh lost'.[32]

The melodies of southern Europe, however, which he believed were the sources of early plainsong, were 'not accompanied by harmony of any kind, neither were they easily susceptible of such accompaniment.' The first examples of melodies that were suitable for harmonisation were found in the north, and have 'not the slightest analogy with the Gregorian or Ambrosian systems, nor yet with the music of the Greeks, or of the oriental nations.' Ouseley speculates that the earliest examples of harmony were found among the Scythians,[33] possibly before the 'Christian era', but he also believed that the Goths, the Scandinavians and the Vandals 'have left traces behind them of a peculiar and harmonized species of music', and that the history of harmony among the 'Celtic inhabitants of our own country' was equally ancient, citing the 'Leges Wallicæ' as evidence. Therefore Ouseley's analysis of the origins of harmony embraces the duality of origins implicit in Giraldus: the ancient Britons were particularly blessed with the gift of natural harmony, but it was also located more generally in the northern tribes of Europe. England is therefore granted its own indigenous musical ability, but in the context of a larger ethnic grouping.

Ouseley saw the seventh to fifteenth centuries as a period of struggle between musical styles, which was not finally resolved until around the time of the Reformation. Organum he considered 'an unsuccessful endeavour to join the harmony of the north to the melody of the south'; he attributes the lack of success to the inherently modal nature of the melodies and to the fact that it was the 'work of monks, skilled indeed in the Cantus Ecclesiasticus, but utterly incapable of appreciating the principles of harmony'. It was only when 'master minds arose in Italy, Germany, France, and England, who dared to write melodies of a sublime character, analogous in style to the old southern tunes, and yet so confined to major and minor modes as to admit freely of the co-operation of harmonic and contrapuntal resources' that composition became possible 'in the true sense of that term'.[34]

---

[31] Ouseley, 'Church Music', 161–2.

[32] Ouseley, 'Ecclesiastical Music', 32. This desire to locate the origins of chant in the Western, rather than Oriental, tradition can be found as recently as 1958 (Treitler, 'Gender and Other Dualities', 29–35).

[33] For a detailed and sophisticated analysis of historical perceptions of ethnicity in the development of national identity, and in particular for possible connections between the Scythians and the Celts, see Kidd, *British Identities*, 188–94.

[34] Ouseley, 'Church Music', 163–5.

Although Ouseley admits that his arguments are 'not altogether in accordance with commonly received opinions', they run parallel with Metcalfe's argument, and are broadly consistent with the general contours of the Galfridean myths and with later Protestant interpretations of the English Reformation.[35] The roots of the plainsong can be traced back to Greco-Roman classical antiquity in the same way that, via Brutus the Trojan, the origins of the British people could. Pre-Reformation music, under the sway of the monks, was unsatisfactory until the natural Northern harmony was wedded to sublime melody, and music was raised to 'its highest pinnacle of earthly perfection'.[36] And again, this marriage is most clearly seen in the harmonised chant of the litany and responses, considered by Ouseley to be the 'the most important and characteristic feature of our choral service' and particularly in Tallis's 'magnificent harmonies'[37]

Macfarren's discussion of Tallis's Preces and Responses in his extensive twelve-part survey of 'The Music of the English Church' published in the *Musical Times* in 1867, while more interested in the historical resonances of the plainchant upon which they are based than the northern origins of harmony, again sees Tallis's harmonies as embodying the complete history of the English church. Macfarren is not, in general, pro-Gregorian, arguing that their restoration is undesirable on artistic, historical and ecclesiological grounds.[38] He believes, however, that the plainsong to which the Preces, Responses and Litany are sung should be retained, due to its 'revered familiarity':

> The knowledge that these identical phrases of melody formed part of the religious rites in the Roman temples which stood upon the very ground now occupied by many of our cathedrals; the knowledge that these identical phrases, appropriated from heathen to Christian use, were sung in the early, if not the primitive Church, were sung when that Church was reformed, and are sung now when, musically speaking, it stands more than ever in need of reform; the knowledge that these identical phrases have, under the rule of classic Rome, of Christian Rome, and of English independence, ever formed the song of religion; this knowledge indeed invests them with associations which fail not to affect all hearers.[39]

---

35 It is of course possible that Metcalfe's article may have been influenced by Ouseley's views.

36 Ouseley, 'Church Music', 165.

37 Ouseley, 'Church Music', 176.

38 Macfarren, 'Music of the English Church', 71.

39 Macfarren, 'Music of the English Church', 69. An essentially similar passage inspired by the plainsong hymns *Urbs beata* and *Te lucis ante terminum* can be found in Charles William Pearce's 'On the Treatment of Ancient Ecclesiastical

The threads of a number of narratives of religious, ethnic and musical identity can therefore be traced through the few simple chords of Tallis's Responses. Harmonised settings of plainsong, which are uniquely English, and of which Tallis's was the prototype, were believed to have their roots in Classical antiquity, but with the addition of the spontaneous and indigenous harmony that was simultaneously distinctly British, and also broadly associated with the tribes of northern Europe. The simplicity of this harmony distinguished it from the artificial, clerical, pre-Reformation counterpoint, and the association of this natural harmony with the ancient Britons reinforced the links with the classical past and the early independent British church. This link was further strengthened by Tallis's association with the Welsh Tudor monarchs,[40] and with heroes of the Reformation, such as Archbishop Parker.[41]

As we have seen, the rhetoric dedicated to Tallis's Preces, Responses and Litany in the nineteenth century appears, to the twenty-first century observer, overblown and decidedly out of proportion to the actual musical interest of these simple phrases. Yet, when it is recognised that these few chords were believed to carry within them the entire history of the English Church, and to provide a link back to Classical antiquity, we can begin to understand their immense popularity.

❧ *The Golden Age*

The significance of the Responses was not, however, located only in the ancient origins of the plainsong and of the 'natural' harmony in which is was clothed. They

Melodies in Modern Instrumental Composition', *Proceedings of the Musical Association* 13 (1886–7): 70–1. Pearce describes standing 'on the grassy heights of old Sarum' contemplating the 'poetical associations' of the melodies, which range from the Briton in his 'rude war-car', through the 'imperial truncheons' of the Romans, the 'dragon standard' of Saxons and the 'magnificent Norman cathedral'.

[40] A similar point was made by John Blacking as recently as 1973 in his *How Musical is Man?* (Seattle: University of Washington Press, 1973), when he argues that 'the remarkable development of polyphonic music in England during the sixteenth century may have been stimulated [...] by the advent of Welsh monarchs [... as] Welsh popular music had been noted for its polyphonic technique since at least the twelfth century' (75, cited in Nixon, 'Giraldus Cambrensis', 285). For more on the Welsh/British associations of the Tudor monarchs, see Peter Roberts, 'Tudor Wales, National Identity and the British Inheritance', in Bradshaw and Roberts, *British Consciousness*, 15–16. The tendency to describe the music of Tallis and his contemporaries as 'Tudor Music' that became common in the early twentieth century also highlights the association.

[41] Dyce had also painted a fresco of the consecration of Archbishop Parker at Lambeth Palace (Pointon, *William Dyce*, 83).

were also valued as one of the first fruits of the Reformation, and of the Elizabethan golden age of English music.

Barnard, in the dedication to his 1641 *Church Musick*, argued that despite the good work of early Christian musicians such as 'Adrian the monk' and

> the good old Bishop *Putta* of Rochester [...] none that we know of, hath committed ought to score which would be much usefull, or pleasing to the eares of our age, till Queene *Elizabeth*. Her reigne brought forth a noble birth, as of all learned men, so of Famous Composers in Church-Musick.

The view that little music of value or interest survived from before the reign of Elizabeth was common until the twentieth century, and was shared by both Metcalfe and Ouseley, who implicitly attributed the inadequacies of pre-Reformation music to the oppressive hand of Roman Catholicism: the monks were 'utterly incapable of appreciating the principles of harmony'; their 'fleshless musical arithmetic' served to 'cramp sweet sounds in the stocks of fugue'.[42] As described above, the English Reformation was believed to have cleansed the English church of Popish corruption, and one of the most valued features of the music of the Reformation was its perceived independence from foreign influence.

The role of Elizabeth I in establishing England's unique and independent heritage of Protestant church music is clearly articulated by Edward Taylor in a lecture given in his capacity as Gresham Professor of Music in the early 1840s:

> The means which Elizabeth adopted and the course of education she prescribed and provided for perpetuating the existence of Church music in its most elevated form had now been tested, and they were found to be fully equal to their designed end. The great artists of the early period of her reign had [...] created a School of Church music which rivalled that of Rome: and England presented the solitary instance of a *Protestant* Church in which Music of the sublimest character was produced and performed by numerous, well-trained and amply endowed Choirs. In Protestant Germany, in Switzerland, in Holland, and among the Protestants of France, singing was reduced to *psalmody*. In England *alone* the art was free to expand its power, and bring its choicest tribute to the altar.[43]

The perceived independence of English music from foreign influence under Elizabeth is a recurring trope in later histories of Tallis and his contemporaries, and can

---

[42] Ouseley, 'Church Music', 165, and Metcalfe, 'Music of the Church of England', 159.

[43] Edward Taylor, 'Lecture V', MS MC 257/124, Norwich Record Office, fols. 1–2 (original emphases).

be seen in the histories of both Burney and Hawkins. Burney justifies his inclusion of two lengthy examples, which 'will require more plates than I can well afford to give', by arguing that

> if foreigners should ever deign to look into my book, it is my wish, for the honour of our nation, they should see, that long before the work and reputation of Palestrina had circulated throughout Europe, we had a Choral Music of our own, which [...] was equal to the best productions of that truly venerable master.[44]

Hawkins argues in a similar vein that Tallis

> may justly be said to be the father of the cathedral style; and though a like appellation is given by the Italians to Palestrina, it is much to be questioned, considering the time when Tallis flourished, whether he could derive the least advantage from the improvements of that great man. It is rather to be believed that Palestrina was co-ordinate with the musicians of England in sustaining the gravity of the ancient ecclesiastical style [...][45]

Jebb cites Burney's claim that 'Bird and Tallis are evidently of the school of an English composer anterior to Palestrina, Robert White', and continues: 'And with all the admiration which I feel for the reformer of the Roman music, I must avow a conviction that the early composers of England, Bird, Farrant and Gibbons, are at least his equals in every essential quality.'[46]

Unfortunately, this state of grace was short lived; the next 200 years of the history of English church music were widely seen as a period of decline and corruption due largely to the seductive lures of Continental Catholicism and theatrical secularism.[47] Within forty years of Elizabeth's death, the decline in church

---

[44] Burney, *General History*, 2:69.

[45] Hawkins, *General History*, 456.

[46] Jebb, *Choral Service*, 339. William Burge also argues that 'It is a mistake [...] to suppose that the school of these great composers [Tye, Tallis, etc] was formed upon the compositions of Palestrina': this appears to a paraphrase of Jebb (*Choral Service*, xliv). Once again, however, S. S. Wesley expressed the contrary view, arguing that Tallis is inferior not only to Palestrina but even to Josquin, who, as he was born earlier, was expected to be less advanced (Wesley, *Few Words*, 45–6).

[47] Nicholas Temperley discusses the widespread belief that English music suffered a 'dark age' in his 'Xenophilia in British Musical History', *Nineteenth-Century British Music Studies*, ed. Bennett Zon, vol. 1 (Aldershot: Ashgate, 1999), 3–19. He argues, however, that 'nobody' dated the beginning of this dark age to before the death of Purcell in 1695, but he focuses on twentieth-century perceptions, and cites no sources prior to 1886.

music was etched, at least according to Macfarren, in the very notes of the Responses themselves.[48] He claims that the deviations from the plainsong in Barnard's version of the Litany and Responses indicate either ignorance or indifference, and lays the blame at the foot of the Stuart kings, claiming that they prove 'that the Plain Song had lost its pre-eminent position as the Church Part, before the Stuart dynasty had been forty years upon the English throne.' Barnard, he argues, is not to be held fully responsible for his lack of respect for, or knowledge of, the chant, but is merely 'representative of the rapid corruption which [...] had crept into one of the most important elements in her Service' under Charles I.[49]

Edward Taylor makes explicit the relationship between the failures of the Stuarts and their openness to foreign influence: Charles II's 'prepossessions were not merely foreign, but, unfortunately for literature as well as for Art in general – French'.[50] He expands upon this argument in the significantly titled *The English Cathedral Service, Its Glory, – Its Decline, and its Designed Extinction*:

> The accession of the Stuart family operated most injuriously upon the interests of music generally in England. The Tudors, themselves all musically educated by the best English masters, fostered and patronized the musical talent of their subjects: with what effect has been seen. James did worse than nothing for Cathedral music. [...] Henry and William Lawes, Locke, Child and Rogers are the only names of any note that occur in the reign of Charles I., who, with the predilection for French musicians which other members of his family displayed, appointed a very sorry composer named Laniere (several of whose productions are, unfortunately for his reputation preserved) to be the master of his music.[51]

While Taylor admits the adverse effect of the Civil Wars upon the state of church music, he argues that 'Everything that Charles [II] could do in order to lower and vulgarize the character of Cathedral music, he did', and supports this claim by noting that Charles 'began by forbidding the performance in the Chapel Royal of all the best compositions for the church, – from Tallis to Gibbons, all were proscribed.'[52]

---

[48] Macfarren appears to have accepted Rimbault's view of the respective merits of the four and five-part versions; their joint editorship of the *Musical Journal* indicates a personal relationship.

[49] Macfarren, 'Music of the English Church', 70.

[50] Taylor, MC 257/124, fol. 4.

[51] Taylor, *English Cathedral Service*, 16–17. This second half of this passage can also be found in Taylor's review of the *Choral Service*, 99.

[52] Taylor, *English Cathedral Service*, 18.

Not only was English church music seen as vulnerable to foreign corruption, but church music in general was believed, at least by the conservative musicians who valued and performed Tallis's music, to have been in a state of decline since the sixteenth century. William Hayes argued that 'the further we look back, the more excellent the Composition will be found, and the most properly adapted to the sacred Purposes of Devotion.'[53] The anonymous writer of the 1849 *Practical Remarks on the Reformation of Cathedral Music* expressed a similar view:

> The point is one of fact, and simply this, that music, which for the most part happens to have been composed previously to a certain date, is for our purpose of the best kind; grave, but cheerful, dignified, solemn, firm, masculine; calculated, not to raise a momentary heat of enthusiasm, but to foster a calm and earnest and permanent devotion.[54]

The belief that music, particularly music for the church, was in a state of decline is also clearly articulated by William Crotch in Chapter 4 of his *Substance of Several Courses of Lectures*, entitled 'The Rise, Progress, and Decline of the Art'.[55] These lectures were intended to provide a method whereby taste could be developed, and 'the principles of just criticism' acquired.[56] Central to this process was the identification of three styles of music: the sublime, the beautiful and the ornamental. The sublime is rated the most highly of the three, 'as requiring the most mind in the person gratified, and in the author of the gratification';[57] Crotch cited Tallis's Litany as 'a perfect specimen of pure sublimity'.[58] Crotch considered a movement

---

53 Hayes, *Remarks*, 45. The limit to the backwards progression set by the Reformation is implied, but not stated.

54 *Practical Remarks on the Reformation of Cathedral Music* (London: John Bohn, 1849), 45. The use of overtly gendered language is a common feature of these discussions, with the older music frequently characterised as pure and manly, while modern music is corrupt and effeminate. Treitler has identified both the frequent appearance of such terms in narratives of corruption, and the correlation between gender and 'dualities of ethnicity, nationality, or race' ('Gender and Other Dualities', 28 and 23).

55 Crotch, *Lectures*, 66–78.

56 Crotch, *Lectures*, 14. Crotch's aesthetic theories have been examined by a number of recent writers, including William Gatens (*Victorian Cathedral Music*, 65–9); Howard Irving (*Ancients and Moderns*, esp. 59–65); Bennett Zon, 'History, Historicism, and the Sublime Analogy', in Zon, *Nineteenth-Century British Music Studies 1*, 23–9; Grant Olwage ('Music and Masculinity', 27–32); and Adelmann, *Cambridge Ecclesiologists*, 40–3.

57 Crotch, *Lectures*, 82.

58 Crotch, *Lectures*, 39.

in any art from the sublime style toward the ornamental to be a 'sure indication of [...] decline and decay' and he saw just such a movement in the history of church music:[59]

> As long as the pure sublime style, – the style peculiarly suited to the church service, – was cherished, which was only to about the middle of the seventeenth century, we consider ecclesiastical style to be in a state worthy of study and imitation, – in a state of perfection. But it has been gradually, though not imperceptibly, losing its character of sublimity ever since. [...] Church music is therefore on the decline.[60]

Jebb argued that the only cure for this disease was the study of the music of the early masters:

> The study of Tallis, as a correct, grave, and religious harmonist, is essential towards any real progress in the knowledge of Sacred Music. And nothing has tended more to debase the art amongst us, than the neglect of such studies, and the substitution of the showy, but thin and imperfect harmonies, of modern composers, and the exaggerated and effeminate melodies, that rather express the morbid sentiment of religious excitement, than the deep-seated energy of a calm but influential devotion of the understanding and of the heart.[61]

Such narratives of purity and decay were not restricted to English music, or English discussions of music. E. T. A. Hoffmann, for example, argued in 1814 that while composers before Palestrina were 'obsessed with harmonic affectations [...] with Palestrina began what is indisputably the most glorious period in church music (and hence in music in general)'.[62] This glorious period was, however,

---

[59] Crotch, *Lectures*, 66. It must be borne in mind that this represents a particularly conservative view: Crotch states that one of the goals of his publication is to 'overturn the absurd and mischievous opinion held by many writers and the generality of professors of the art, that music is continually improving from every invention, innovation, and addition, that her successive cultivators choose [...] to make' (p. 15).

[60] Crotch, *Lectures*, 73. E. H. Gombrich points out, however, that once perfection has been attained 'the only alternatives are imitation or decline' (*The Ideas of Progress and their Impact on Art* (New York: Cooper Union School of Art and Architecture, 1971), 10, 46).

[61] Jebb, *Lectures on the Cathedral Service*, 137, reproduced as 'Value of Tallis's Harmonies', *Parish Choir* 1 (1846): 4.

[62] Hoffmann, 'Old and New Church Music', *E. T. A. Hoffmann's Musical Writings: Kreisleriana, The Poet and the Composer, Music Criticism*, ed. David Charlton, trans. Martyn Clarke (Cambridge: Cambridge University Press, 1989), 356–7.

followed by a period of decline during which 'the old authenticity and strength gradually degenerated into the present affectation and sickliness.'[63] Jebb suggests that 'the gravity of the ancient ecclesiastical style' had actually 'degenerated on the Continent much more than in England'.[64]

While this narrative of a golden age followed by an inevitable decline is not unique to England, the stylistic differences between pre- and post-Reformation music in England were particularly sharp, and the English Reformation formed a dramatic point of rupture that could not easily be circumvented. In these constructions of the history of English music there was no room for the appreciation of pre-Reformation music, even by much loved composers such as Tallis, except as academic curiosities. This antipathy to pre-Reformation music can be seen in the negative reviews of *Spem in alium*, which dismissed it as representative of the 'barbarous age' that preceded the Reformation (although it is now generally believed to date from the reign of Elizabeth). The frequent mechanical metaphors used in these reviews (the rusty, creaking machine, the 'table made of a million pieces of wood') reflect the widely held perceptions of music of this earlier period as 'grim and ecclesiastical' science.[65]

Towards the end of the nineteenth century, however, as we saw in Chapter 2, a group of predominantly Roman Catholic musicians began to tell new stories about the history of English music. In his 1899 article 'Tallys, Byrde and, and Some Popular Fictions' Terry explicitly challenges the idealisation of the Elizabethan golden age, arguing that the Reformation actually marked the end, rather than the beginning, of 'the English school of Church music'.[66] Similarly, the title 'Father of English Church Music', which not only claimed Tallis as an Anglican but effectively dismissed all sacred music composed before the Reformation, was challenged; Tallis was reconfigured instead 'as one of the last of the Catholic composers'.[67]

---

[63] Hoffmann, 'Old and New Church Music', 361. The nineteenth-century German reception of Palestrina is discussed by James Garratt in 'Mendelssohn's Babel: Romanticism and the Poetics of Translation', *Music & Letters* 80 (1999): 23–49 and at greater length in *Palestrina and the German Romantic Imagination: Interpreting Historisicm in Nineteenth-Century Music* (Cambridge: Cambridge University Press, 2002), 42–7. Garratt has noted that Palestrina reception 'privileged' homophony over polyphony in a way analogous to the nineteenth-century English preference for Tallis's homophonic music that I have described.

[64] Jebb, *Choral Service*, 339.

[65] *Daily Telegraph*, 19 May 1879. Rev. H. R. Haweis paints a particularly evocative picture of the union of science with 'wild and beautiful' art, although he argues that the results of this 'perfect marriage' were first seen in the music of Carissimi (*Music and Morals*, 16th ed. (London: W. H. Allen, 1892), 130–1).

[66] Terry, 'Tallys, Byrde', 75.

[67] Terry, *Catholic Church Music*, 187.

The superficially similar title that Anderton bestows upon Gibbons – 'Father of pure Anglican Music' – allows the music of Tallis (and Byrd) to be constructed as other than purely Anglican, and opens up the possibility of English church music that pre-dates the Reformation.

In these new stories the simplicity of the service music composed for the English liturgy was constructed not as purity, but as poverty. The restrictive metaphors that Metcalfe and others had used to describe pre-Reformation music were now applied to the music of the new English liturgy: Tallis is described as 'fettered' and 'hampered' by the new regulations. Similarly, it is no longer the simple harmony of the Responses that is described as natural, but the polyphony of the *Cantiones sacrae*.[68] The language of seduction used by Whittaker in his discussion of *Spem in alium* – he speaks of his 'irresistible desire' to 'penetrate its mysteries' – stands in stark contrast to the earlier references to puzzles and machines.

New ways were sought to provide continuity between the pre- and post-Reformation periods: one of the most frequent was the suggestion that pieces previously believed to have been composed for the English liturgy were arrangements of earlier Latin works. Rockstro, for example, argued that the Versicles were, 'in all probability, set originally to the old Latin words'.[69] From 1899 Terry took this argument a step further, claiming:

> all (I say advisedly *all*) the best of this early music – whether it has been sung and admired in Anglican cathedrals, as it has been for three hundred years, or buried in libraries and museums – is Catholic in spirit, and Catholic in origin; written by Catholics for the services of the Catholic Church. It is our heritage – our birthright; and the fact that our claims to it have lain so long in abeyance does not make it any the less ours, or its revival any less a duty which we owe to the memory of our Catholic forefathers.[70]

Terry's arguments were widely accepted in the early years of the twentieth century: Bumpus, for example, although not himself a Catholic believed that 'with a few exceptions, all the anthems by Tallis printed with English words are adaptations from his Latin pieces'. He claims that *Hear the voice and prayer* and *If ye love me* are based upon the Latin originals *Christe, qui lux es et dies* and *Caro mea vera est cibus*.[71]

---

[68] Davey, *English Music*, 147, and Bumpus, *Cathedral Music*, 45–6.

[69] Rockstro, 'Versicle', 257.

[70] Terry, *Our Church Music* (London: Catholic Truth Society, 1901), 16, also *Catholic Church Music*, 199. Terry cites Davey's *English Music*, 126–7, as the source of his arguments.

[71] Bumpus, *Cathedral Music*, 46. Myles Birket Foster, in his *Anthems and Anthem Composers* (London: Novello, 1901), 20, claimed that *Caro mea vera est cibus* had

By challenging the prevailing belief that the greatest English choral music post-dated the Reformation, and indeed arguing that the best known Anglican music of the Elizabethan golden age was indebted to earlier Latin models, Terry and his Catholic colleagues opened up pre-Reformation choral music for reassessment and reclamation in a way that had not been possible under the older constructions of the history of English music and the English church.

The narratives constructed by Metcalfe, Ouseley and Macfarren in the 1860s were in many ways just a more complex version of the view that had been dominant since at least 1641 that English choral music had reached its apogee in the late sixteenth century (the length and complexity of these arguments hints, however, that this attitude may have been in need of defence). Not only did they extol the virtues of early Anglican music, but they also effectively closed off the possibility of reviving music from earlier periods. The music-historical narratives of Terry *et al*, on the other hand, introduced a new set of cultural values that had a profound effect upon musical life in the early twentieth century, and led to the rediscovery of the musical riches of pre-Reformation polyphony. Both of these 'discourses of myth' were in their own ways flawed, but they played a powerful role in shaping responses to early English sacred music.

been published, although I have not been able to locate this publication. His debt to Bumpus as a source of much of his information is clearly acknowledged. Terry also published a Latin version of *If Ye Love Me*, but to the text 'Bone Pastor' in about 1905 in his series of Downside Motets. The sectarian implications of this argument are made explicit in the correspondence in *The Times* between Royle Shore and Terry about whether Orlando Gibbons's *Hosanna to the son of David* was originally composed in English or Latin ('Church Music', *The Times* 26 Mar 1910, 9; S. Royle Shore, 'Orlando Gibbons's "Hosanna"', *The Times*, 29 Mar 1910, 9, and R. R. Terry, 'Orlando Gibbons's "Hosanna"', *The Times*, 30 Mar 1910, 10).

Conclusion

ONLY a fraction of Tallis's compositional output was discussed, published or performed in the nineteenth century, and that fraction cannot, at least by current criteria of judgement, be considered his best; of this fraction only *If ye love me* can be said to have 'stood the test of time'.[1] The setting of *All people that on earth* attributed to him at that time is competent but uninspiring; the *Veni Creator* is unworthy of even such faint praise. The Responses are inherently slight, and the four-part arrangements, particularly as advocated by Rimbault, reduce their interest still further; the Dorian Service is today infrequently performed. The one work that would now be judged to be of significant musical interest, *Spem in alium*, was, in the nineteenth century, met with critical incomprehension.

The figure of Tallis, however, enjoyed a prominence that extended far beyond this limited engagement with his music, and a detailed examination of the nineteenth-century reception of his music highlights the significant changes in attitudes towards the music of the past that took place during the nineteenth century, and particularly in its closing decades.

These changes were comprehensive and extended well beyond a simple re-evaluation of the Latin polyphony at the expense of the English homophony. Perceptions of the role of the composer in the creative process, the nature of the engagement with the biography of the composer, and of the function and meaning of the music were all subject to fundamental change. The shifting fortunes of the Responses and *Spem in alium* serve to illustrate these changes. The Responses were valued in the nineteenth century as the first fruits of the English Reformation, setting the standard for the English liturgy. They were perceived as a type of crystallisation in music of the history of the English Church and, by extension, of the English people. Tallis played an essential role in this process, as a conduit of the divine will (or possibly the will of the 'Pious Reformers of our Church'), but the Responses were not generally seen as an expression of Tallis's inner life. In the early years of the twentieth century, however, while interest in the Responses declined, *Spem in alium* and the Lamentations began to be valued in exactly these terms; by the 1920s *Spem in alium* was acknowledged as a 'work of genius'. This status was, however, largely achieved without stripping the music of its religious function.

---

[1] Peter Phillips, for example, judges it a 'masterpiece', although even this assessment takes place in the context of an argument that such music should not be assessed (and by implication, often is) in terms of 'imperfection' due to 'clerical intervention' (*English Sacred Music*, xiii).

While Whittaker's performance of the Song of Forty Parts took place in the secular context of a concert, Collins's discussion reads an overtly religious meaning into the work that had been missing from earlier responses.[2] Likewise Terry's advocacy of the music of both Tallis and Byrd is directed specifically at the church musician: he suggests, for example, that 'if it is yet too early to expect appreciation of Tallis from Catholic choirmasters', 'others' – presumably Anglicans – might like to adapt some of the Latin music to English texts.[3]

Indeed the importance of Roman Catholicism as the driving force behind the late nineteenth-century interest in Tallis's music – and in pre-Reformation polyphony in general – is one of the most significant findings of this study. The contribution of R. R. Terry to the revival of early English polyphony has been acknowledged,[4] and there is no doubt that he was a major influence on the thinking of later Catholic writers, and, indeed, upon general perceptions of the history of early English music. But the extent to which his activities were a direct result of his Catholicism, and of the changing status of English Catholicism generally, has been largely overlooked.[5] The relationship between Catholicism and the revival of early English polyphony is considerably more complex than has generally been assumed.

Furthermore, the careful examination of the reception of Tallis's music over an extended period suggests that the beginnings of the new interest in sixteenth-century English polyphony can be traced back to the early 1880s, nearly twenty years before Terry began to work in the area. Although the antiquarian revival of the 1840s has been recognised, the shift in attitude around 1880 remains largely unexplored.[6] Timothy Day, for example, argues that, as early polyphony was little known in the nineteenth century, and as Pope Pius x's *Motu proprio* on church music was not issued until 1903, 'it was by no means obvious' that Terry would

---

[2] Collins's interpretation of the Latin text restores a religious function that had been absent in the English translation for centuries. Indeed, many of the reviews of the nineteenth-century performances failed even to mention whether the Latin or English words had been sung.

[3] Terry, 'Some Unpublished Tallis', 91.

[4] See, for example, Timothy Day, 'Sir Richard Terry', Roche, '"Great Learning, Fine Scholarship, Impeccable Taste" and Andrews, *Westminster Retrospect*.

[5] Stradling and Hughes, for example, suggest that the discovery that Tallis and Byrd were 'crypto-Catholics' was made in the late twentieth century, and somehow undermines the role of Tudor models in the construction of a 'national music' (*English Musical Renaissance*, 211).

[6] Stradling and Hughes claim that the revival of Tudor music was a direct result of the publication of Grove's *Dictionary* (*English Musical Renaissance*, 76), but like many other assertions in this book, little evidence is provided in support of this argument. This is a subject deserving of much more detailed examination.

perform this type of music at Downside Abbey in the late 1890s. Day then notes that Terry performed Byrd's three Masses and Tye's 'Euge bone' Mass at Westminster Cathedral from 1901. It is true that Terry was largely responsible for reviving these works in performance – although the Byrd four-part Mass had been performed a decade earlier under Thomas Wingham at the Brompton Oratory[7] – but editions of Tye's Mass and of Byrd's Mass for Four Voices had been published by Godfrey Arkwright in 1896 and by William Barclay Squire and W. S. Rockstro in 1890 respectively, indicating an interest in this music that significantly pre-dates Terry.[8] While the scope of Terry's contribution to the revival of early music may have been unprecedented, his interest in it was not. And again, while Day acknowledges that Terry's Catholic faith was the 'focal point round which his aesthetic, moral and spiritual pre-occupations' revolved, he fails to identify the extent to which the early polyphony revived by Terry at Westminster was perceived as exclusively Catholic.[9] It is, I believe, no coincidence that William Rockstro, one of the first voices to question the dominant view of Tallis as the Anglican composer of the Dorian Service, had also recently converted to Roman Catholicism.

The claim that Roman Catholicism became a driving force behind the revival of early English polyphony towards the end of the nineteenth century raises several other questions worthy of further study. If, as I suggest in the previous chapter, the prevailing Victorian Protestantism had effectively precluded the revival of pre-Reformation polyphony, why is this effect not observed in similar revivals in other arts, most notably architecture? The 'Middle Pointed' or 'Decorated' style, dating from between 1260 and 1360, was considered the epitome of Christian architecture by Catholics and Anglicans alike. Although Augustus Welby Pugin, one of the driving forces behind Gothic Revival architecture, converted to Catholicism largely as a result of his antiquarian studies,[10] this idealisation of fourteenth-century architecture was also embraced by Anglican bodies such as the Cambridge Ecclesiologists. Adelmann has noted that the Ecclesiologists justified the inconsistency of their advocacy of fourteenth-century architecture and sixteenth-century music by arguing that 'every art form had an infancy, maturity, and

7 'Byrd's Mass at the Brompton Oratory', *Musical Times* 32 (1891): 26.

8 Christopher Tye, *Mass to Six Voices 'Euge bone'*, ed. G. E. P. Arkwright, Old English Edition 10 (London: Joseph Williams, 1893); Gulielmo Byrd, *Missa ad quatuor voces inaequales*, ed. Gulielmus Smith Rockstro and Gulielmus Barclay Squire (London: Novello, 1890).

9 Day, 'Sir Richard Terry', 300–1.

10 B. Ferrey, *Recollections of A. N. Welby Pugin and his Father Augustus Pugin* (London, 1861), 90, cited in S. Lang, 'The Principles of the Gothic Revival in England', *Journal of the Society of Architectural Historians* 25 (1966): 262.

degeneracy',[11] but I believe that the sectarian subtexts of these debates warrant further examination. A thorough investigation of the contribution of Roman Catholicism to the revival of early English polyphony towards the end of the nineteenth century would also need to examine the disparity between these musical and architectural golden ages, and the reasons why the renewal of interest in 'medieval' music took place so much later than similar movements in the other arts.

Although they must, for the moment, remain unanswered, these questions are a direct result of the methodology of this study. The decision to concentrate upon a single composer has its limitations: in particular the not inconsiderable differences in the reception of Tallis and his contemporaries, particularly Byrd and Gibbons, remain unexplored,[12] and this study is no substitute for a general history of early music in nineteenth-century Britain. But the narrow focus has allowed the reception of individual works, and particularly little-known works, works that have failed the 'test of time', to be examined in much greater depth than would have been possible in a more general study. By examining this music over an extended period and across a broad range of performing contexts, including church services, festivals, lectures, concerts and private performances by antiquarian societies, and by taking it seriously in both aesthetic and social terms, substantial differences in reception, even amongst the works of this single composer, have been identified. By the beginning of the twentieth century Tallis's English service music was seen as the embodiment of established Anglicanism, while the revival of his Latin polyphony was not just a departure from but a direct challenge to that tradition. An understanding of these differences, and a recognition that there is no single monolithic meaning that can be assigned to early choral music, is essential to a fuller understanding of the widely accepted, yet largely unexplored, role of 'Tudor' music in the so-called English Musical Renaissance of the late nineteenth and early twentieth centuries. To take just one example: in 1983 Richard Turbet wondered why so many predominantly early twentieth-century composers, such as Vaughan Williams, Darke and Howells, composed works on themes from the music of Tallis rather than Byrd.[13] Without wishing to challenge the validity of Turbet's conclusions, which are based upon his critical assessment of the composers' relative

---

[11] Adelmann, *Cambridge Ecclesiologists*, 2, 26–7, 39. This disjunction between the preferred models for music and architecture was not unrecognised at the time: Adelmann cites a complicated scheme by the Rev. Samuel Stephenson Greatheed to draw parallels between the different styles of early music and gothic architecture. (pp. 133–5).

[12] A comparison of the reception of Tallis and Byrd can be found in Cole, 'Who is the Father?'

[13] Richard Turbet, 'Friends of Cathedral Music: Tallis and Byrd', *Musical Opinion* 106 (1983): 301.

strengths, an understanding of the cultural resonances of Tallis's music in the early twentieth century is at the very least pertinent to such questions.

The social locatedness of all music has been increasingly recognised over the last twenty-five years. Richard Taruskin's review of the Cambridge *Histories* of nineteenth and twentieth-century music, 'Speed Bumps', in which he distinguishes 'Romantic' musicology, devoted to the ideal of the autonomous work of art, and the 'Realist', which views music as an integral part of the 'reality of worldly activities', is just one recent and particularly trenchant example.[14] Taruskin's 'Realist' position maintains that no music can be fully understood in isolation from the social context in which it was produced or performed, and this study has shown that this is particularly true of the understanding of the music of Tallis and his contemporaries in the nineteenth century. At this time the principle of aesthetic autonomy was less firmly entrenched, particularly with respect to early music, and the church was still a substantial cultural force. Recognition of the distinct religious and cultural meanings carried by this music is essential to understanding the role of early choral music in musical life in the nineteenth and early twentieth centuries.

Harry Haskell's history of the early music movement, *The Early Music Revival*,[15] begins with Mendelssohn's revival of the St Matthew Passion in 1829, when music that was written for the church was, in Goehr's words, taken 'away from the church and put into the concert hall'. It is, I think, no coincidence that this event is chosen by Haskell as the beginning of his story. The early music movement can be seen as a campaign to bring an increasingly wide range of music under the concept of the autonomous musical work,[16] and the secularisation and aestheticisation of early sacred music are a direct consequence of this. This study suggests, however, that these two processes are not necessarily identical. At least some of the music of Tallis appears to have been seen in aesthetic terms as works of art despite a continued religious function. It is only well into the twentieth century that the music of Tallis was 'stripped' of its religious meanings: prior to this, the reception of this music, even in secular contexts, can only be fully understood when its religious meanings are taken into account. And by extension, a full understanding of the revival of this music can only be achieved when the religious function is considered alongside the aesthetic function, and when we leave aside our desire for the music of Tallis and his contemporaries to be 'just very good music'.

---

[14] Richard Taruskin, 'Speed Bumps', *19th Century Music* 29 (2005): 189.

[15] Harry Haskell, *The Early Music Revival* (New York: Thames & Hudson, 1988).

[16] See, for example, Goehr, *Imaginary Museum*, 245–9.

Bibliography

☙ *Published books and articles*

Adelmann, Dale. *The Contribution of Cambridge Ecclesiologists to the Revival of Anglican Choral Worship, 1839-62*. Aldershot: Ashgate, 1997.

Anderton, H. Orsmond. 'Thomas Tallys'. *Musical Opinion* 37 (1914): 282–3. Reproduced in *Early English Music*, 104–10. London: Musical Opinion, 1920.

Andrews, Hilda. *Catalogue of the King's Music Library, Part 2: The Miscellaneous Manuscripts*. London: British Museum, 1929.

———. *Westminster Retrospect*. London: Geoffrey Cumberlege; Oxford University Press, 1948.

Anglo, Sydney. 'The *British History* in Early Tudor Propaganda'. *Bulletin of the John Rylands Library* 44 (1961): 17–48.

Aplin, John. 'The Origins of John Day's "Certaine Notes"'. *Music & Letters* 62 (1981): 295–9.

Arkwright, G. E. P. *Catalogue of Music in the Library of Christ Church Oxford, Part 1: Works of Ascertained Authorship*. 1915. [Wakefield, Yorkshire]: S.R. Publishers, 1971.

Ashbee, Andrew, and John Harley, trans. and ed. *The Cheque Books of the Chapel Royal: With Additional Material from the Manuscripts of William Lovegrove and Marmaduke Alford*. 2 vols. Aldershot: Ashgate, 2000.

Aspden, Suzanne. ' "Fam'd Handel Breathing, tho' Tranformed to Stone": The Composer as Monument'. *Journal of the American Musicological Society* 55 (2002): 39–90.

Avison, Charles. *An Essay on Musical Expression*. London, 1752.

B[urge], W[illiam]. *On the Choral Service of the Anglo-Catholic Church*. London: George Bell, 1844.

Baptie, David. *A Handbook of Musical Biography (1883)*. Intro. Bernarr Rainbow. Classic Texts in Music Education 17. Clarabricken: Boethius Press, [1986].

Barczewski, Stephanie L. *Myth and National Identity in Nineteenth-Century Britain: The Legends of King Arthur and Robin Hood*. Oxford: Oxford University Press, 2000.

Barrett, Philip. 'English Cathedral Choirs in the Nineteenth Century'. *Journal of Ecclesiastical History* 25 (1974): 15–37.

———. 'The Tractarians and Church Music'. *Musical Times* 113 (1972): 301–2, 398–9.

Bashford, Christina. 'Learning to Listen: Audiences for Chamber Music in early-Victorian London'. *Journal of Victorian Culture* 4 (1999): 21–55.

Bayley, Stephen. *The Albert Memorial: The Monument in its Social and Architectural Context*. London: Scolar Press, 1981.

Bennett, John. 'A Tallis Patron?' *Royal Musical Association Research Chronicle* 21 (1988): 41–4.

[Bennett, Joseph]. *A Short History of Cheap Music*. London: Novello, Ewer & Co, 1887.

Blacking, John. *How Musical is Man?* Seattle: University of Washington Press, 1973.

Bradshaw, Brendan, and Peter Roberts, eds. *British Consciousness and Identity: The Making of Britain, 1533–1701*. Cambridge: Cambridge University Press, 1998.

Brett, Philip. 'Facing the Music'. *Early Music* 10 (1982): 347–50.

Bumpus, John S. *A History of English Cathedral Music*. 2 vols. London: T. Werner Laurie, 1908.

Burkholder, J. Peter. 'Museum Pieces: The Historicist Mainstream in Music of the Last Hundred Years'. *Journal of Musicology* 2 (1983): 115–34.

Burney, Charles. *A General History of Music: From the Earliest Ages to the Present Period (1776–89)*. Ed. Frank Mercer. 2 vols. London, 1935. Repr. New York: Dover, 1957.

Butler, Charles. *The Principles of Musik (1636)*. Amsterdam: Da Capo, 1970.

A Catalogue of Books … Now on Sale at Robert Triphook's, 37, St James's Street, London. London, 1815–17.

Catalogue of Books, Pictures, Prints, etc., Presented by Mrs Laetitia Hollier to, and also of Books and Music in, the Library of Gresham College London. London, 1872.

A Catalogue of an Extensive and Valuable Collection of Music Books … Part of which were the Property of the Late Mr G. E. Williams Organist of Westminster Abbey … London, 1820.

Catalogue of Music and Musical Literature. No. 9. London: William Reeves, 1882.

Catalogue of Music and Musical Literature Contained in the Library of St Martin's Hall. London: Parker, 1850.

Catalogue of Printed Books and Manuscripts Deposited in Guildhall Library. London: Corporation of London, 1965.

Catalogue of the Important Musical Collections Formed by the Late Thomas Oliphant, Esq. … London, 1873.

Catalogue of the Music Library of Charles Burney (1814). Intro. A. Hyatt King. Amsterdam: Frits Knuf, 1973.

Catalogue of the Music Library of Edward Francis Rimbault sold at London, 31 July – 7 August 1877, with the Library of Dr. Rainbeau. Intro. A. Hyatt King. Amsterdam: Frits Knuf, 1975.

A Catalogue of the Very Valuable and Celebrated Library of Music Books, Late the Property of James Bartleman, Esq. London, 1822.

Church Music Society. *Forty Years of Cathedral Music, 1898–1938.* London: SPCK, 1940.

Clifford, James. *The Divine Services and Anthems usually sung in His Majesties Chappell, and in all Cathedrals and Collegiate Choires in England and Ireland.* London, 1663, 1664.

Cole, Suzanne. 'Who is the Father?' Changing perceptions of Tallis and Byrd in Late Nineteenth-Century England', *Music & Letters* (forthcoming).

Colley, Linda. 'Britishness and Otherness: An Argument'. *Journal of British Studies* 31 (1992): 309–29.

Collins, H. B. 'Thomas Tallis'. *Music & Letters* 10 (1929): 152–66.

Collinson, Patrick. 'A Chosen People?: The English Church and the Reformation'. *History Today* 36 (1986): 14–20.

Cook, Nicholas, and Mark Everist, eds. *Rethinking Music.* Oxford: Oxford University Press, 1999.

Cooper, Victoria Lee. *The House of Novello: Practice and Policy of a Victorian Music Publisher, 1829–1866.* Aldershot: Ashgate, 2003.

Coover, James. B. 'William Reeves, Booksellers/Publishers, 1825–'. In *Music Publishing and Collecting: Essays in Honor of Donald W. Krummel*, edited by David Hunter, 39–67. Urbana-Champaigne: Graduate School of Library and Information Science, University of Illinois, 1994.

Craufurd, J. G. 'The Madrigal Society'. *Proceedings of the Royal Musical Association* 82 (1955–6): 34–46.

Crosby, Brian. 'A 17th-Century Durham Inventory'. *Musical Times* 119 (1978): 167–70.

———. *A Catalogue of Durham Cathedral Music Manuscripts.* Oxford: Oxford University Press, 1986.

———. 'A Service Sheet from June 1680'. *Musical Times* 121 (1980): 399–401.

Crotch, William. *Substance of Several Courses of Lectures on Music (1831).* Intro. Bernarr Rainbow. Classic Texts in Music Education 16. Clarabricken: Boethius Press, 1986.

C[rowdy], J[ohn]. 'On the Choral Treatment of the Litany'. *Musical Standard* 5 (1866): 144–5.

Cummings, William H. 'Tallis – Waltham Abbey'. *Musical Times* 17 (1876): 649–50.

———. 'Tallis and Waltham Abbey', *Musical Times* 54 (1913): 789–91.

Dahlhaus, Carl. *Esthetics of Music.* Trans. William H. Austin. Cambridge: Cambridge University Press, 1982.

———. *Foundations of Music History.* Trans. J. B. Robinson. Cambridge: Cambridge University Press, 1983.

———. *The Idea of Absolute Music.* Trans. Roger Lustig. Chicago: University of Chicago Press, 1989.

———. *Nineteenth-Century Music*. Trans. J. Bradford Robinson. Berkeley: University of California Press, 1989.

Daniel, Ralph T., and Peter le Huray. *The Sources of English Church Music, 1549–1660*. Early English Church Music Sup. Vols. 1/1 and 1/2. London: Stainer & Bell, 1972.

Darnton, Robert. *The Great Cat Massacre and Other Episodes in French Cultural History*. New York: Basic Books, 1984.

Davey, Henry. *History of English Music*. London: J. Curwen & Sons, 1895.

Dawson, William. 'Church Music in Kent'. *Parish Choir* 1 (1847): 123–4.

Day, Thomas C. 'A Renaissance Revival in Eighteenth-Century England'. *Music Quarterly* 57 (1971): 575–92.

———. 'Old Music in England, 1790–1820'. *Revue belge de musicologie* 26–7 (1972–3): 27–37.

Day, Timothy. 'Sir Richard Terry and 16th-Century Polyphony'. *Early Music* 22 (1994): 297–307.

de Montmorency, James. *A Brief History of the Church of St Alfege*. London: Charles North, 1910.

Dearnley, Christopher. *English Church Music, 1650–1750, in Royal Chapel, Cathedral and Parish Church*. London: Barrie & Jenkins, 1970.

Dibble, Jeremy. 'Grove's Musical Dictionary: A National Document'. In *Musical Constructions of Nationalism*, edited by Harry White and Michael Murphy, 33–50. Cork: Cork University Press, 2001.

Doe, Paul. *Tallis*. 1968. 2nd ed. London: Oxford University Press, 1976.

———. 'Tallis's "Spem in alium" and the Elizabethan Respond-motet'. *Music & Letters* 51 (1970): 1–14.

'Dotted Crotchet'. 'The Abbey Church of Waltham Holy Cross'. *Musical Times* 47 (1906): 594–602.

Druitt, Robert. *A Popular Tract on Church Music with Remarks on its Moral and Political Importance and a Practical Scheme for its Reformation*. London: Francis & John Rivington, 1845.

Duncan, J. M. 'The Preces, Responses and Litany of the English Church: A By-Way of Liturgical History'. *Musical Times* 61 (1920): 551–52, 625–7, 692–4.

Ellinwood, Leonard. 'Tallis' Tunes and Tudor Psalmody'. *Musica Disciplina* 2 (1978): 189–203.

Erauw, Willem. 'Canon Formation: Some More Reflections on Lydia Goehr's Imaginary Museum of Musical Works'. *Acta Musicologica* 70 (1998): 109–15.

Fellowes, E. H. *Catalogue of Manuscripts in the Library of St. Michael's College, Tenbury*. 2nd ed. Paris: Éditions de l'Oiseau Lyrc, 1933.

———. *English Cathedral Music*. London: Methuen, 1941.

Fenlon, Iain, and Hugh Keyte. 'Memorialls of Great Skill: A Tale of Five Cities'. *Early Music* 8 (1980): 329–34.

Fenlon, Iain, and John Milsom. ' "Ruled Paper Imprinted": Music Paper and Patents in Sixteenth-Century England'. *Journal of the American Musicological Society* 107 (1984): 139–63.

Flood, W. H. Grattan. 'New Light on Late Tudor Composers – Thomas Tallis'. *Musical Times* 66 (1925): 800–1.

Foster, Elizabeth. *Proceedings in Parliament 1610*. Vol. 1. New Haven, CT: Yale University Press, 1966.

Foster, Myles Birket. *Anthems and Anthem Composers*. London: Novello, 1901.

Frogley, Alain. 'Rewriting the Renaissance: History, Imperialism, and British Music since 1840'. *Music & Letters* 84 (2003): 241–57.

Garratt, James. 'Mendelssohn's Babel: Romanticism and the Poetics of Translation'. *Music & Letters* 80 (1999): 23–49.

———. *Palestrina and the German Romantic Imagination: Interpreting Historicism in Nineteenth-Century Music*. Cambridge: Cambridge University Press, 2002.

Gatens, William J. *Victorian Cathedral Music in Theory and Practice*. Cambridge: Cambridge University Press, 1986.

Goehr, Lydia. *The Imaginary Museum of Musical Works*. Oxford: Clarendon Press, 1992.

———. *The Quest for Voice: On Music, Politics, and the Limits of Philosophy*. Berkeley: University of California Press, 1998.

———. 'Writing Music History'. *History and Theory* 31 (1992): 182–91.

Gombrich, E. H. *The Ideas of Progress and their Impact on Art*. New York: Cooper Union School of Art and Architecture, 1971.

Gregory, Jeremy. 'Christianity and Culture: Religion, the Arts and the Sciences in England, 1660–1880'. In *Culture and Society in Britain, 1660–1800*, edited by Jeremy Black, 82–109. Manchester: Manchester University Press, 1997.

Grier, James. *The Critical Editing of Music: History, Method and Practice*. Cambridge: Cambridge University Press, 1996.

Grove, Sir George. *A Dictionary of Music and Musicians*. 4 vols. London: Macmillan, 1879–90.

Hadow, Sir W. H. *English Music*. London: Longman, Green & Co., 1931.

Haskell, Harry. *The Early Music Revival*. New York: Thames & Hudson, 1988.

Haweis, Rev. H. R. *Music and Morals*. 1871. 16th ed. London: W. H. Allen, 1892.

Hawkins, John. *A General History of the Science and Practice of Music (1776)*. Intro. Charles Cudworth. 2 vols. 1853. Repr. New York: Dover, 1963.

[Hayes, William]. *Remarks on Mr. Avison's Essay on Musical Expression*. London, 1753.

Heighes, Simon. *The Lives and Works of William and Philip Hayes*. New York: Garland, 1995.

Hepokoski, James. 'The Dahlhaus Project and its Extra-Musicological Sources'. *19th Century Music* 14 (1991): 221–46.

Hobsbawm, Eric, and Terence Ranger. *The Invention of Tradition*. Cambridge: Cambridge University Press, 1983.

Hoffmann, E. T. A. 'Old and New Church Music' (1814). In *E. T. A. Hoffmann's Musical Writings: Kreisleriana, The Poet and the Composer, Music Criticism*, edited by David Charlton, 351–76. Trans. Martyn Clarke. Cambridge: Cambridge University Press, 1989.

Hofman, May, and John Morehen. *Latin Music in British Sources, c. 1485–1610*. London: Stainer & Bell, 1987.

Hogwood, Christopher, and Richard Luckett, eds. *Music in Eighteenth-Century England: Essays in Memory of Charles Cudworth*. Cambridge: Cambridge University Press, 1983.

Holman, Peter. ' "Evenly, Softly, and Sweetly Acchording to All": The Organ Accompaniment of English Consort Music'. In *John Jenkins and His Time: Studies in English Consort Music*, edited by Andrew Ashbee and Peter Holman, 353–82. Oxford: Clarendon Press, 1996.

Holub, Robert. *Reception Theory: A Critical Introduction*. New York: Methuen, 1984.

Hughes, Meirion. *The English Musical Renaissance and the Press, 1850–1914: Watchmen of Music*. Aldershot: Ashgate, 2002.

Hullah, Frances. *The Life of John Hullah*. London: Longmans, Green & Co., 1886.

Illing, Robert. 'Tallis's Psalm Tunes'. *Miscellenea Musicologica* 2 (1967): 21–74.

———. *English Metrical Psalter 1562: A Catalogue of the Early Editions, an Index to their Contents, and a Comparative Study of their Melodies*. 3 vols. Adelaide: n.p., 1983.

Ingarden, Roman. *The Work of Music and the Problem of its Identity*. Trans. Adam Czerniawski. Ed. Jean G. Harrell. Berkeley: University of California, 1986.

Irving, Howard. *Ancients and Moderns: William Crotch and the Development of Classical Music*. Aldershot: Ashgate, 1999.

Jauss, Hans Robert. *Toward an Aesthetic of Reception*. Trans. Timothy Bahti. Intro. Paul de Man. Minneapolis: University of Minnesota Press, [1982].

Jebb, John. *The Choral Service of the United Church of England and Ireland; being an Enquiry into the Liturgical System of the Cathedral and Collegiate Foundations of the Anglican Communion*. London: Parker, 1843.

———. *Three Lectures on the Cathedral Services of the Church of England (1841)*. 2nd ed. Leeds: T. W. Green, 1845.

Johnson, David. 'The 18th-Century Glee'. *Musical Times* 120 (1979): 200–2.

Johnson, Samuel. 'An Essay on Epitaphs' (1740). In *Samuel Johnson*, edited by Donald Greene, 96–102. Oxford: Oxford University Press, 1984.

Johnstone, H. Diack. 'The Genesis of Boyce's "Cathedral Music"'. *Music & Letters* 56 (1975): 26–41.

——— and Roger Fiske, eds. *Music in Britain: The Eighteenth Century*. Blackwell History of Music in Britain 4. Oxford: Blackwell, 1990.

Joyce, F. W. *The Life of Rev. Sir F. A. G. Ouseley, Bart.* London: Methuen, 1896.

Judd, Cristle Collins. *Reading Renaissance Theory.* Cambridge: Cambridge University Press, 2000.

Kenyon, Nicholas, ed. *Authenticity and Early Music: A Symposium.* Oxford: Oxford University Press, 1988.

Kerman, Joseph. 'A Few Canonic Variations'. *Critical Inquiry* 10 (1983): 107–25.

———. 'A Tallis Mass'. *Early Music* 27 (1999): 669–71.

Kidd, Colin. *British Identities before Nationalism.* Cambridge: Cambridge University Press, 1999.

King, A. Hyatt. *Printed Music in the British Museum.* London: Clive Bingley, 1979.

———. *Some British Collectors of Music, c. 1600–1960.* Cambridge: Cambridge University Press, 1963.

Krummel, D. W. *The Memory of Sound: Observations on the History of Music on Paper.* Washington, DC: Library of Congress, 1988.

Kumar, Krishan. *The Making of English National Identity.* Cambridge: Cambridge University Press, 2003.

Lang, S. 'The Principles of the Gothic Revival in England'. *Journal of the Society of Architectural Historians* 25 (1966): 240–67.

Langley, Leanne. 'Roots of a Tradition: The First *Dictionary of Music and Musicians'*. In *George Grove, Music and Victorian Culture*, edited by Michael Musgrave, 168–205. London: Palgrave Macmillan, 2003.

———. 'The Musical Press in Nineteenth-Century England'. *Notes* 2nd ser. 46 (1990): 583–92.

le Huray, Peter. *Music and the Reformation in England.* London: Herbert Jenkins, 1967.

Leavis, Ralph. 'Tallis's 40-Part Motet'. *Musical Times* 122 (1981): 30.

Lee, Sidney, ed. *Dictionary of National Biography.* London: Smith, Elder & Co., 1895.

Leppert, Richard. 'Imagery, Musical Confrontation and Cultural Difference in Early 18th-Century London'. *Early Music* 14 (1986): 323–45.

———. *Music and Image: Domesticity, Ideology, and Socio-Cultural Formation in Eighteenth-Century England.* Cambridge: Cambridge University Press, 1988.

Lindgren, Lowell E. *Nicola Francesco Haym: Complete Sonatas Part 1.* Recent Researches in Music of the Baroque Era 116. Middleton, WI: A-R Editions, 2002.

Lovell, Percy. ' "Ancient" Music in Eighteenth-Century England'. *Music & Letters* 60 (1979): 401–15.

Macfarren, G. A. 'The Music of the English Church'. *Musical Times* 13 (1867): 69–71.

Mason, William. *Essays Historical and Critical, on English Church Music*. York, 1795. Reproduced as 'Essays on English Church Music'. *Musical Standard* 7 (1867): 112–13; 144–5; 206–7; 238–9; 305–6.

Metcalfe, J. Powell. 'The Music of the Church of England, as Contemplated by the Reformers'. *Musical Times* 12 (1865): 157–60.

Milsom, John. 'A New Tallis Contrafactum'. *Musical Times* 123 (1982): 429–31.

———. 'Sacred Songs in the Chamber'. In *English Choral Practice, 1400–1650*, edited by John Morehen, 161–79. Cambridge Studies in Performance Practice 5. Cambridge: Cambridge University Press, 1995.

———. 'Songs, Carols and *Contrafacta* in the Early History of the Tudor Anthem'. *Proceedings of the Royal Musical Association* 107 (1980–1): 34–45.

———. 'Tallis, Byrd and the "Incorrected Copy": Some Cautionary Notes for Editors of Early Music Printed from Movable Type'. *Music & Letters* 77 (1996): 348–67.

———. 'A Tallis Fantasia'. *Musical Times* 126 (1985): 658–62.

———. 'Tallis's First and Second Thoughts'. *Journal of the Royal Musicological Association* 113 (1988): 203–22.

Monson, Craig. 'Authenticity and Chronology in Byrd's Church Anthems'. *Journal of the American Musicological Society* 35 (1982): 280–305.

———. 'The Preces, Psalms and Litanies of Byrd and Tallis: Another "Virtuous Contention in Love." ' *Music Review* 40 (1979): 257–71.

———. 'Thomas Myriell's Manuscript Collection: One View of Musical Taste in Jacobean London'. *Journal of the American Musicological Society* 30 (1977): 419–65.

Moroney, Davitt. 'Alessandro Striggio's Mass in Forty and Sixty Parts'. *Journal of the American Musicological Society* 60 (2007): 1–70.

Mukařovský, Jan. *Aesthetic Function, Norm and Value as Social Facts*. Trans. Mark E. Suino. Michigan Slavic Contributions. Ann Arbor: University of Michigan, 1970.

———. *Structure, Sign, and Function*. Trans. & ed. John Burbank and Peter Steiner. New Haven, CT: Yale University Press, 1978.

Murdoch, Anna King. 'A Vocation of Intoxication'. *Age*, 7 July 1995, 18.

Naumann, Emil. *The History of Music*. Trans. F. Praeger. Ed. F. A. Gore Ouseley. Vol. 2. London: Cassell, [1882].

Nettel, Reginald. 'The Oldest Surviving English Music Club'. *Musical Quarterly* 34 (1948): 97–108.

Nettl, Bruno. 'Mozart and the Ethnomusicological Study of Western Culture: An Essay in Four Movements'. In *Disciplining Music: Musicology and its Canons*, edited by Katherine Bergeron and Philip V. Bohlman, 137–55. Chicago: University of Chicago Press, 1992.

Newman, Gerald. *The Rise of English Nationalism*. New York: St Martin's Press, 1997.

Nichols, John. *The Progresses, Processions, and Magnificent Festivities of King James the First*. Vol. 3. London, 1828.

Nixon, Paul J. 'Giraldus Cambrensis on Music: How Reliable are his Historiographers?' In *Proceedings of the First British-Swedish Conference on Musicology: Medieval Studies, 11–15 May 1988*, edited by Ann Buckley, 264–89. Stockholm: Royal Swedish Academy of Music, 1992.

Oliphant, Thomas. *A Brief Account of the Madrigal Society from its Institution in 1741, up to the Present Period*. London: Calkin & Budd, 1835.

Olleson, Philip, and Fiona M. Palmer. 'Publishing Music from the Fitzwilliam Museum, Cambridge: The Work of Vincent Novello and Samuel Wesley in the 1820s'. *Journal of the Royal Musical Association* 130 (2005): 38–73.

Olwage, Grant. 'Hym(n)ing: Music and Masculinity in the Early Victorian Church'. In *Nineteenth-Century British Music Studies*, edited by Peter Horton and Bennett Zon, 3:21–44. Aldershot: Ashgate, 2003.

Order of Service. 'Tallis' Commemoration Service Held in St. Alfege Church, Greenwich, November 23rd, 1885 … Greenwich: H. Richardson, [1885].

Ouseley, F. A. Gore. 'Considerations on the History of Ecclesiastical Music of Western Europe'. *Proceedings of the Musical Association* 2 (1875–6): 30–47.

———. 'The History and Development of Church Music'. *Church Congress Reports*, Manchester 1863, 161–70.

[Peace, John]. *An Apology for Cathedral Service*. London: John Bohn, 1839.

Pearce, Charles William. 'On the Treatment of Ancient Ecclesiastical Melodies in Modern Instrumental Composition'. *Proceedings of the Musical Association* 13 (1886–7): 63–82.

Pearce, Rev. E. H. *Sons of the Clergy, 1655–1904*. London: Murray, 1904.

Phillips, Peter. *English Sacred Music, 1549–1649*. Oxford: Gimell, 1992.

———. 'Sign of contradiction: Tallis at 500'. *Musical Times* 146 (2005): 7–15.

Pine, Edward. *The Westminster Abbey Singers*. London: Dennis Dobson, 1953.

Pointon, Marion. *William Dyce, 1806–1864: A Critical Biography*. Oxford: Clarendon Press, 1979.

Powers, Harold. 'A Canonical Museum of Imaginary Music'. *Current Musicology* 60–1 (1996): 5–25.

Practical Remarks on the Reformation of Cathedral Music. London: John Bohn, 1849.

Pugin, A. W. *Contrasts or a Parallel between the Noble Edifices of the Middle Ages, and Corresponding Buildings of the Present Day: Shewing the Present Decay of Taste*. 1836. 2nd ed. London, 1841.

Pulver, Jeffrey. *A Biographical Dictionary of Old English Music*. London: Kegan, 1927.

Puttick & Simpson Sales Catalogue, 29 Feb 1876.

Rainbow, Bernarr. *The Choral Revival in the Anglican Church (1839–1872)*. London: Barrie & Jenkins, 1970.

———. *The Land without Music: Musical Education in England, 1800–1860, and its Continental Antecedents*. London: Novello, 1967.

Rees, Owen. 'Adventures of Portuguese "Ancient Music' in Oxford, London, and Paris: Duarte Lobo's "Liber Missarum" and Musical Antiquarianism, 1650–1850'. *Music & Letters* 86 (2005): 42–73.

Reeves' Catalogue of Music and Musical Literature. Vol. 9. London: Williams Reeves, 1882.

Rennert, Jonathon. *William Crotch (1775–1847): Composer, Artist, Teacher*. Lavenham, Suffolk: T. Dalton, 1975.

Ribiero, Alvaro, ed. *The Letters of Dr Charles Burney*. Vol. 1. Oxford: Clarendon Press, 1991.

Rimbault, Edward F., ed. *The Old Cheque-Book or Book of Remembrance of the Chapel Royal*. 1872. Repr. New York: Da Capo, 1966.

Roche, Elizabeth. ' "Great Learning, Fine Scholarship, Impeccable Taste": A Fiftieth Anniversary Tribute to Sir Richard Terry (1865–1938)'. *Early Music* 16 (1988): 231–6.

———. 'Tallis's 40-Part Motet'. *Musical Times* 22 (1981): 85.

St Paul's Cathedral, London, Music Bills, 1875–91. 3 vols. London, British Library.

Samson, Jim, ed. *The Cambridge History of Nineteenth-Century Music*. Cambridge: Cambridge University Press, 2001.

———, 'Chopin Reception: Theory, History, Analysis'. In *Chopin Studies 2*, edited by John Rink and Jim Samson, 1–17. Cambridge: Cambridge University Press, 1994.

———. 'Myth and Reality: A Biographical Introduction'. In *The Cambridge Companion to Chopin*, edited by Jim Samson, 1–8. Cambridge: Cambridge University Press, 1992.

Schofield, Bertram. 'The Manuscripts of Tallis's Forty-Part Motet'. *Music Quarterly* 37 (1951): 176–83.

Scholes, Percy. *The Great Dr Burney*. 2 vols. London: Oxford University Press, 1948.

———. *The Mirror of Music, 1844–1944*. 2 vols. London: Novello, Oxford University Press, 1947.

———. *The Oxford Companion to Music*. Oxford: Oxford University Press, 1938.

Schor, Esther. *Bearing the Dead*. Princeton: Princeton University Press, 1994.

Shay, Robert. ' "Naturalizing" Palestrina and Carissimi in Late Seventeenth-Century Oxford: Henry Aldrich and his Recompositions'. *Music & Letters* 77 (1996): 368–400.

———. 'Purcell as Collector of "Ancient" Music: Fitzwilliam MS 88'. In *Purcell Studies*, edited by Curtis Price, 35–50. Cambridge: Cambridge University Press, 1995.

——— and Robert Thompson. *Purcell Manuscripts: The Principal Musical Sources*. Cambridge: Cambridge University Press, 2000.

Sheppard, H. Fleetwood. 'Tallis and his Song of Forty Parts'. *Musical Times* 19 (1878): 97–8.

Shillingsburg, Peter. *Scholarly Editing in the Computer Age: Lectures in Theory and Practice*. Duntroon, ACT: Royal Military College, 1984.

Smiles, Sam. *The Image of Antiquity: Ancient Britain and the Romantic Imagination*. New Haven, CT: Yale University Press, 1994.

Solomon, Maynard. 'Thoughts on Biography'. *19th Century Music* 5 (1982): 268–76.

Spencer, Charles Child. 'Historical doubts as to the Genuineness of Tallis'. *Parish Choir* 1 (1847): 121–2.

Spink, Ian. *Restoration Cathedral Music, 1660–1774*. Oxford: Clarendon Press, 1995.

Stafford, William C. *A History of Music (1830)*. Intro. Bernarr Rainbow. Classic Texts in Music Education 18. Clarabricken: Boethius Press, 1986.

Stevens, Denis. 'A Songe of Fortie Partes, Made by Mr. Tallys'. *Early Music* 10 (1982): 171–81.

Stockigt, Janice B., and Michael Talbot. 'Two More New Vivaldi Finds in Dresden'. *Eighteenth-Century Music* 3 (2006): 35–61.

Stow, John. *A Survey of the Cities of London and Westminster … Brought Down from the Year 1633 to the Present Age by J. Strype*. London, 1720.

Stradling, Robert, and Meirion Hughes. *The English Musical Renaissance*. Routledge: London, 1993.

Stuhr-Rommereim, John. 'Thomas Tallis's *Spem in alium* and the "Ultimate Musical Experience"'. *Choral Journal* 33 (1993): 21–6.

Talbot, Michael, ed. *The Musical Work: Reality or Invention?* Liverpool Music Symposium 1. Liverpool: Liverpool University Press, 2000.

Taruskin, Richard. 'Speed Bumps'. *19th Century Music* 29 (2005): 185–207.

———. *Text and Act: Essays on Music and Performance*. New York: Oxford University Press, 1995.

Taylor, Edward. Review of *The Choral Service*, etc. *British and Foreign Review* 17 (1844): 83–116.

———. *The English Cathedral Service, Its Glory, – Its Decline, and Its Designed Extinction*. London: Simpkin, Marshal & Co., 1845.

———. 'Works Printed for the Members of the Musical Antiquarian Society'. *British and Foreign Review* 16 (1844): 397–419.

Temperley, Nicholas. *The Lost Chord*. Bloomington, IL: Indiana University Press, 1989.

———. *The Music of the English Parish Church*. 2 vols. Cambridge Studies in Music. Cambridge: Cambridge University Press, 1979.

———, ed. *Music in Britain: The Romantic Age, 1800–1914*. Blackwell History of Music in Britain 5. London: Athlone Press, 1981.

Terry, Richard Runciman. 'Anglican Church Music'. *The Chord* no. 3 (1899): 17.

———. *Catholic Church Music*. London: Greening Co., 1907.

———. *A Forgotten Psalter and Other Essays*. London: Oxford University Press, 1929.

———. *Our Church Music*. London: Catholic Truth Society, 1901.

———. 'Some Unpublished Tallis'. *The Chord* no. 5 (1900): 64–72.

———. 'Tallys, Byrde, and Some Popular Fictions'. *Downside Review* 19 (1900): 75–81.

Treitler, Leo. 'Gender and Other Dualities of Music History'. In *Musicology and Difference: Gender and Sexuality in Music Scholarship*, edited by Ruth Solie, 23–45. Berkeley: University of California Press, 1993.

———. 'History and Ontology of the Musical Work'. *Journal of Aesthetics and Art Criticism* 51 (1993): 483–97.

———. *Music and the Historical Imagination*. Cambridge, MA: Harvard University Press, 1989.

———. 'The Politics of Reception: Tailoring the Present as Fulfilment of a Desired Past'. *Journal of the Royal Musicological Association* 116 (1991): 280–98.

———. 'Toward a Desegregated Music Historiography'. *Black Music Research Journal* 16 (1996): 3–10.

Turbet, Richard. 'An Affair of Honour: "Tudor Church Music", the Ousting of Richard Terry, and a Trust Vindicated'. *Music & Letters* 79 (1995): 593–600.

———. 'Byrd Throughout All Generations'. *Cathedral Music* 35 (1992): 19–24.

———. 'Friends of Cathedral Music: Tallis and Byrd'. *Musical Opinion* 106 (1983): 301.

———. 'Horsley's 1842 Edition of Byrd and its Infamous Introduction'. *British Music* 14 (1992): 36–45.

———. ' "A Monument of Enthusiastic Industry": Further Light on "Tudor Church Music" '. *Music & Letters* 81 (2000): 433–6.

———. 'The Musical Antiquarian Society'. *Brio* 29 (1992): 13–20.

———. 'Quack Doctor'. *Musical Times* 137 (1996): 4.

———. 'Thomas Tallis and Osbert Parsley (Died 1585)'. *Brio* 22 (1985): 50–5.

———. 'William Dyce and the Motett Society'. *Aberdeen University Review* 56 (1996): 442–6.

Turnbull, E. 'Thomas Tudway and the Harleian Collection'. *Journal of the American Musicological Society* 8 (1955): 203.

Vodička, Felix. 'The Concretization of the Literary Work: Problems in the Reception of Neruda's Works'. In *The Prague School: Selected Writings, 1929-1946*, edited by Peter Steiner, 105-34. Trans. John Burbank. Austin: University of Texas Press, 1982.

———. 'The History of the Echo of Literary Works'. In *A Prague School Reader on Esthetics, Literary Structure, and Style*, edited and translated by Paul L. Garvin, 71-81. Washington DC: Georgetown University Press, 1964.

Walker, Ernest. *A History of Music in England*. Oxford: Clarendon Press, 1907.

Weber, William. 'Mass Culture and the Reshaping of European Musical Taste, 1770-1870'. *International Review of the Aesthetics and Sociology of Music* 8 (1977): 5-21.

———. *The Rise of Musical Classics in Eighteenth-Century England*. Oxford: Clarendon Press, 1992.

———. 'Thomas Tudway and the Harleian Collection of "Ancient" Church Music'. *British Library Journal* 15 (1989): 187-205.

Wesley, S. S. *A Few Words on Cathedral Music (1849)*. London: Hinrichsen, 1965.

White, Harry. ' "If It's Baroque, Don't Fix It": Reflections on Lydia Goehr's "Work-Concept" and the Historical Integrity of Musical Composition'. *Acta Musicologica* 69 (1997): 94-104.

White, James F. *The Cambridge Movement: The Ecclesiologist and the Gothic Revival*. Cambridge: Cambridge University Press, 1962.

Whittaker, W. Gillies. 'An Adventure'. *Dominant* 2 (May-June 1929): 40-2. Reproduced in *Collected Essays*, 86-9. London: Oxford University Press, 1940.

Willetts, Pamela J. 'Musical Connections of Thomas Myriell'. *Music & Letters* 49 (1968): 39-42.

Williams, Glanmor. 'Some Protestant Views of Early British Church History'. *History* 38 (1953): 219-33.

Wolffe, John. *God and Greater Britain: Religion and National Life in Britain and Ireland, 1843-1945*. London: Routledge, 1994.

Woodfield, Ian. ' "Music of Forty Several Parts": A Song for the Creation of Princes'. *Performance Practice Review* 7 (1994): 54-64.

Wordsworth, William. 'Essays on Epitaphs' (1810). In *Selected Prose*, edited by John O. Hayden. Harmondsworth: Penguin, 1988.

Young, Percy M. *George Grove, 1820-1900: A Biography*. London: Macmillan, 1980.

———. 'Music in English Cathedral Libraries'. *Fontes Artis Musicae* 36 (1989): 252-61.

Zon, Bennett. *The English Plainchant Revival*. Oxford Studies in British Church Music. Oxford: Oxford University Press, 1999.

———, ed. *Nineteenth-Century British Music Studies*. Vol. 1. Aldershot: Ashgate, 1999.

❧ *Dissertations*

Langley, Leanne. 'The English Musical Journal in the Early Nineteenth Century'. 2 vols. PhD diss., University of North Carolina at Chapel Hill, 1983.

Morehen, John. 'The Sources of English Cathedral Music, *c*. 1617–*c*. 1644'. PhD diss., Cambridge University, 1969.

Moroney, Michael Davitt. 'Under Fower Sovereygnes: Thomas Tallis and the Transformation of English Polyphony'. PhD diss., University of California at Berkeley, 1980.

Sipe, Thomas. 'Interpreting Beethoven: History, Aesthetics, and Critical Reception'. PhD diss., University of Pennsylvania, 1992.

❧ *Published editions of music*

The Byrd Edition. Gen. ed. Philip Brett. London: Stainer & Bell, 1977–.

  1. *Cantiones Sacrae (1575)*. Ed. Craig Monson. 1977.

  10a. *The English Services*. Ed. Craig Monson. 1980.

Early English Church Music. London: Stainer & Bell, 1962–.

  12. *Thomas Tallis: English Sacred Music: I. Anthems*. Ed. Leonard Ellinwood. Rev. Paul Doe. 1971; rev. ed. 1973.

  13. *Thomas Tallis: English Sacred Music: II. Service Music*. Ed. Leonard Ellinwood. Rev. Paul Doe. 1972; rev. ed. 1974.

Tudor Church Music. London: Oxford University Press, 1922–9.

  6. *Thomas Tallis, c. 1505–1585*. Ed. P. C. Buck, A. Ramsbotham, E. H. Fellowes and S. Townsend Warner. 1928.

All People that on Earth do Dwell. Musical Times 1 (1845): 127–30.

Barnard, John. *The First Book of Selected Church Musick … (1641)*. 10 vols. Farnborough: Gregg, 1972.

Barnby, Joseph, ed. *Tallis's Preces and Responses, with Harmonized Confession (Ely Use) Arranged for Four Voices …* London: Novello, 1893.

Bishop, John. *Choral Responses at Morning and Evening Prayer*. London: R. Cocks, 1859.

———. *The Order of the Daily Service of the United Church of England and Ireland, as Arranged for Use 'In Quires and Places where they Sing' by Thomas Tallis …* London: R. Cocks, 1843.

Boyce, William. *Cathedral Music: Being a Collection in Score of the Most Valuable and Useful Compositions for that Service, by the Several English Masters of the Last Two Hundred Years (1760)*. 2nd ed. 1789. Repr. London: Kraus Reprint, 1975.

Byrd, Gulielmo. *Missa ad quatuor voces inaequales*. Ed. Gulielmus Smith Rockstro and Gulielmus Barclay Squire. London: Novello, 1890.

Crotch, William, ed. *Tallis's Litany, Adapted to the Latin Words with Additions by Dr. Aldrich* … Oxford, 1803.

Dyce, William. *The Order of Daily Service, the Litany and Order of the Administration of the Holy Communion with plain tune, according to the use of the United Church of England and Ireland*. London, 1843.

Elvey, George I., ed. *Tallis's Litany and Responses. Arranged for Daily Use of Cathedral and Collegiate Churches* … London: R. Mills, 1846.

The Festal Preces and Responses … from the Best Known Editions. London: SPCK, 1901.

Havergal, Henry E., ed. *The Preces & Litany Set by Thomas Tallis for Four Voices … from MSS. of Dean Aldrich*. Oxford: I. Shrimpton, 1847.

Hopkins, Edward J., ed. *Tallis's Festival Responses Consisting of the Versicles, Preces, &c., and Litany, the Plainsong being Restored Throughout, and the Whole Reduced to the Original Number of Four Parts*. London: Weekes, [1868].

H[unter], L[yon], R[obert], ed. *The Order for Chanting the Morning and Evening, Wednesday and Friday, and Eucharistic Services, Arranged Chiefly from Tallis* … London, 1847.

Jackson, Francis, ed. *Anthems for Choirs 1: 50 Anthems for Mixed Voices*. Oxford: Oxford University Press, 1973.

Jebb, John. *The Choral Responses and Litanies of the United Church of England and Ireland*. Vol. 1, London: Bell, 1847; Vol. 2, London: Stainer, 1856.

Joule, Benjamin S. John Baptist. *Directorium Chori Anglicanum: The Choral Service of the United Church of England & Ireland, Compiled from Authentic Sources*. London: Novello, 1849.

Lowe, Edward. *A Short Direction for the Performance of Cathedrall Service* … Oxford, 1661.

——. *A Review of Some Short Directions for Performance of Cathedral Service* … Oxford, 1664.

Mann, A. H., ed. *Motet for 40 Voices by Thomas Tallis*. London: Weekes, 1888.

Martin, George C., ed. *Tallis's Festal Responses and Litany as Sung at St Paul's Cathedral*. London: Novello, 1903.

Merbecke, John. *The Book of Common Prayer with Musical Notes: The First Office Book of the Reformation*. Ed. Edward F. Rimbault. 2nd ed. London: Novello, Ewer & Co., 1871.

Novello, Vincent, ed. *Cathedral Music … Selected and Revised by W. Boyce … Revised and the Organ Accompaniment Added by V. Novello*. 3 vols. London: Novello, 1849.

Oliphant, Thomas, ed. *The Full Cathedral Service as Used on the Festivals and Saints' Days of the Church of England, Composed by Thomas Tallis …* London: C. Lonsdale, 1841.

The Order for Morning Prayer and the Litany, Noted by Thomas Tallis. London: Novello, 1854.

Pearsall, Samuel, ed. *The Hymns of the Church, Pointed as they are to be Sung or Chanted: with the Versicles, Creed of S. Athanasius, Litany, Commandments, etc. as Set to Music by Thomas Tallis*. 2nd ed. London: James Burns, 1843.

Pettman, Edgar, ed. *Tallis's Responses: A Simplified Arrangement as Sung at St James's Church Piccadilly*. London: Houghton, 1900.

Preces, Responses, & Litany by Thomas Tallis for Festivals and Special Services (From the Society's Common Prayer with Plain Song). London: SPCK, 1869.

Rimbault, Edward Francis, ed. *The Book of Common Prayer with Musical Notes as Used in the Chapel Royal of Edward VI, Compiled by John Marbeck*. London: J. A. Novello, 1845.

———, ed. *The Full Cathedral Service as Used on the Festivals and Saint's Days of the Church of England, Composed by Thomas Tallis*. London: D'Almaine, 1845.

———, ed. *The Order of Chanting the Cathedral Service; with Notation of the Preces, Versicles, Responses, &c., &c., as Published by Edward Lowe, A.D. 1664*. London: Chappell, 1845.

———, ed. *The Order of Morning and Evening Prayer with the Musical Notation in Harmony of Four Parts, the Plainsong of the Church being in the Tenor …* London: Novello, 1850.

———, ed. *The Order of the Daily Service of the United Church of England and Ireland, as Arranged for Choirs by T. Tallis*. London: D'Almaine, [1846].

Shaw, H. Watkins, ed. *Settings of the Preces and Responses by Byrd, Morley, Smith, Tomkins*. Church Music Society Reprints No. 48. Croydon: RSCM, 1985.

———. *Two Setting of the Preces and Responses at Morning and Evening Prayer by Thomas Tallis …* London: Novello, 1957.

Stainer, John, ed. *Tallis's Preces and Responses, with Harmonized Confessions (Ely Use) in the Key of F. …* London: Novello, 1900.

Tallis, Thomas. *Missa sine titulo*. Ed. Ricardus R. Terry. Leipzig: Breitkopf & Härtel, 1906.

———. *Spem in alium*. London: Oxford University Press, [1928].

———. *Spem in alium nunquam habui: A Motet in Forty Parts*. Rev. ed. Philip Brett. London: Oxford University Press, 1966.

——— and William Byrd. *Cantiones quae ab argumento sacrae vocantur (1575)*. 12 vols. Leeds: Boethius Press, 1976.

Thompson, C. *The Plain-Song of the Versicles & Responses at Morning and Evening Prayer … From Tallis's Festal Service. …* London; New York: Novello, 1891.

Tye, Christopher. *Mass to Six Voices 'Euge bone'.* Ed. G. E. P. Arkwright. Old English Edition 10. London: Joseph Williams, 1893.

Veni, Creator Spiritus. Musical Times 5 (1853): 183–5.

———. Supplement to *Parish Choir*, 1846.

The Versicles and Responses at Morning and Evening Prayer, with the Festal Harmonies after Tallis Edited for Use at the Festivals of the South Shropshire Choral Union. London: Novello, 1888.

Warren, Joseph, ed., *Cathedral Music … Selected by Dr. William Boyce, Newly Edited and Carefully Collated and Revised …* London: R. Cocks & Co., 1849.

Wesley, S. S. *A Morning and Evening Service.* London, [1845].

Westbrook, W. J., ed. *Tallis's Preces and Responses, Arranged for Three Treble Voices, with Accompaniment for the Organ, Harmonium or Pianoforte.* London: Alfred Whittingham, 1865.

🎵 *Manuscript sources*

Accounts of the Madrigal Society, 1832–81. Mad. Soc. F.17–19. British Library, London.

Taylor, Edward. 'Lecture v'. MC 257/124, fol. 4. Norwich Record Office, Norwich.

'Syllabuses of Gresham Lectures'. Guildhall Library, London.

🎵 *Music Manuscripts*

Cambridge, Pembroke College [*GB-Cpc*] MSS Mus. 6.1–6.

———, Peterhouse [*GB-Cp*] MSS 33, 34, 38, 39.

London, British Library [*GB-Lbl*] Add. 23624.

———, ——— Add. 38541.

———, ——— Add. 33239.

———, ——— Add. 29968.

———, ——— Egerton 3512.

———, ——— Harleian 7337–42.

———, ——— Mad. Soc. H.114.

———, ——— R.M.4.g.1.

———, ——— R.M.24.c.11.(26).

———, Gresham College [*GB-Lgc*] MS G.Mus.420.

———, Royal College of Music [*GB-Lcm*] MS 722.

——— ——— Mss 1045–51

Oxford, Bodleian Library [*GB-Ob*] Tenbury MS 836.

———, ——— Tenbury MS 1270.

———, Christ Church [*GB-Och*] Mus. 9.

———, ——— Mus. 11.

———, ——— Mus. 16.

———, ——— Mus. 48.

———, ——— Mus. 614.

———, ——— Mus. 1229.

———, ——— Mus. 1230.

———, ——— Mus. 1235.

———, ——— Mus. 1220–4.

Windsor, St George's Chapter Library [*GB-WRch*] MS 45.

❧ *Websites*

The Andertons and Religion. Accessed 23 May 2003. <http://freepages.genealogy.rootsweb.com/~anderton/religion.html>.

Handlo Music. Accessed 7 Aug 2003. <http://www.handlo-music.com/>.

Thomas Tallis: The Complete Works, Volume 6 - Music for a Reformed Church, Accessed 6 Jan 2007. <http://www.signumrecords.com/catalogue/sigcd022/reviews.htm>.

Tupper, John Lucas. 'Henry Hugh Armstead'. *English Artists of the Present Day: Essays by J. Beavington Atkinson, Sidney Colvin, F. G. Stephens, Tom Taylor, and John L. Tupper*. London: Seeley, Jackson & Halliday, 1872. Reproduced on The Victorian Web. Accessed 21 Mar 2003. <http://65.107.211.206/victorian/sculpture/armstead/bio1.html>.

Index

References to musical examples and illustrations appear in italics